Duel for the Crown

Duel for the Crown

Neil Harman

André Deutsch

First published in Great Britain in 1999 by
André Deutsch Limited
76 Dean Street
London W1V 5HA

www.vci.co.uk

1 3 5 7 9 10 8 6 4 2

ISBN 0 233 99489 0

A catalogue record for this book is available from the British Library

Typeset by Derek Doyle & Associates
Mold, Flintshire
Printed in the UK by
MPG Books Ltd, Bodmin, Cornwall

Jacket photographs from Allsport and Action Images

Extracts from the *Express* and the *Sunday Express*
reprinted by kind permission.

Acknowledgements

To all those in the international tennis family who helped and encouraged me along the way, who showed interest in the subject, who were willing to talk and were as enthused as I was about the idea of chronicling an unprecedented period in British tennis history, thank you.

To the former tennis correspondent of the *Daily Mail*, Laurie Pignon and *The Times*, Rex Bellamy, and the present correspondent of the *Daily Telegraph*, John Parsons, for their love of the game, which rubbed off on a callow youth.

To all at publishers André Deutsch, especially my editor Nicky Paris, who kept me on my toes throughout the year and was never less than 100 per cent committed and managing director Tim Forrester for giving me the opportunity to put an idea into print. To my sports editor at the *Sunday Telegraph* Colin Gibson, who realized how important the project was to me and was full of the enthusiasm, advice and experience which makes him such a highly-regarded journalist.

And finally, to my family, both on this side of the Atlantic and in the United States, who were extremely supportive. I just wish my dad was still alive to have read this book. I know how proud he would have been.

Contents

	Prologue	1
Chapter 1	Birth Signs	12
Chapter 2	The Man with a Passport of Gold	26
Chapter 3	Telford, Tashkent, Teacher and Tribulations	36
Chapter 4	The Desert Song and an Aussie Lament	53
Chapter 5	Split Personalities	62
Chapter 6	Paradise Lost, Paradise Regained	69
Chapter 7	Feet of Clay	77
Chapter 8	Oh to be in Paris	92
Chapter 9	The Pressure Begins to Show	97
Chapter 10	The Championships	108
Chapter 11	After the Lord Mayor's Show	150
Chapter 12	If I Can Make It There . . .	163
Chapter 13	The Davis Cup	175
Chapter 14	The Long and Winding Road to Hanover	186
Chapter 15	The ATP World Championships	223
Chapter 16	Year's End	235
	Epilogue	244
	Tim Henman Tour Statistics	254
	Greg Rusedski Tour Statistics	264

Prologue

The BBC's Sports Personality of the Year awards has been a not-to-be-missed celebration in the armchair theatre of a British winter for nigh-on half a century – an evening of nostalgia, of moments that lift, touch and sometimes break the heart. It is an occasion to wrap oneself in sentiment, to wallow in the sporting archives.

A relaxing glass of the finest Cabernet Merlot in hand on the evening of Sunday 7 December 1997, I was as eager as the next man to indulge in the guessing game as to who would be presented with the famous trophy designed in the shape of a camera upon a tripod. My vote would have gone to Steve Redgrave, the world's pre-eminent oarsman. There was not a hint that the final outcome would have such profound repercussions for the victor's sport.

At a touch past 10.30p.m., the rather bulkier cameras inside London's Queen Elizabeth II Conference Centre swung around to scan the rows of the famous sportsmen and women before focusing on an upturned crescent-moon smile – conjure the image of Cesar Romero as Batman's rival The Joker and you get the basic shape – lighting up in the manner which had become so disconcertingly familiar.

The formal announcement was seconds away but Greg Rusedski, the new darling of British tennis, had a goose-pimply sense of the moment he could hardly have foreseen when he first heard that his mother had been born in Dewsbury, West Yorkshire. Rusedski was on the threshold of becoming BBC Sports Personality of the Year, following the likes of Chataway, Cooper, Cousins and Coe to an accolade of monumental significance. Tim Henman tried his best to force a smile of his own, but he was to discover that in the hearts and minds of the sporting public, in 1997 at least, he would be a silver medallist for the second time in his career. But there was no Olympic-like podium upon which to climb this time, he simply had to accept the prize and then stand to one side.

Richard Lewis, then the Director of International and Professional Men's Tennis at the Lawn Tennis Association (LTA), was in the audience, enjoying the applause for Henman when a passing thought made him freeze. 'I thought to myself, I don't believe it, Greg's been overlooked, it's going to be Tim second, someone else first,' Lewis said. 'I turned away deliberately so I didn't have to come into eye contact with Greg. I didn't want to see the look on his face.'

Lewis, so powerfully supportive of Rusedski's desire to switch national allegiance from the moment he learned of the intriguing prospect in 1993, wondered who the winner might be. It was not long before he was relieved to discover that the British people had chosen Greg as their man of the year. Not bad for a man who had been 'British' for only two-and-a-bit years. Cue a resounding fanfare for a sport which, on these shores, had been trapped in such terminal paralysis it thought it would never hear such acclaim again. As he lapped up the applause and that eerie signature tune played across the final credits, the realization dawned that tennis in Greg's adopted country might never be the same. The sea change in the sport's standing had been achieved by two people who stood side by side, but remained, in so many ways, an ocean apart. Not for the first time since Rusedski decided to assert that British was best, a lot of people in tennis didn't quite know how to feel.

Henman for one. In 1997 he had reached the Wimbledon quarterfinals for the second consecutive year and won his first Association of Tennis Professionals' (ATP) Tour title, but that was way back in January and happened half the world away, in Sydney, Australia. Come December, the memory of such a breakthrough triumph was too distant and its impact rendered vague by the passing of the months.

Henman had also been declared the most popular player at Wimbledon by a survey of more than 1,500 visitors commissioned by the All England Club. One assumed that the people who nominated him first, Pete Sampras second, Boris Becker third and Rusedski fourth, just in front of ladies' champion Martina Hingis, were the same respectable folk who responded to the BBC's invitation to cast their votes at Sports Personality time.

But tennis had moved relentlessly on and Rusedski had battled his way with phenomenal courage and self-belief to the men's singles final at the United States Open in September, the same month he sky-rocketed into the top-ten tennis players in the world. He was to reach a career-best No.4 in October, and had to be regarded as a genuine international force. The accent had long since ceased to matter.

Tim, aka Gentleman Tim, said all the right things on presentation night, but beneath his cultivated and dignified veneer, he must have been gently smouldering. Lightning struck twice inside a matters of days. Rusedski was named as recipient of the 'Services to Tennis' Award at the annual dinner of the Lawn Tennis Writers' Association but before the ink had dried on his two acceptance speeches there appeared a newspaper article by Henman under the headline 'You're Really Getting On My Nerves, Greg'. Here was a column whose underlying thrust was that Rusedski 'sits there grinning, collecting all the prizes'. Here was proof of the earnestness of the rivalry.

Henman continued: 'The memory of seeing Greg rather than me, rise from his chair to receive award after award has made me more committed than I have ever been in my life. I've never attached much importance to coming second, it's not a position I've ever enjoyed.

'If I have ever needed a motivation to get out there in the gym and on the practice court to work hard for the year ahead, then it's seeing Greg collect all those prizes and sitting there grinning at No.6 in the world rankings. There is not a problem between us, there's no animosity although everyone knows Greg and I are hardly best of friends. You won't find us going out to dinner together and contrary to what he's been saying, I can't remember any friendly football kick-abouts, either.

'It's a case of me going my way and he going his. But the fact we aren't close is only natural because such an intense rivalry has developed between us. It's just that I want to be better than Greg. That's why my two major aims for 1998 are to reclaim the title of British No.1 and emulate what he did by getting into the world's top ten for the first time.

'Greg reached the final at the US Open and that was a marvellous achievement but I have to say I wouldn't have minded his draw. He only had to beat one seed to get to the final. What he achieved throughout the year did come as a surprise to me. Never in my wildest dreams did I expect him to make No.4 in the world and reach a Grand Slam final.

'And nobody needs to remind me that in our only match this year, he beat me in straight sets in the semi-finals in Vienna. There was much more on that match than it just being a semi-final. In terms of how we played, it was a real anti-climax because the court was so fast and I wouldn't say either of us performed particularly well. There was no way he played at a standard more than average and it would be nice to play again on a more interesting surface. After all, I'd beaten him three out of three in our previous matches.'

Although Henman was to tell Rusedski later that the article's presentation embarrassed him (according to Rusedski) every word attributed to him had been read back to him by his co-writer, and he was happy with each and every one of them. The facade about the lack of a personal rivalry was fundamentally exposed.

Followers of the development of their careers could understand the depths of the Englishman's anger. A newcomer – a foreigner at that – had achieved a major public relations triumph.

Henman himself had not been immune to castigating critiques. One newspaper described the reaction to his 'successes' on Wimbledon's Centre Court – where he had reached consecutive quarter-finals and been involved in a memorable 1997 People's Sunday victory over Dutchman Paul Haarhuis, as 'nauseating middle-class hysteria'. At Nottingham in the summer, Rusedski hadn't helped his own cause when he sarcastically suggested that if he ever reached a final of a tournament in England in which Henman had lost in the semis, the headline would read 'Henman in Shock Defeat'.

These feelings portrayed the underlying suspicion in the Rusedski camp that he was still a second-class Brit, a sensation intensified when they discovered how many blue-chip sponsors Henman's management company were able to turn down, while they struggled to attract similar levels of support. It was like being in Canada all over again.

And if he needed an extra spur, there was one staring back at him from the back of a cornflakes packet. Henman's face was everywhere, identified with the best brand names, while Rusedski had to keep chipping away, knowing deep down it was likely that Tim, the 'true' Brit, would find it easier to attract sponsors who were sold on his pleasing Michael Owen-like brand of mega talent and homely personality. Greg, as ever, would have to work that much harder to be loved.

Each time their rivalry was played down, something, or someone, came along to fan its flame. Here was a contest both on court and off which knocked spots off anything experienced in tennis before, generated by the arrival of a twenty-two year old with the wrong inflection, the wrong background but the proper papers.

When they met in the locker rooms or in the back of a courtesy car, as they did most weeks of the year given the intimacy of the tennis world, they passed the time convivially enough. They didn't see the need to fit in with the media perception of fervent rivals, but then things that each of them did or didn't do riled the other. And, though they insisted they were delighted when the other achieved, it would hurt like hell if the other should win Wimbledon, the French (no, come on, don't be silly), or reached No.1 in the world first. Being British No.1 had once been something their own press derided – now it was taken with utmost seriousness. Jealous of each other's talent? No. Determined to be more successful? Absolutely.

Their playing careers were entwined to the extent that it was almost impossible to unravel them. As Simon Barnes of *The Times* wrote perceptively: 'Perhaps the most interesting thing about Henman is Rusedski; perhaps the most interesting thing about Rusedski is Henman. The success and failure of each of them is connected in the most extraordinary and intimate fashion.'

When questioned individually, the two players kept insisting there was no competition within a competition, they didn't feed off the other's glories and despairs, they were good for each other, they respected each other, there was no innate bitterness – but, surely, Henman's first-person article in December 1997 with its personal undertones squashed that pretence. The two players didn't hit it off, were never going to hit it off, and why should they? The world they frequented made dolts of nice guys. As John McEnroe said to me more than once during the year: 'Nice guys might get into the top twenty, but they don't hang around there too long.'

It was clear that the public had been smitten by Greg's determination to smile in the face of adversity, both emotional and physical. They loved a winner – even if he hadn't actually won anything yet. In reality, he had been little more than a glorious loser, but the Brits had always had a soft spot for those. Greg Rusedski had become the nation's strawberries and cream and the British couldn't get enough of him, especially those flashing incisors.

Yet this was the guy whose defection from Tennis Canada many in Britain had wanted to block, either through a deep-seated suspicion about the player's intentions, or because they felt the LTA had ridden roughshod over the wider implications for the sport.

Placing personal antipathy to one side, what was clear was that British tennis was in the limelight for something other than its annual staging of the most famous championship in the world, and this was a rare moment indeed. When, before the advent of Rusedski and the blossoming of Henman, had the sport been burnished with two such high-profile successful athletes? You had to flick back through sixty years of history, to the halcyon days of the 1930s, when Fred Perry and Bunny Austin were resplendent, awe-inspiring heroes of the long-trousered age who regularly laid waste to the opposition.

On 1997's Review of the Year night, for the first time in twenty years, tennis occupied the best camera angle seats at the QEII Centre, for once supplanting the Olympians, the Formula One drivers, footballers, boxers, and Test cricketers. The BBC used to invite the odd representative from tennis merely to make sure there were no embarrassing empty spaces in the audience. Not since 1977, when Virginia Wade won the Centenary ladies' singles title at Wimbledon and you couldn't move at the Television Centre for LTA insignia, had anyone representing British tennis double-checked with the ushers to confirm they hadn't been placed in the front row by mistake.

An irony of the ceremony was the absence of Ian Peacock, chief executive of the LTA through many of the leaner years, who missed the presentation for the first time since 1985. Peacock had been the most influential individual in persuading an organization not noted for proactivity to take Rusedski on when the pressure reached its height a decade later.

As the Christmas tree lights were being switched on in early December 1997, British tennis wallowed in a warm glow of satisfaction. Peacock's successors at the LTA were patting their own backs, because the sport was beginning to make enormous inroads into the public consciousness but the celebrations had a hollow ring. Had the association been significantly involved in the rise of Henman and Rusedski to such distinctive prominence? The answer was no. Rusedski had landed on their doorstep with a resounding thud, while they were miffed that Henman only came to their attention via a scheme outside their control.

Henman sometimes had to get on *despite* the LTA. Australian Warren Jacques, who became Britain's Davis Cup captain in 1988, had kept a close eye on Henman's development and in 1990, when he took a team of wannabees to Australia for a series of qualifiers and junior tournaments, he decided he wanted to give sixteen-year-old Tim Henman some critical experience. 'It was an important period in his life,' said Jacques. 'I could tell he had that something special, even though it looked as though a puff of wind might blow him over. The lad had guts, talent and he was desperate to learn. I told the LTA he should come to the Australian with me.' Jacques's bosses decided they wouldn't pay the full fare for a kid who hadn't been raised in one of their schemes and so it was left to his parents to subsidize their son's travel, with Jacques paying the rest out of his training budget.

The problem for the LTA in 1998 was that there wasn't any sign of another Henman, or Rusedski on the horizon. And there was precious little apart from them, in terms of playing success, to show for the megabuck success of Wimbledon which annually delivered the LTA a cheque the size of which would alleviate much of Third World debt. Wimbledon's astonishing profits helped generate plenty of smart, red-brick office buildings, a much needed spurt in facilities (even if the number of indoor courts had reached a paltry one per 63,000 of the population by December 1998) but very few players, who on the highest stage, were able to hit the ball over the net and, most importantly, hit it back a second time once it had been returned to them.

The LTA told everyone they were setting up Task Forces but the record suggested they couldn't identify or retain the interest of a potentially gifted player. In the mid-1980s Rex Bellamy, then correspondent of *The Times,* hit the nail on the head when he wrote: 'Britain can obviously make money out of tennis players. If only we could make tennis players out of the money.' Nothing had changed.

The image of the British tennis professional was someone too easily satisfied with a third-tier existence, who drove a sponsored car before they'd learned the rudiments of a topspin forehand, whose mental attitude was questionable and yet was handed invitations each summer to compete at Wimbledon – a free pass known in tennis-speak as a wild card. No one argued that the British didn't have a right to offer their own a leg-up in the world, but the basis for such assistance had long since demanded a closer examination.

Ian Barclay, the man who coached Pat Cash to his 1987 Wimbledon singles triumph and was now in charge of the LTA's National School at Bisham Abbey, described our malaise as 'The Satellite Syndrome.' He said: 'Before I came to Britain in 1991 and since I've been here, this country must have set the world record for players on the satellite circuit [one rung below the full Tour]. 'They are jammed in, stuck there forever. They can get a fair enough world ranking, get a wild card into Queen's or Wimbledon, win a couple of rounds, their ranking jumps up and they wait for the same thing to happen the next year.'

This was the real state of British tennis. Henman and Rusedski were window dressing.

The wild cards exposed the inferior British players to the levels of competition they could only enjoy on grass because their rankings were too lowly for direct entry into the other three Grand Slam events where most were reluctant to put their pride on the line and try to qualify. And they exposed a lot more than that. Thrust into the limelight, one or two warmed the Wimbledon crowd into a polite frenzy but, by and large, they shrivelled, soon to return to the small print of the results sections.

'We don't want a nanny state,' said John Crowther, who succeeded Peacock as chief executive of the LTA, in 1997, when pressed on the touchy subject of payments to players. 'We recognize that financial support can be counter-productive by making life too easy.' But what alternative did the LTA have, trapped as they were by the need to encourage, yet wary of being seen as little more than the equivalent of a cash withdrawal machine any time a player wanted new balls?

Further down the scale, there was little promise of building on the success of the top two. For a start, the level of facilities, though lauded by the LTA, were appalling in comparison with, say, Holland and France, our nearest neighbours in terms of geography and climate. And did their associations have £31 million each year? No. Britain has 5,000 fewer indoor courts than France, and almost 2,000 fewer than the Dutch. Of France's 6,400 indoor courts, 1,400 are indoor clay courts which is the only surface on which to teach the rudiments of tennis. The LTA said it was 'thinking' about building indoor clay courts. The whole thing was scary.

More than once during 1998 it was suggested to me that the governing body was petrified by the success of Henman and Rusedski. It had knocked them (and the players they represented) out of a once cosy, comfortable existence and a few sinecures were threatened because there was no one in the organization who had any experience of handling genuine superstars. To have two at once was completely unnerving.

Ion Tiriac, the Romanian mastermind behind Boris Becker's rise to international superstardom and one of the most influential characters in the sport, had once approached the LTA with an offer they shouldn't have refused. In 1990, the then president of the association, Ron Presley, was told that Tiriac would accept £250,000 to run the entire squad system. If he couldn't get a player in the top ten within three years, the LTA would get their money back.

Tiriac didn't want any of the current LTA people involved. He would employ the men to coach the players; he would supervise their itineraries; he would decide where they should and shouldn't play. Presley thought it was a magnificent idea, but he couldn't get it through the appropriate committee. Another blind eye had been turned to an opportunity for progress.

In 1998 Tiriac recognized Henman's achievements. 'Henman is a man on his own, he is professional, a man with decent morals if what I see is right,' he said. 'The LTA may have a lot of money, more money than they really know what to do with, but that's not the point here because Henman gives them something their money can't buy. It's the identification of the English people with a potential champion. That cannot be bought.'

Elsewhere, the story was much less upbeat. A couple of the Brits in their mid and late twenties, who had forced their way into the public's consciousness at Wimbledon, were debating retirement while a few more were considering a coaching career. Mark Petchey was one of the never-quites – a twenty-eight-year-old who should have done more as a player, who was thinking now of bowing out. Petchey had learned how to survive the rigours of the international circuit, he had been there, experienced the 'satellite syndrome' and had broken into the world's top 100 – no mean achievement at any time. If Petchey had decided to go into coaching he should have been high on the LTA's list of people to inspire a generation uncertain of how to take the opportunities that the sport offered. But there was little chance of that, even when several of the country's supposedly promising tyros were being rebuked for their lackadaisical approach to the profession at the time.

In November 1998 the National men's title was won by Danny Sapsford, a twenty-nine-year-old doubles specialist who only decided to enter at the last minute because Henman and Rusedski weren't there, who had quit tennis for three years earlier in the decade, who was a smashing bloke but, in tennis terms, an honest grafter.

So who would be left to pick up the pieces if either of the top two either faded away, lost interest, or simply buckled under the pressures generated by the relentless lifestyle of the modern tennis pro? The chances were that Rusedski and Henman could look forward to another five or six years at the top by which time the LTA would have to have discovered someone out there, or run the risk of total ridicule.

John Lloyd, the last golden boy of the British game – who had been brought back into the domestic fold as coach to the Davis Cup team under the captaincy of his elder brother David – underlined the gravity of the situation. 'When you think that Greg wasn't raised in England, we have one home-produced male player in the top 100 and if you take into consideration the amount of money that's been spent on development – regarding it purely as a business proposition – then people should be looking out for their jobs,' he said. 'The profile of the top two is such that people who are in powerful positions have been getting away with the horrendous situation that exists below them.'

The conservative British press, which had been against Rusedski when his switch from Canada was first mooted had, by and large, been converted the moment they realized they were on to a winner. I returned to the mainstream of the sport in 1998 after seven years at the sharp end of football reporting, to find tennis more exhilarating, more exhausting, and, vitally for a journalist, a hundred times more relevant.

For years, the British tennis writers had been treated on the sport's circuit as one would a slightly dotty relative. The ten or so full-time correspondents were able to travel extensively and the tournaments across the vast spread of the sport greeted us with open arms, because we were *de facto* representatives of the greatest championship in the world. Having the British press, with their inextricable link to Wimbledon, in town, was seen as a means of giving their events greater credibility. What the foreigners couldn't work out was what we actually wrote about. When we told them we were just there to cover the tennis, they looked at us as if we'd landed from Mars.

Henman and Rusedski changed that perception. From the mid-1990s, the British press had no reason to frown when they were shown the ranking lists. We had decent players. Top-ten players. Potential champions. People looked up to us. Tim and Greg made us feel we were much more than an idiosyncratic bunch who took some grim, masochistic pleasure in chronicling the nation's sporting inadequacies before turning our attention to the latest McEnroe outburst.

For the first time in years, the American journalists weren't able to deride their British colleagues with their less than subtle brand of ironic cynicism – for a start, even though they had had the No.1 men's player in the world for the past five years, Americans didn't even appreciate him, so who were they to preach? It was the same with other countries. The great Swedes, Borg, Wilander and Edberg, had gone. Noah and Forget were past tense in France. The German duo Becker and Graf were apparently on the wane and the Italians didn't have a player to frighten anyone. Only the Spaniards gave as much as a suggestion of dominating the game.

For Britain however, Henman and Rusedski were vibrant. They were winning more matches than they lost and they were fiercely competitive in a world where you put yourself on the line the minute you walked out on court, with nothing to protect you save the graphite gadget in your hand. It could be a savage, uncompromisingly isolated existence. Step into that rectangle, peer over the net and do it on your own.

Every Monday, in common with the rest of the 1,300 or so tennis professionals, the position of the British pair in the world order was despatched across the wires, it flashed up on Ceefax, it was often the lead item on the half-hourly BBC radio sports news. 'What would there be to talk about in tennis if it wasn't for Henman and Rusedski?' asked Sky TV's veteran anchor man Bob Friend to one of his sports news readers in November 1998. 'Nothing,' came the reply.

And yet, was there a genuine understanding of what the two were achieving? From not having had a tennis player within a country mile of the top ten for decades, the public had little or no idea how to relate to Henman and Rusedski. They weren't helped by the few increasingly fanciful spin doctors who ran the sports sections of the national press going overboard at every minor shift in the pair's rankings. What did they know of the circuit's relentless grind? If Henman was No.12 one week and No.15 the next, it was supposed there was a terminal failure with his game; if he went back up the following week, he was the next Wimbledon champion for sure. This knee-jerk stupidity betrayed the real truth and the depth of the drama which unfolded with the year.

The ranking system itself isn't ideal, being based upon a player's best fourteen tournament performances over the fifty-two-week cycle but it would have to do for now. The bigger the championship (Wimbledon, Roland Garros, the United States Open and Australian Open the biggest, the ATP Tour's World Championships and Mercedes Super Nine tournament series not far behind), the more points at stake, and the further you progress in these, the more points you earn. Bonus points are awarded to take into account the level of the player you beat – for instance, a win over Pete Sampras is worth an awful lot more than if you defeat Chris Wilkinson. If you do well at a tournament one year the points accrued there are deducted on the anniversary of your success, so it is crucial to achieve a consistency across the months. A lapse of form or a bad injury at a time when you have points to defend, and your ranking can suffer terrible damage.

It is damned hard to break into the top twenty players in the world, even harder to stay there. At the onset of 1998, Rusedski was ranked No.6 – there had never been a British player higher since official rankings were introduced a quarter of a century ago – and Henman was No.17. There was an awful lot to play for. The first Grand Slam of the year, the Australian Open, was bearing down fast.

Would either of them prevail? Could one of them win a major championship? Both were content with their lot and their English coaches, Henman with David Felgate whom he had first met in 1992; Rusedski with Tony Pickard, the former coach to Stefan Edberg. Rusedski had come closest in 1997, reaching the final at Flushing Meadows before losing to Australia's Patrick Rafter in four sets. Henman and Rusedski both had their sights set higher. They believed that nothing was beyond them.

1   Birth Signs

Greg Rusedski was born on 6 September 1973 and, precisely a year later, Tim Henman popped into the world. Both Virgos, of course, but so far removed in background, character, personality, attitude, everything, it was difficult to believe they were under the influence of the same star sign.

Rusedski was born in Montreal to Tom and Helen Rusedski, whose antecedents were Ukrainian, though Helen was born in Dewsbury, Yorkshire, so charmingly referred to by Greg in his whiplash Canadian accent as Dooseberry. Henman was born in Weston-on-the-Green, Oxfordshire, to Jane, a dress designer and Tony, a solicitor, a family with tennis coursing through its genes.

Tim didn't appreciate being continually reminded that his maternal great grandmother, Ellen Stanwell-Brown, was the first woman to serve overarm at Wimbledon and that grandmother Susan Billington was the last to serve underarm. (How ironic, then, that Henman's service would become the most debated component in his tennis armoury in the year ahead.) His grandfather, Henry Billington, a farmer by trade, represented Britain in the Davis Cup in the late 1940s and quite often played against a young Oxford scholar, Geoffrey Cass, who was to become both a knight of the realm and president of the Lawn Tennis Association. 'Henry had a terrific fluency, he was a great match player, a great fighter and I'm sure whatever Tim inherited from his father and mother, who were both excellent sports people in their

own right, he definitely had his grandfather's determination, talent and
will to win,' said Sir Geoffrey.

The Henmans, a polite, good-natured, upper middle-class family,
are about as truly representative of the English Home Counties tennis
ethos as it is possible to find. Jane Henman played in the old National
junior championships at Wimbledon, Tony was of county standard and
from the time they could walk, their three sons, Michael, Richard and
Timothy, played on the grass court in the back garden of the family
home.

It was a scenario far removed from the Rusedskis. Greg was first
bitten by the tennis bug when he was six, watching his father play at
the Clear Point Tennis club in the Montreal west-island community of
Pointe Claire. Helen and Tom Rusedski encouraged Greg and his elder
brother by three years, Bill, to attend art classes and take music lessons,
but also to try their hand at as many sporting activities as they could fit
in. Both boys loved tennis. Baseball and soccer were second and third
favourites (though whether it was in Canada that Greg first became a
devotee of Arsenal FC and a loyal Gooner – which aggravated the hell
out of David Felgate, who had been a season-ticket holder at Highbury
for years – isn't known).

Greg had a natural affinity for tennis and started to enter tournaments at the age of ten, but at home, he frequently lost to his brother,
who knew how to exploit his younger sibling's temper and impatience.
It was difficult to see from where Greg got his build, for Mum was five
foot three, Dad five foot nine, while Greg sprang to six foot three.
Mum didn't play the game but was the left-handed one while Dad
played moderate club tennis, and it was he who first recognized the
potential in his younger son and determined to make the utmost of it.

The two of them would spend hours perfecting every single facet of
Greg's game. Dad would set up tin cans as targets – his younger son
would have to try to knock them over. Tom Rusedski kept meticulous
notes on all Greg's shots, and strove to make them better. The two
formed an unbreakable bond. Greg's father, more than anyone, took the
credit for laying the foundations of a serve which would become the
single most powerful shot in the world.

Starting out in competition, Greg lost in the final of his first two
provincial under-12 tournaments to someone who was to become a
long-time rival, Sebastian Lareau of Boucherville, Quebec, going
down 6–0, 6–1 and 6–0, 6–0. A couple of years later, stiffened rather
than demoralized by the emphatic nature of those defeats, he had
improved enough to win the Canadian under-14 championship,

beating Robert Janecek in the final. But the physical growth spurts between the ages of fifteen and seventeen which fashion many a sporting career caused Greg to be hampered both by injuries and an awkwardness in mobility.

These twin considerations were enough for the selectors to choose Lareau, Janecek, Sebastian LeBlanc and Daniel Nestor as the Canadian side for the 1989 world junior team championship, the Sunshine Cup. When Lareau and LeBlanc paired to win the French Open and Wimbledon junior doubles titles a year later, Rusedski again felt left on the sidelines. These decisions undoubtedly prepared him for the isolation he would find as his career developed. Undaunted, he defeated Nestor later that summer to become Canada's under-18 champion.

In 1991, he made his first appearance at the All England championships winning the boys' doubles with Karim Alami of Morocco, and reaching the semi-finals of the singles, a performance he was to repeat at the US Open in New York.

It was on his eighteenth birthday, 6 September 1991, that he decided to turn professional and head for his first satellite tournament, in Israel. He was beaten early in both singles and doubles. What was to come of him? 'It was so demoralizing at the time and I remember thinking, what am I going to be like on the main tour if I can't even win a satellite? I wondered if I should continue to play, or go back to school,' he said.

'I was utterly despondent, I was in a nowhere tournament, in a nowhere town, I didn't know anyone and I was already out of everything. I was ready to quit and take the next flight home.' The words of encouragement he required – 'take a couple of days off, go to the beach, then see how you feel' – came from the first in his long line of coaches, Bud Schultz of Boston, Massachusetts, sports psychologist Wayne Halliwell, from Montreal, and his own family. 'The following week I reached the final, I won the last two tournaments,' he said, 'and ended up winning the satellite circuit.'

That upsurge in fortunes meant trips to Guam, the United States, France and China. 'Apart from the fact that winning the satellite gave me a lot of experience, it also made me hungrier and tougher and that carried me through,' Rusedski said. 'My parents supported me, underwriting the cost of travelling, coaching and hotels and although they never said anything, I knew they were taking a big risk and that made me fight even harder. I didn't have the support of the tennis federation at home either. There's nothing like knowing that if you don't win you don't eat to make you practise and play harder. If it's handed to you on a plate like it is with some of the younger players, where's the motivation? It's not a disaster if they lose. It was for me.'

At the end of 1991, Rusedski was No.603 on the computer rankings, and a year later, he was No.158, partly on the strength of a victory in a $75,000 Challenger on the grass in Newcastle in mid-July. Sensing he may have started off on a steep upward curve, Rusedski flew to Toronto for the Canadian Open where he had to play his first-round match within hours of stepping from the plane. He was probably high on adrenalin – or perhaps the in-flight service was too good to be true – for he defeated fellow Canadian Martin Laurendeau 7–6, 3–6, 7–5, then upset the reigning US collegiate champion Steve Bryan in straight sets the following day.

'I was on such a high after that Newcastle victory, and playing on the grass doesn't punish the body that much for someone with my style of game,' he said, relishing the praise he was receiving in Canada. That style was to become the Rusedski hallmark: the sweeping left hander's serve and the rushing of the net. Sometimes naïve and headstrong, he was too bold, and he had to learn to curb his wildness. On the third day of his Toronto adventure, however, he was to confront the best returner in men's tennis, Andre Agassi. It was only three weeks since the American – who still had a flowing mane of flaxen hair – had won Wimbledon to such unadulterated acclaim. Rusedski's effort was gallantry personified, but he lost 6–4, 6–1.

It was then that the pace of the game, the travelling and the demands of trying to live up to his family's expectations caught up with the teenager. 'After Toronto, I was injured for about two months. My back and my hips were especially sore,' he said. 'I'd been on the road for five months, with just a single day at home, and I'd played too much. My body had to mature, I had to get physically stronger, and I took the time off to strengthen myself with a new physical trainer.'

Pat Etcheberry was not a bad catch. The American had had two No.1s, Pete Sampras and Jim Courier, on his client list before now, and if anyone could get Greg in shape, he was the man. The arrival of Etcheberry was the first in the fascinating series of examples as to how Tom Rusedski would influence every aspect of his son's career. Rusedski Snr had also asked Australia's former Wimbledon singles finalist Fred Stolle and the legendary Pancho Segura to take an interest in Greg and the response was favourable, although their contributions were relatively short-lived.

Tom Rusedski made sure Greg was exposed to the toughest competition, which meant playing in the juniors on the USTA circuit – in

America, not Canada. 'When I was younger, I always went to the States to play,' Greg recalls, 'because of the competition. You would get 128 draws with about fifty kids who could all play at your level, which made a big difference.'

Exposure to this kind of rivalry was fine, but it came at a price. The Rusedskis weren't rich by any means. Tom was a project development officer with Canadian Pacific Railroad in Montreal while Helen worked in market research. They had a modest home in Pointe Claire, hardly the means to support a son who needed to trot the globe for weeks on end if he was to fulfil his undoubted promise. Financial help was essential but, fortunately, Greg's personality was a saleable commodity.

Dad Tom knocked on the door of corporate heavyweights such as the late Paul Paré, the chairman of Imasco Ltd (a Canadian conglomerate, and parent company of Imperial Tobacco, sponsors of the Canadian Open) and Charles Bronfman, vice-chairman of Seagram, to ask if they would help set up events at which notable Montrealers, such as hockey legends Henri and Maurice Richard would attend. Greg met them there, and went into charm overdrive, not for the last time in his life.

Paré and Bronfman also put their hands in their own pockets, forking out well into six figures for the Rusedskis. They believed in Greg; they were thrilled that Canadian tennis could benefit from such a potential hero. They wanted to help subsidize his future.

All of these fiscal efforts helped the cause but the Rusedskis still had to mortgage and re-mortgage their home and take out substantial loans to support their son's tennis. Red ink was everywhere in the Rusedskis' financial forecasts; and although Greg earned $151,345 in 1993, there was the never-ending toll of expenses to be met. And, if Greg was really going to make it, he needed full-time assistance. Tom Rusedski decided that Keith Diepraam, a native of Houston, Texas, who reached the quarters of Wimbledon in 1965, was the right man. Diepraam had served Wayne Ferreira, an up-and-coming South African, for three years and Ferreira had reached No.9 in the world in 1992. But the Rusedskis wanted higher than that.

'My goal isn't to stop at No.50, it's to get into the top twenty by the end of the year,' Greg said. 'Realistically, I won't have a chance of that if I don't have somebody experienced like Keith with me. The financial demands of hiring a coach are really high for me and my family. But if I don't take that chance, I'll never know whether I could have gotten into the top twenty.'

By July 1993, the omens were good, certainly on the playing side.

Greg was twenty years old now, fearsome and formidable, afraid of no-one, and was being courted as the 'best Canadian in men's tennis history'. His serve was clocked at 127 mph (among the ten fastest on the circuit) and he became the first of his countrymen to win a tour event since 1967 by claiming the Hall of Fame title in Newport, Rhode Island.

Like the Kennedy dynasty in American politics, most of whose remaining family members had holiday homes in the town, Newport was a perennial survivor on the men's circuit. The tournament had as much tradition as Wimbledon, and the grass courts were so good they could have been dug up and transported from London SW19. The week of tennis there served as a throwback to less ostentatious times. The International Tennis Hall of Fame, a place to which Rusedski aspired, had its headquarters in this quaint Rhode Island resort.

Rusedski arrived in buoyant mood, determined to make as many waves as he could. The Newport grass perfectly suited his game and he bulleted through, beating Argentine Javier Frana, ranked No.78, in the final. The world was beginning to become the Canadian's oyster.

Rusedski then defeated Richard Krajicek and Michael Chang to reach the semi-finals of the $1 million Seiko Super Indoor in Tokyo, Japan. The following week, in Beijing, he defeated Brad Gilbert and Sweden's Magnus Gustafsson, before losing in the final of the $300,000 Salem Open in Hong Kong to Chang, the Orient's favourite American.

It was there that the much-respected British journalist Richard Evans learned of Rusedski's dual nationality, and wrote a couple of articles suggesting the LTA should act because here was a player capable of winning and there weren't many of those about. 'I was ringing a bell, it was like "Hello, anybody there, anybody listening?" ' Evans said. 'I couldn't believe it – or maybe I could – when the LTA, instead of leaping at the chance, put out a statement saying they couldn't possibly get involved in paying anyone to come and play for Britain. Their reaction was laughable.'

On Rusedski's arrival at Montreal's Dorval Airport, he was treated to a hero's welcome. A mob of local media thirsted on his every word. Meanwhile, Tom and Helen Rusedski wondered how they would afford the next overseas trip. Helen Rusedski, not averse to letting the authorities have the sharp end of her tongue, thought aloud. 'The media has been fantastic,' she said. 'If we'd had as many offers from companies as we've had interest in the press, we'd probably have had at least three solid sponsors by now.'

Her son took up the theme. 'I've had four or five meetings with companies but none of them have come through,' Greg said. 'Some of the meetings I've gone to, they've actually said things were guaranteed and then nothing happened. You think to yourself, sure there's a recession going on in Canada, but there's a recession going on everywhere in the world, but you see guys like Thomas Enqvist who's now ranked No.50 and when he came out of juniors a few years ago, he had made about $250,000 in contracts. Now, he's making $250,000 a year just from clothing and rackets.

'I'm not looking for massive sums like that. I'm just looking for half of my expenses, I can take care of the other half. If I was an American like David Witt coming out of the juniors, in the top ten – which I was – I'd have half a million dollars and the USTA sponsoring me fully and paying my expenses.'

Air Canada, for instance, had refused to come through on a deal for Greg that the family had set their heart on. Tom Rusedski was infuriated. 'We're not looking for handouts, just to give the kid some passes to help him out,' he said. 'We're as normal as a family can be and in the circumstances, we're just trying to do as best we can. We're not an elite family like the Bassetts [Carling Bassett from the famous brewery house reached a career-high No.11 in the world in 1984] who had their child spend three years in Florida at Nick Bollettieri's academy, or whatever.'

Initially, the problem for the Rusedskis was way beyond their control. It was down to timing. John Beddington recognized their problem. Beddington had moved to Canada in the late 1970s and had become, to all intents and purposes, the man who made Canadian tennis tick. He was to rise to the heights of executive vice president of Tennis Canada and he was tournament director of the Canadian Open, both the men's and women's, which were staged with great success in Montreal and Toronto each August, as part of the build-up to the US Open. He knew the Rusedskis well.

In the late 1980s, the recession was biting the Canadian economy hard. 'When it struck in Canada,' Beddington recalled, 'it really hurt. They say when the United States catches a cold, Canada gets pneumonia – this was one of those times. It was also much harder coming out of the recession in Canada, to the extent the sponsorship in sport took a very big hit. Then, at the 1988 Olympics in Seoul, Ben Johnson won the gold medal and broke the world record for the 100 metres, but was almost immediately embroiled in a drugs scandal. When we knew that he had cheated, it was a terrible moment for sport in Canada. A lot of companies had sponsored Johnson and got burned. Most of them decided it would take a long time before they trusted individual sportsmen, and that really hurt Greg, who was just trying to make his way in the world.

'It is fair to say he didn't get the level of commercial support within Canada he could have done in other countries for the No.1 player. At the same time, tennis had never been flavour of the month as a sport in the country, and through the 1980s it had dropped in popularity, even when attendances at the Canadian Open were on the increase.

'It is arguable that Tennis Canada didn't support Greg as much as they should but, on the other hand, they had policies they were determined to adhere to. They weren't convinced, either, that Greg was going to be any better than any of the rest of the Canadian players. You could see the guy was going to be good, but just how good? There were half-a-dozen players around at the time, and it was decided they should be all treated equally.'

The Rusedskis weren't happy with that. Over the years, they constantly reminded Tennis Canada about the possible use of the British option while trying to seek a financial settlement which would have sustained the status quo. The Canadians weren't prepared to play ball.

Beddington said: 'Tennis Canada were asked to come up with a figure somewhere in the region of $250,000 a year for a three-year deal for which Greg would play the Canadian Open, play Davis Cup and be available to promote the sport in Canada. It wasn't that Tennis Canada wouldn't come up with the money, they couldn't. It is money that would have had to have been be taken out of a lot of other programmes – making all of it available to the Rusedskis just couldn't be justified, whatever Greg's promise. Greg playing Davis Cup for Canada would have been very helpful – as for the Open, I had been running it for seventeen years and I'd never had problems getting a good field, so Greg's appearance wouldn't have made any difference. He wouldn't have sold any more tickets.'

Beddington recalled telephoning and meeting Ian Peacock, the LTA's chief executive, frequently over a period of a couple of years about 'The Rusedski Matter'. 'Ian was very straight about it,' Beddington said. 'He told me that the LTA had made no offers, and if Greg chose to move to England, they would embrace him, but there would be nothing extra on the plate.'

Beddington went on to discuss Rusedski's decision to change his domicile. 'I personally believe that, as much as it had to do with tennis, Greg was enamoured of Lucy Connor (the English girl with whom he

became smitten when she was a ballgirl at a junior tournament in 1990).
He was in love and that was crucial. Of course, there was a large oppor-
tunistic element in the move, which would have been there had Lucy
existed or not. But love definitely played its part. And, also whereas
Tennis Canada couldn't come up with anything else to persuade the
Rusedskis to stay – there was a lot of encouragement from a lot of
people in Britain to Tom and Greg.

'It is ironic that had Greg decided to stay and represent Canada, I
undoubtedly believe he would have done better for himself in terms of
endorsement deals, made a lot more money, and been a real hero in the
country. I don't believe he'll ever achieve the same level of income from
endorsement deals in Britain. He could have been earning between
$500,000 and $1 million off court – which he isn't doing here [in
England].'

That, of course, was one man's supposition, but a man who had been
involved in tennis on all sides – Beddington worked for Mark
McCormack's hugely influential International Management Group
(IMG) in the Cleveland headquarters in the 1970s – and knew how the
tennis machinery worked. There were others in the personal management game who argued vehemently that Rusedski would never have
been as powerful, personality wise, or financially, if he had stayed in
Canada. Rusedski himself just wanted to play, and repay.

'My parents have given everything and it hasn't been easy on my
older brother either,' Greg said. 'He's had to give up a lot. Bill wanted
to try tennis himself and my parents had to make a decision when I was
thirteen, and he was sixteen, as to whom they would offer financial
support for tennis. It's difficult to choose one kid over another at such
a young age. My brother has been very understanding. If I can get into
the top twenty and make half a million dollars, I'd get rid of my
parents' debts and give something back to Bill.

'But I decided to give myself a cut-off point. If I wasn't in the top
twenty by the time I was twenty, I was going to quit and get a job, or
go to university and study the law.'

Rusedski opened 1994 – the year in which he turned twenty-one –
with a world ranking of No.48, but by the end of it, he had slipped to
No.117 and needed sorting out.

Rusedski was still aiming tennis balls at tin cans in his back garden
when Tim Henman first came to national attention. At the age of ten,
he was selected among the initial intake for a tennis scheme funded by
renowned businessman Jim Slater, who found a willing soulmate and
investor in David Lloyd, the former British Davis Cup player who was

later to become team captain. Lloyd had embarked on the journey to multi-millionaire status by constructing a series of tennis centres within easy reach of the M25, giving him enormous influence in the sport and beyond. Slater and Lloyd became a dream ticket for the British game.

In many eyes – certainly those at LTA HQ – Lloyd was a trouble-maker, always sniping at the tennis authorities and claiming – with what many regarded as good reason given the paucity of tennis success – that he could do their jobs better than they could. Now he was taking an opportunity to add some substance to the bravado.

Lloyd had long believed that junior tennis in Britain was in a disas-trous state and needed a fresh sense of direction. Slater had initially spoken to Paul Hutchins, then British Davis Cup captain, about setting up such a scheme under 'official' auspices, but his offers of help had been politely declined. When the Slater Scheme was announced in 1984 with Lloyd at its helm, a lot of people inside the establishment hoped it fell flat on its face.

Hutchins didn't reckon on the need for pushy outside influences. It wasn't the stuff of LTA *realpolitik*. Lloyd said: 'The negativity he received from the LTA got Jim Slater riled. He had had phenomenal results when he put money into promoting chess and he felt he could do the same for tennis. His was what I called the "laser-beam approach". He pinpointed his target, cutting away at all the peripheral rubbish – i.e. if there was only one person good enough, just work with him.

'All he wanted to do in tennis was to act as the catalyst for change. We were so successful in our little way that it did alter the thinking inside the LTA, but to this day, no-one says "Oh, by the way, the reason we look at kids as young as nine or ten these days is because Slater and Lloyd proved it was the right approach." I remember being told we couldn't possibly succeed with kids that young, that we couldn't know how good they would be at nine or ten. I disagreed totally. All you had to do was go and look at the results of the Orange Bowl [World Youth championships] under-12s and I bet 50 per cent of the kids became world-class players, the list was like a *Who's Who* of tennis. You didn't have to be a brain surgeon to work it out, you only had to look. It was fact.

'These were under-12s, so why were we picking kids at fourteen when every single sport psychologist since the year dot said that the way they were moulded started when they were nine years old?' The LTA's official reaction was that the scheme was all right in its way, but that it probably wouldn't work. Give it a couple of years and the loud-mouthed Lloyd would get his comeuppance and good riddance.

While there was undeniably a hint of 'I'll show 'em' in Lloyd's planning, the plain fact was he did show 'em. He began by employing the best tennis coaches available, the New Zealander Onny Parun, Donald Watt, Nick Brown, Roger Becker and his younger brother Tony. ('Who did the LTA have in those days? No one,' Lloyd insisted.) Academic excellence was also considered vital, and Reeds School in Cobham, Surrey was selected, where the boys would be boarders. They would play tennis at dawn, follow a normal school timetable, and then practise in the evenings. There would be no place for skivers.

The original intake was eight kids with stars in their eyes. Lloyd selected the nine-, ten- and eleven-year-olds he believed had the most natural talent, as well as the heart and spirit to want to excel at tennis players, to stay the course. 'I was quite brutal in the method of selection, we wanted those who wouldn't fold at the first sign of hard work,' he recalls. 'We brought in an army sergeant from Sandhurst who was even more brutal, the kids were absolutely cream crackered at the end of the day and that's the way it should be. I wanted them to leave every training session almost on their knees, but wanting to come back the next day.

'The choice of school was vital, and Reeds was excellent. We wanted a boarding school so the boys would be mixing with other kids, to make them more well-rounded as people. If they had just been ten isolated kids, it could have been boring as hell, but they integrated well, and played other sports too. Everything except rugby – we didn't want them battered and bruised. Tim was a smashing all-rounder, I think he would have been good at anything.'

Lloyd had wanted to cast his net wider through the British population, looking for those kids who had never picked up a racket but who had an innate athletic ability. 'The reason we aren't as good at tennis as we should be,' he said, 'is because too many second-class athletes play tennis. I wanted to get in amongst those kids where tennis had never been brave enough to jump before. But, when I gave it more thought, I decided we should narrow the field and we chose those youngsters who had at least shown a tendency towards tennis.'

If Lloyd had been climbing trees in an orchard seeking the crunchiest, crispest fruit, he couldn't have come up with ten better apples. In the first year of the Slater Scheme, Lloyd's inductees won every single under-12 and under-14 national title going. In time, Jamie

Delgado, regarded as the pick of the bunch, would win the under-14 Orange Bowl in Miami, Florida, the most prestigious title in junior tennis.

The LTA panicked, not for the first time. 'They said "we've got to do something about this",' Lloyd recalled, 'and suddenly, it became harder to pick kids, because they (the LTA) started to make it plain to parents that they wouldn't get into their teams if they joined us. Coxy (Mark Cox) and Richard Lewis definitely made it harder for me to persuade parents that their kids should join our scheme. That was short-sighted and stupid. The Slater Scheme cost me x thousands of pounds, it cost Jim Slater x number of thousands, we weren't getting anything back, so why did they think we were doing it? Because we loved tennis. Jim believed in our cause and so did I.

'I asked Ian Peacock if he would give it an LTA sanction and he said he would if the LTA's coaches would become involved. I told him that the reason the scheme was successful was because there weren't any LTA coaches involved. That was it, quite straightforward. I wasn't asking for financial support from the LTA, just their stamp of approval. I said, "Ours is working, yours isn't, why can't you see that?" '

Not all the Slater Kids made the grade, but Lloyd was delighted that they turned out, all of them, to be decent human beings. James Baily burst into the cosmos when he won the Australian junior title in 1993 (before deciding less than a year later to quit the game); Martin Blackman went to university, got his degree, and played to high county standard. 'They're not all burned out, washed up layabouts, none of that crap,' said Lloyd. 'They are all decent members of society, exactly the way we wanted them to turn out.

'I just wanted the LTA to try something different, experiment, change their ways. We showed them the way it could be done. If they kept doing the same thing and it didn't work, as had been the case for years, then it couldn't be right. There was a breakdown somewhere in junior development, so why not examine it and come up with new ideas. That's what we did.' While the scheme was a success, nobody realized that it would be Henman's star that was to burn the brightest.

'There were probably only ten lads out there who would be any good at tennis, so don't have 100 on the course, have ten. In fact, have eight, so two don't get on until they've worked their arses off. The LTA's defence is that they do things for the good of the game and that's fine in its way, but if you want better players, I don't agree that you should put all standards of people in the same class and the top brings up the bottom. I believe the bottom brings down the top. Jim and I believed in pin-pointing an elite, because then you'd get an elite and more people would want to achieve.'

When Henman's parents first read about the Slater Scheme, they might well have thought it was too radical, too risky for their ten-year-old son to be allowed to join. But Tim was showing the first signs of the independent streak which was to hold him in such excellent stead as his career progressed. He knew that this was what he wanted.

With a tinge of reluctance, his parents let him go; largely because they were satisfied that at Reeds School, he would receive an excellent education and the right pastoral care. Lloyd recalls: 'We had world class coaches, excellent facilities and the boarding-school back up and the kids would get to play other sports at the same time. We weren't just bombarding them with tennis. And, at that stage, we were the only ones with such a scheme for kids so young.'

In the case of Henman, Lloyd was encouraged with the ten-year-old's attitude. 'In my opinion, he had what it took to be good. He was selfish – in a nice way – and I knew he would have been good at any sport because he had that ability to think, to try, never to give in and the ability, fundamentally, to do the right thing under the most intense pressure. He believed in himself, he had a massive heart and it hurt him badly to lose.

'He was injured for a year at the age of eleven and we kept him going, even though he couldn't play. He came to my club for nine months but couldn't hit a ball because of the damage to his right arm. We took him to the gym, we trained him mentally, trained his legs, but there was no way the doctors would allow him to hit a ball. He saw the other kids playing and it used to break his heart, it really hurt. I'm not sure, in retrospect, that the whole episode didn't make him a better, hungrier player.

'His desire grew, I'm sure. He wanted to succeed badly enough anyway and that was good to see. I believe you can spot that really young. He never put in a bad practice session and Tim was always first off the bus in the morning, first to be changed, and first on to the court, wanting to play.'

'However difficult it was to let him go at the age of ten, it was probably even harder when he reached 14,' Lloyd recalled. 'At that stage, the family had to make the choice between Tim staying with us or going on to concentrate more fully on his education. They believed in my assessment that their son had it in him to be very good at the sport and I remember Tim being adamant that this was what he wanted to do. He had as much influence over his parents at that stage of his life than I did.'

Yet, perhaps blinded by the need to give the scheme major credibility, Lloyd concentrated much of his time and energies on Delgado, who had been picked out as his real hope of a breakthrough. As a player himself in the 1960s and 1970s, Lloyd wasn't blessed with the natural flair of his brother John, and Delgado wasn't the most fluent stroke maker in the group but he had spunk. Lloyd liked his Latin temperament, the brooding, brilliant, slightly arrogant style. 'If you have a talented one who is a trier as well, like McEnroe,' he said, 'you have an 80–90 per cent chance of having a champion. I felt we could harness Jamie's Latinesque abilities, and to a degree we succeeded. He won the Orange Bowl at fourteen, but we didn't capitalize on that and I felt we failed there. I think he has gone on too long now, flirting around the edges of the professional game. In terms of being right up there, he's history.

'Tim, on the other hand, has surprised me. I really didn't think he would get to where he has in the world. It just goes to show that even I'm not always right about everything.'

It was when Lloyd was channelling all his efforts into Delgado that the Henman family began to wonder whether their son's best chance to fulfil his potential was inside the Slater Scheme. Around that time, Tony Pickard, Stefan Edberg's coach and one of the most respected tacticians in the game, was in contact with Jane and Tony Henman, suggesting that he might take an interest in their youngest son's development.

The Henmans, who had long known Pickard, fretted about the overtures, but had been persuaded by their son's enthusiasm and desire to stay with Lloyd's Lads. They weren't to know that Pickard was to play a significant part in Tim's future progress – though never as intimately as he would have liked.

2 The Man with the Passport of Gold

The French national sports paper *L'Equipe* did not mince its words. '*L'homme au passport en or,*' it trumpeted. He was born a Canadian and, *voilà*, today he's English. It was for the best, the paper said. And for his bank balance.

An article, penned by correspondent Philippe Maria, traced Rusedski's story back to October 1993 when he was to be found seated on the terrace of the sports palace in the Chinese capital, Beijing, during one of his first tournaments as a professional. He was laughing a lot, almost uncontrollably. Maria remarked: 'In a French accent which smelt of the St Lawrence River, which reminds the writer of Charlebois [a famous singer from the French-speaking province of Quebec] Rusedski took his audience, from first to last, through the terms used by the Quebecois to describe certain tennis shots. Laughter filled the air.

'With his face like Courtemanche [a native of Quebec, who made his reputation in France with his ability to stretch his facial muscles into incredible contortions], Rusedski had everything going for him to become the most favoured player of all the Francophones in the world.' That was then.

The readers were transported forward to Tuesday 1 July 1997, to a corridor near the press interview room at Wimbledon, where Rusedski was responding to questions thrust at him after his defeat of American

Richey Reneberg, which meant a place in the quarter-finals against Cedric Pioline of France. One of the many microphones stuck beneath the famous grin was held by the journalist from the French radio station Inter, who asked whether Rusedski would mind saying a couple of words about his next opponent in French.

The refusal was categorical. 'Excuse me,' said the man of the moment, 'but I don't speak very good French.' Was Rusedski trapped by amnesia, Maria demanded to know? Was this the same man who had kept his French audience enthralled in Beijing four years earlier? Was this the bilingual Greg Rusedski?

Back 'home' in Canada, they wouldn't have been taken aback at Rusedski's reluctance to speak a language which came so naturally to him, given what they perceived as his determination to cut all links with the land where he'd grown up. Tom Tebbutt, the tennis correspondent of the *Toronto Globe and Mail* contributed to the argument with his sentiments that Rusedski wanted to 'erase the past from his mind.' It was as deep as that. 'It was Greg's right to make that choice,' Tebbutt said, 'but he didn't have to deny Canada so much. To become a real Brit, and to make profit from all the money on offer before Tim Henman arrived, he played the British card for all it was worth and that was very hard for Canadians to take.'

Maria's article in *L'Equipe* picked up the thread of financial motivation which was to dog Rusedski's move to Britain: 'When he realizes that his mother Helen was born in Dewsbury, a small locality in Yorkshire, it is too good to miss. Too good for Rusedski, who was looking for a country which could help him financially. Too good also for England, which has been looking with increasing desperation for a player who can wear the national colours with pride, and get results. In a few months, the deal is done. From this moment, Greg Rusedski did everything he could to become more English than he really is. He will hesitate for nothing, not even playing his first Wimbledon with a Union Jack bandanna on his forehead. England fell in love, Rusedski took the money.

'At this moment, Tim Henman pokes his nose in. Between the imported product and the pure juicy certified "Brit" from Oxford, England didn't hesitate. The sponsors put their money on the native. Greg Rusedski had to face a new rival. Rusedski, of course, had then to do more and more.

'Since the start of this [1997] Wimbledon, the young English who have watched his matches, have bought their cardboard visors, but not put them across their foreheads, but above their mouths, with two big teeth drawn on them, like a vampire. The pro-Rusedskis prefer to see this as a player with a great appetite. For the others – we will let you guess.'

Tom Rusedski had been having misgivings about the way Canada treated his son for a long time. If Greg was to have the opportunity to reach his fullest potential, he had to stretch his wings and – at home – the family's opinion was that they were constantly being clipped.

Rusedski junior was, as *L'Equipe* intimated, living in England and loved the place. He felt it brought the best out of him, and, with a piece of exquisite timing, he set eyes on Lucy Connor across a tennis court when she was a ballgirl, and was entranced. Everything was falling into place. Their first official date was at the Wimbledon Champions' Dinner at The Savoy in 1991 after he had won the junior doubles with Morocco's Karin Alani. England was coming alive for him. Rusedski was seventeen, Lucy fifteen – 'even though she said she was older,' Greg remarked. An English girlfriend might have made the potential transition a whole lot easier for him to bear, but what made him so attractive was that he had that precious something British tennis had long lacked in a professional player. He won.

Back at Barons Court in south-west London, a lot had been heard of Rusedski. The powers-that-be knew of his British leanings but they couldn't be seen to be trying to influence a decision. The first move had to come from the Rusedskis, the LTA would not dare to make a pass in his direction – overt or otherwise – or the stench would never clear.

When it was discovered that Rusedski had paid back to Tennis Canada the $30,000 they had given him as a down payment on his talent – and thus cleared all his dealings with them – it was assumed that there was no going back. The call the LTA had been hoping for was put through to the office of Ian Peacock in the spring of 1995. Would the LTA be willing to support the Rusedski family's desire to apply to the International Tennis Federation (ITF) for clearance for Greg to switch his allegiance from Canada to Britain?

Peacock could easily answer for himself, for this was manna from heaven for a man in his position. Whether he could rally everyone at headquarters and keep tethered together an association which was certain to have stridently diverse opinions on such a controversial decision remained to be seen. It was bound to be difficult for Peacock as the LTA was an organization steeped in an amateur ethos, even though it needed a coherent commercial objective, charged as it was with transforming the huge sums earned from Wimbledon's phenomenal success into tangible evidence of progress. And, what better way to make the whole picture look good than a player who could survive and thrive in the cut-throat environment of professional tennis?

Here, in a Canadian brandishing a British passport, was a ready-made potential top thirty player on the doorstep, waiting to be welcomed across the threshold. What would the answer be – would he be embraced like a prodigal son or would the curtains be drawn, as if the occupants were sheltering from a Saturday afternoon visit from the Jehovah's Witnesses?

The resident British players were muttering from their positions of privilege. Who was this guy arriving from out of nowhere, claiming that Britain meant everything to him? Those who spoke out and others who kept their thoughts to themselves saw a carpetbagger, who was a little too eager to spout his love for Queen and country, while wresting away a few lucrative contracts which would, otherwise, have been theirs.

Previous experience of these situations in Britain suggested Rusedski would probably be off and out before the money well ran dry. But two men who couldn't afford to look such a gift horse in the mouth, had no doubts both about Rusedski's sincerity and that he would provide the kick up the backside the sport required. The buck stopped at Peacock, and he found a willing ally in former professional and now the Director of International and Professional Men's Tennis, Richard Lewis, who knew this was a God-sent opportunity, if the process was handled properly.

During Lewis' playing career, Colin Dowdeswell had decided to take up British nationality, having played for both Rhodesia and Switzerland. Dowdeswell met the criteria for switching countries, landed at the LTA, pledged unswerving allegiance to the Union Jack and became Britain's No.1 ranked player in 1984. He stayed for next to no time before unhitching the caravan, watering the ponies and heading for France.

Lewis didn't want the same situation to happen again. And there were already hints of unhappiness, especially among those players who didn't accept Rusedski's motives at grinning face value. Any suggestion that the Rusedski's had demanded money for Greg to come over and play for Britain, an allegation that the family, that Lewis – once treasurer and a member of the ATP Tour board – Peacock and everyone else connected with the move vehemently refuted.

'Never in a million years,' Lewis said as we sat in his Barons Court office, flanked with pictures of Tim and Greg. 'I couldn't have lived with myself, or faced anyone else in tennis if we had decided to pay money for Greg to come here. Imagine what horrendous problems it would have caused at the time, and would continue to cause now. And what's more, to put the record straight, money was never asked for either. The Rusedskis did everything completely right.'

Lewis, though, wanted to make sure there could never be recriminations. He needed to be assured that Rusedski wasn't going to accept British nationality and then dump on his new nation. He knew the established players would have to be convinced and that it wouldn't be the easiest task he had ever undertaken.

'I was able to make the case to the players that Greg would do them all a lot of good,' said Lewis. 'Actually, he's done them the world of good. I don't believe a single one of them lost out with his arrival. Sure, they might have gone down the Davis Cup pecking order, but he's given British tennis, and thus British tennis players, a higher profile and taken the game here to a higher level.

'If British tennis had stayed where it was much longer – and it was quickly going down in the public's esteem even though the rankings of our leading players were being maintained and, in some cases, improved – the sponsors would have been less and less inclined to stay involved. I don't even think Wimbledon would have been as successful as it has been in the past few years and, who knows, maybe Tim wouldn't have come through to be the force he is. Greg has helped Tim, and Tim knows that.'

Rusedski had taken the attic in Lucy's parents' house, so he was domiciled in Britain and he routinely practised at Queen's Club. He was much more comfortable in England than in Canada and he carried a British passport. He was a client of Mark McCormack's prestigious IMG after a spell with Advantage International, and when the move to London had to be smoothed out, IMG turned to their London-based tennis specialist Jan Felgate. The surname was intriguing. Jan Felgate was the American wife of David, Tim Henman's coach.

It had to be said that Canada didn't exactly bid Rusedski farewell with tears streaming down its cheeks. Daniel Nestor was one Canadian who was thrilled to see him go. Nestor was a better than decent player – ten years on the Tour was testament to that. He had, ironically, been born in Belgrade, Yugoslavia, and raised in Ontario. It suited Nestor for Rusedski to leave in 1995, so he wasn't distressed at the parting, only in its manner. 'I think he could have handled his departure a little better,' recalled Nestor. 'He said that he had felt

British his whole life. I grew up with him from the under-12 age group and I don't ever remember him mentioning Britain until three months before he left.

'He was a Canadian player on the ATP Tour, but he didn't play for his country in the Davis Cup when he could have, so the rest of the guys felt that something was up. There were rumours flying around for a while. It wasn't so much of a shock when it actually happened. What upset so many of us was that he never explained himself.

'I don't think he was that sorely missed as far as the guys were concerned. He kept himself very much to his own group of people, his parents and his girlfriend. The Canadian players respected him as a player, he had shown what he was about. Personally, I didn't really care what he did, it didn't affect my life at all. I just felt bad for those who had helped him through his career in Canada.

'I know that the British guys didn't exactly welcome him with open arms. The locker room talk was that he was taking their spots, and he wasn't an easy guy to have around.'

Nestor went on, 'I have a lot of respect for Tim Henman, both on and off the court, a nice guy, a gentleman as you guys like to call him. He will joke around, he doesn't get caught up in his own success, he's the same guy if he's winning or losing.'

It was Greg's desire which so entranced the British public, for they hadn't had a player with both desire and talent for years. Ian Peacock recalled all those tough – or should that be trough – times.

'It was obvious that if Greg was going to fulfil his potential, England was the place to do it,' Peacock said to me in the middle of 1998. 'The opportunities to cash in were excellent, far greater than Canada. The opportunity to have a British player in the top fifty was like a miracle. Jeremy [Bates] was briefly in the top forty, but the idea of a player capable of sustaining a top fifty spot was tremendous and would enable him to earn a lots of rewards in terms of sponsorships, endorsements and the like.

'There were all these things going on in Greg's mind. He was locked into a family living in Lucy's parents' home in Purley, he had a strong relationship with his girlfriend, he liked Britain, there were excellent facilities at Queen's Club, with all the medical mod-cons. I talked a lot of this over with Tom, and Greg was really keen to make the move permanent.

'I had been through agonies before with Monique Javer [who came from the United States in the late 1980s, armed with a British passport] which looked such a good idea at the time, and then all went pear-shaped. There were problems for as long as she was British, we never really sorted them out. The Colin Dowdeswell experience had also left a bitter taste in a lot of mouths at the LTA. We were assured it wouldn't happen this time.

'So, yes, the background of people changing nationalities and taking over the Union Jack had not been good and, in truth, it wasn't very LTA to do it in the first place. I have to admit that personally, I was always very committed to Greg, in encouraging him to come because I felt we needed him. Tim Henman wasn't even a twinkle in David Felgate's eye, and the thought of having someone who would be a flag-bearer for the game was something we really needed to drive on everything else we were trying to do.

'I went over to the States [on behalf of the LTA] and talked to Tom and even that journey caused ructions inside the LTA. They thought we were going overboard. I had to make them see sense. Some of our coaches felt like the youth team manager at Chelsea must feel when Vialli goes out to sign another megastar from Inter Milan – "here I am working with a group of talented young players, trying to get them into the first team and somebody else comes along from another country and takes my spot."

'I think Ian Barclay [the Australian who had coached Pat Cash to his memorable 1987 Wimbledon triumph and was now working for the LTA at the National School at Bisham Abbey] felt he had a group of young players including Martin Lee and James Trotman, and that this was a kick in the teeth for them. That instead of them being able to go on and try to get the No.1 spot, we were importing someone to take that on.

'Throughout the LTA at that time, there was a good deal of animosity. There was a feeling that it smacked of desperation, that we couldn't develop a No.1 of our own, so we had to go out and find a Canadian with a British passport. I thought that that was so negative. I thought it was worth giving it a go. I didn't see a top fifty player in the ranks, and here was a chance. It merited all the criticism.'

But the LTA's chief executive and Director of International and Professional Men's Tennis alone couldn't make the move a reality. This wasn't a click your fingers and everything would turn out fine job. It had to be sanctioned by the ITF, the governing body of world tennis, and it wouldn't be the cake-walk many people had hoped for.

The ITF wanted to look into every detail of Rusedski's move before it granted him its equivalent of the green card. Rusedski had lived in Purley for three years – the requisite time for someone to show they meant to stay – he had rejected Canada's overtures for him to represent the country of his birth in the ITF's baby, the Davis Cup, so there was nothing holding him there; he had a British passport and his mother had been born in 'Dooseberry', Yorkshire. He met all the technical criteria.

Rusedski's case came up in May 1995 at the ITF executive meeting held in Rome. The LTA – showing unusual prescience – had drafted a PR handout for the media to inform them that the ITF was going to sanction Rusedski's move and had handed it to a couple of noted journalists to give them time to work on their stories. *Daily Telegraph* correspondent John Parsons was reading the message when Ian Barnes, then ITF Director of Media Relations, happened to walk by and snatched a glance of the document over his shoulder.

Barnes, doing what a good professional should, immediately reported to his boss, ITF president Brian Tobin, that the LTA was assuming that Rusedski's move was already signed, sealed and delivered. Tobin took umbrage. 'He went spare,' said Peacock. 'It was a very difficult moment for me. I had to explain that the statement was something we wanted to have ready for publication in the papers the minute the announcement was made. We weren't trying to take the ITF for granted. But I really feared we might have blown it. Brian was a bit iffy about the whole idea anyway and our statement made him mad.'

Peacock remembers Tobin's tone. ' "We've got to vote on this," he said, "you shouldn't assume, very naughty etc., etc." I could understand his annoyance, nobody likes their decisions to be pre-empted. It was clumsy on our part. I couldn't tell you what a great relief it was when I got the call to say that Greg had got through.'

Back in Montreal, happiness contrasted with feelings of treachery and on this side of the pond it was time for the most important charm offensive of them all to move into overdrive.

Rusedski was being managed from IMG's Cleveland office at that time, but the switch in his affairs meant a change in his personal agent. Jan Felgate was assigned the reins. 'There was a transition time long before the final decision was made,' she said. 'I wanted to help the family meet the right people in Britain, I needed to try to help Greg win the media over, both the print and TV people.

'The family asked us to make all the right introductions, so they could make sure they were going to be happy with the arrangement and we wanted to do whatever we could to support Greg over here. If

I was going to be managing his day-to-day affairs, I wanted to be sure it would be a nice state of affairs for everyone. I used all the influences I had on behalf of IMG and Greg to put his case forward.'

But she discovered, to her dismay, a cross section of views as mixed as those when the idea of Rusedski's defection to Britain was originally mooted at Barons Court. 'The forward thinkers loved the thought of having such a talented player on British books, but certain players didn't think it was a good idea. They made their views known publicly and they took the hits for those views,' she said. 'I think, on the whole, people wanted to be receptive. It didn't take long for them to come around once they met the player himself.'

Absolutely. Rusedski was good grace and pleasant manners personified. Jan Felgate remembers the initial press conference in the grand clubhouse at Queen's Club, called to introduce Rusedski to his new compatriots. 'Greg was totally wonderful,' she recalls, 'charming to everyone. And, in turn, he was met with open arms. I was really proud of how he came across that day, I was proud to have been associated with him. If I had still to be convinced, I was convinced that day.

'I got to know his girlfriend Lucy and his family who are lovely people, I was assured that he wanted to live in Great Britain, raise a family here, that this was where he wanted to make his home. His motives were absolutely secure, no doubt about them. My job was very easy, because it wasn't difficult to open doors for Greg and do what I could to help him be accepted.'

Rusedski, who has continued to go through coaches and agents like a knife through butter, decided to switch management companies a couple of years after coming to Britain, leaving Jan Felgate and IMG for another firm which had a dynamic reputation in tennis, ProServ, which was to become part of the Marquee Group in 1998. Ian Peacock recalls: 'It was difficult for Jan Felgate to take care of Greg's management, but there were plenty of other talented people at IMG who could have taken him on. It was a case of him wanting to be the No.1 player somewhere else. ProServ didn't have much of a British operation at the time and I think Greg needed a stronger set-up to see him through his subsequent ups-and-downs rather more effectively.'

But Rusedski, as ever, was determined. 'If I saw Greg after we parted company, we always tried to have a quick chat,' said Jan Felgate. 'My kids think Greg's wonderful but we didn't really see him much after we split up unless our paths crossed at tournaments.'

Largely because she had her hands pretty full dealing with the burgeoning career of a client IMG rated a good deal higher than Rusedski, one Tim Henman.

3 Telford, Tashkent, Teacher and Tribulations

The National Tennis Championships would be written off as a nonsensical ritual in most corners of the world. And if Britain persisted with holding such an idiosyncratic event, couldn't the Lawn Tennis Association find somewhere with a bit of a tennis pedigree to stage it? The advertisements stacked around Centre Court in November 1998 read 'Discover Telford', 'Decide Telford', 'Think Telford.' I didn't see one for 'Why Telford?'

We were certain there had to be inhabitants of Shropshire's answer to the sixties New Town craze which appeared to the nominal visitor to be all car parks and roundabouts. A few of them managed to wend their way to the Tennis and Racket Club, just across the way from the Ice Rink, to take note of what was happening in British tennis each autumn, but as the years dragged on, the championship had lost its sponsors, TV had fallen out of love, press coverage had all but evaporated – even the die-hards must have wondered why they took the trouble. Especially when, in 1998, Tim Henman and Greg Rusedski decided the event was an irrelevance for millionaires. So, did 'The Nationals' have a place in an increasingly congested calendar? Absolutely not.

There was an eccentric mystique about it, but that was about all. The players got together and did a cabaret and the press responded with a party piece of their own. The year that Australian Warren Jacques was appointed British Davis Cup captain, the press prepared a spoof *This is Your Life*. The look on his face when he turned up to be greeted with the strains of the famous signature tune and yours truly carrying a big red book remains vivid to this day.

Well, you needed a sense of humour when you visited Telford, otherwise you'd cry. In 1996, there were seven British players in the top 200 in the world. A year later, there were five. By the end of 1998, it was down to three. And these had been 'successful' years for the game, courtesy of Henman and Rusedski. The timing of the event wasn't perfect either – the championships were held a week after the Wimbledon surplus was announced.

The scenes of apathy at the Nationals and the fraying of the edges of the British game, gave the newspapers plenty of ammunition for their annual ritual of 'Let's put the boot into the LTA.' It was a bit like kicking a man when he was down. But there was a serious meaning behind the negative inferences, as there had been for years. What was the LTA going to do with 1998's record £33 million on top of the previous year's £31 million, on top of £29 million before that, with more carriages being hooked onto the gravy train each year? Look around and what did we see of Britain's tennis future? Not much.

No Tim and no Greg meant no sponsor, and no sponsor meant that it would cost the LTA £165,000 to stage the event to reward a litany of players who – though many had shown progress as juniors – stopped progressing or simply gave up the ghost once they crossed the threshold into the senior ranks. It was a case of throwing good money at not very good players. Yet, despite the fact that the whole thing bordered on a farce, there was no sign that the event would be scrapped. The BBC turned up for the 1998 women's final, but they didn't stick around for the men's. No Tim, no Greg, no interest.

Greg Rusedski first stepped into this anachronistic torture chamber in October 1995, beaming bonhomie. It was a championship that, for nine of the previous ten years, had been won either by Andrew Castle or Jeremy Bates. Rusedski couldn't have known what he was letting himself in for.

There were those in the British camp who had already made their views on his arrival crystal clear. Mark Petchey had been around the British top five for several years, without ever breaking through as vibrantly on the international scene as his talents suggested he should. When Petchey first heard of Rusedski's move to Britain, he was outraged. And he didn't hide behind non-attributable whispers. He

came right out and said how he felt. A few years down the line hadn't
changed his strident views.

'The public seem to have responded well to him for the most part
and if that's good for British tennis, then that's great,' said Petchey.
'From a personal level, it's tough to relate to him because he's had
nothing to do with us. He just came in, out of the blue, and that was
tough for me, certainly.'

It was a feeling shared by many of Petchey's contemporaries.
Rusedski was an outsider, who didn't really try to be one of the boys –
and if he had, the boys would have made it difficult for him.

After the furore over his move to Britain, Rusedski had wanted to
settle as quickly as he could into a normal existence but the fates
conspired against him. His first appearance on 'home' soil as a 'home'
player was in the Stella Artois championship at Queen's in June and
wouldn't you know, the draw pitched him up against Petchey, his most
vociferous critic.

Petchey emerged from three tight, nervy sets with one of the most
satisfying victories of his life. 'Greg palmed off my reaction to him
coming to Britain, saying that I had the right to my opinion, which I
suppose was the smart thing to say,' Petchey said. 'I don't think he
would have put himself under more pressure by being critical of a
British player when he had just come. It was, though, an absolute pleasure to thump him.'

That year was Rusedski's first at Wimbledon under the British
banner, a real moment to cherish. On 26 June 1995, he arrived a touch
nervously on Court Three – Wimbledon was clearly making him wait
before making him feel at home. There, according to Paul Hayward of
the *Daily Telegraph*, 'he was greeted with the kind of low rippling
applause that attends the showing of a reasonably large marrow at a
horticultural show.'

After his third-round victory over Olivier Delaitre of France, he
was introduced to the press as 'Sir Gregory'. Andre Agassi commented
on how Rusedski's use of the words 'brilliant' and 'super' had shown
how much he had acclimatized. One suspected Agassi was being
sarcastic; Rusedski's change of tone, attitude and nation, was not
exactly cherished in the men's locker room.

Nevermind, in the open, he was totally proper. 'The British are a
very fair public,' he said. 'I just love the way the people are so nice and
polite. I love everything about Britain, the whole picture so to speak.
The culture, everything.' When it was put to Rusedski that not
everyone in Canada had been so well disposed to his decision, he

answered that other athletes in other sports had gone 'where their heart had been'.

At the same time as Rusedski's arrival on the British scene Tim Henman was just beginning to make his mark. David Felgate hadn't been expecting that much when he was called by Billy Knight in 1992 and asked if he might like to help with a second-string team of juniors at the LTA. Felgate, who had been in and around the pro circuit for years without representing much more than a blip on the ATP computer, was hoping to change his work definition. He spent a couple of years in the United States, but missed England and came back to assist Ian Barclay with the coaching at Bisham Abbey. When Knight, the manager of Men's National Training, called to say he was putting together a group of four players and wanted a coach to travel with them, it seemed just the job Felgate had coveted.

The 'first' team squad, sponsored by Laing, the building company, and under the tutelage of former Davis Cup player Nick Brown, included Andrew Richardson and Andrew Foster, a couple of six-foot plus players who had never really capitalized on their physical advantage. The group to which Felgate was assigned, was Nick Gould, Dan Sanders, Barry Cowan, and a fresh-faced stripling named Tim Henman.

Knight had asked David Lloyd if he wanted to keep the seventeen-year-old Henman in his Slater Scheme and the reply was that although Lloyd saw some potential in the player, the time was probably right for a change. Lloyd didn't see Henman breaking into the top 100. When Felgate met the teenager for the first time, he registered a big fat zero on the ATP computer and lost in the first round of Junior Wimbledon that year, 6–0, 6–1, to a Mexican kid who was never heard of again. From little acorns . . .

Of the four players in the Felgate group, Gould made the first spurt forward, showing the most promise. But there was something about Henman that Felgate hadn't seen in a British player for a long time. The kid had such a burning desire, a thirst for knowledge and a determination to better himself which wasn't the norm among his contemporaries. Without even thinking about it, Felgate found himself working more and more with Henman and, slowly, from the group situation, a one-on-one partnership evolved.

Tony Pickard who so coveted the chance seemed destined never to work specifically with Henman. When the young man broke his leg in three places in September 1993 and started a long period of enforced absence and rehabilitation, Pickard's term as Davis Cup captain was reaching its hiatus. The controversial coach had long been at logger-heads with the LTA and they parted company in 1994, after a hostile tit-for-tat exchange in the national press.

Knight was asked to step into the breach while a permanent successor was found and he agreed. Not surprisingly, his first move was to call on the fully-recovered twenty-year-old Tim Henman for his Davis Cup singles debut against Slovakia on clay in Bratislava. Talk about a bruising introduction. There was little way such an inexperi-enced player – and his even more inexperienced partner Miles Maclagan – could help prevent the 5–0 defeat (against two players, Karol Kucera and Jan Kroslak, hardly known at the time) which meant that Britain was hanging on to international credibility by its fingertips.

When Knight stepped aside, the new choice as captain – one widely welcomed as the LTA finally decided it would rather have him working from within than shouting the odds from outside – was David Lloyd. The man who had bequeathed Henman from the Slater Scheme, because he didn't believe he had quite enough about him to succeed at the highest level, was now given the chance to build a team around his blossoming potential. For the next tie, there was also to be a new name in the Great Britain team. Greg Rusedski.

Rusedski's Davis Cup debut was in a Euro–Africa Zone relegation tie against Monaco on the grass courts of Devonshire Park, Eastbourne. 'Davis Cup or the Olympics is the highest honour you can put on anybody,' he said. 'It's a dream come true to be a part of the British team'. [He had been unavailable through injury to Canada in 1992, when he was under contract to their Davis Cup squad]. I wanted to become British to play in the Davis Cup. I believe it's just a question of talent and time before we get back into the World Group.'

He revealed that there had been a constant stream of supportive letters filling his Wimbledon pigeon-hole. Well, forty-five to be precise, of which forty-two were on his side. One of the 'not so nice' ones suggested he get back on the next plane to Montreal. Rusedski demurred. He reached the fourth round at Wimbledon, losing to Pete Sampras, who had accounted for Henman a couple of stages earlier. But both had had a sample of what awaited them if they truly turned the corner.

But there was bad taste ahead. Much mileage was made of Rusedski arriving on court in a Union Jack bandanna – which had been presented to him to wear by the *Sun*, a paper which never fought shy of whipping up unashamed jingoism, even when the stooge had been born over 3,000 miles away. Whether the *Sun* or Rusedski knew that they had chosen Canada Day to milk the applause and support of his new found country, we don't know; but the hedonistic tone of his celebrations that afternoon went down like a plunge of bitter Arctic air in Montreal.

Rusedski was changing, more than slightly, in terms of his personality. He was one of the big boys now, and it was noted. When he had first played at Wimbledon as a Canadian junior back in 1991, he used to make a point of going into the referee's office and speaking in bubbling, charming tones to the girls there. Nothing was too much trouble for him. They thought he was wonderful because he was so natural and unaffected. He smiled, he made small talk and he was delighted when the girls presented him with the yellow board with his name on it to take home as a souvenir.

Time was to change that. The small talk days were coming to an end. Publicly, or at least when they turned on the switch, he was that grin personified; privately, he was becoming a consumate professional – some of those who had befriended him on the way up found that a little hard to take. Rusedski was to find that out for himself when he returned to Montreal in July 1995 for the Canadian Open.

Sebastian Lareau was a Rusedski contemporary in the juniors, had battled with him all the way through from the under-twelves to the under-eighteens. The crux of the matter was that Tennis Canada believed they had Rusedski under a three-year contract to represent the country in the Davis Cup, but they could do nothing to prevent his departure to Britain when the chips had been placed on the table.

'I hope the reception he receives this week will be very, very cold,' said Lareau. 'He does not deserve the support of the people he rejected.' Rusedski tried to play down Lareau's invective. 'That's his opinion and he's entitled to say what he wants. I hope the people cheer for me but I realize that that might not happen. I still have family and friends here and didn't think twice about coming.' You could not fault Rusedski for his courage, nor his manners.

Equally, you could hardly fault the likes of Diane Francis, the editor of Canada's business daily, the *Financial Post*, who wrote that Rusedski was a 'turncoat – a Brit of convenience. His reception in Montreal is sure to be icy. It is one thing to be ambitious and aspire to be world class. It's quite another matter to compete on behalf of a country of convenience.

'Greg Rusedski deserves the cold shoulder here in Montreal, where he was nurtured and coached and coddled by the tennis community. He has offended Canada.'

Most offence was taken at the way Rusedski had flaunted the Union Jack at Wimbledon that year. He apologized once again for his actions. 'It was a spontaneous gesture and I didn't think about how it would upset people,' he said. 'The flag was given to me by a journalist. It's not like I planned it, I didn't bring it on to court with me.' And once again, though his voice never raised above its usual courteous level, he had to defend himself against charges that he had only run to Britain for the money. 'It was a personal decision,' he said, repeatedly. He did well to get out of Canada with dignity intact.

Meanwhile, Henman was moving up the ranking list. There was a blip at Wimbledon in 1995, when he lost in the second round of the singles to Sampras and was then greeted with shrill headlines after being disqualified from the doubles with Jeremy Bates. His crime? To strike a ball in anger at losing a vital point just as a ballgirl was running across the net to field one that had landed on Henman's side. The ball caught her flush on the side of the head, stunning her and leaving referee Alan Mills with no alternative but to disqualify the pair and fine Henman $3,000.

The next day, a bunch of flowers in one hand and a piece of humble pie in the other, Henman made his apologies and was pictured across the front pages planting a smacker on the ballgirl's cheek. Young Prince Charming had done it again.

So, the indelible imprints of Wimbledon '95 were of Rusedski and Henman both saying sorry. Neither would apologize any more for their actions. Henman, who admitted to not thinking much of Rusedski's game when he first heard of the player's move onto his patch, now recognized that his own game had someway to go before it could threaten the most talented players in the world. He knew he had the technique, he certainly had the self-belief, but he didn't have one major weapon which might unnerve the opposition. Greg did. That leftie serve was potential dynamite.

It was not in Henman's nature to glory in being the most talented player in Britain, he accepted that such an accolade meant little in international terms; but while his contemporaries in the country moaned and groaned about the Canadian taking their slots, Henman was determined to take the fight to the foreigner. He wouldn't rest on his laurels. There was big game to be shot at, and the biggest incentive was to make sure Rusedski didn't get anywhere first.

David Lloyd said: 'When Greg first came over, Tim didn't have much respect for his ability, though he respected his ranking. Tim didn't think Greg could sustain it and for a while, he didn't. Tim overtook him quickly but he realised later that Greg would always be working at his game and that he had the determination to build himself into a world-class player. I'm sure Tim would admit he made a mistake by not taking Greg seriously enough from the outset. If you had asked Tim three years ago where he thought Greg would be, he'd have said 40, maybe 30. I suspected he was top ten material, simply because of his desire – the desire he hides behind that smile. It's there, don't worry. Tim knows it now.'

The autumn of 1995 was relatively uneventful for both (Rusedski lost in the first round of the US Open, Henman in the second) until the year burst back into life when the National trailer hit the M54 back to Telford.

The two players fought their way through to the final. This was what the public and the press wanted, a real showdown, a genuine Battle of Britain. The experience proved to be as shattering an experience for the new arrival as had been his reverse to Petchey at Queen's, the bad bandanna at Wimbledon or his ball-pelting return to Montreal.

Everyone inside the sport was on Henman's side. The other British players were gagging for him to win. Rusedski was alone. Well, almost. Warren Jacques, who had established himself as one of the most popular personalities on the circuit before, during and after his harshly curtailed spell as the National Team Manager at the LTA, was on his side. To Jacques, it was clear that when Rusedski entered the British bearpit, he would need someone at his shoulder. He could remember what it had been like with some of the younger, bolshier Davis Cup players when, as captain of the team, he had said he wanted to bring the thirty-something John Lloyd back for doubles in 1987. If they were going to be that mean-minded about a popular British player being summoned from semi-international retirement to help the national cause, how would they react to a foreigner queering their pitch?

Jacques said: 'It wasn't easy for Greg. I got a call from his father asking me to be a friendly face, to offer some support. I warned him that it would be tough for his son. I worked a couple of the indoor tournaments with him in 1995 where we did OK and I told him he had to play Telford. I knew it would be tricky for him, I went through all the petty jealousies he would face from players and officials, that he would probably find it difficult to find practice partners, that he'd get the cold shoulder. I just wanted him well prepared for everything.'

Rusedski, ignoring as best he could the cold shoulders, reached the final, where he met the English favourite. Playing superbly, Rusedski led Henman by a set, 2–1 and 40–15, before the fear of winning gripped him around the throat. 'I don't think I'd ever seen anyone choke on quite such a grand scale,' said Jacques. 'There are ten ways to choke, and he managed to produce all of them in one match. He had a complete mental collapse, serving double faults all over the place, and donated the match to Henman, whose confidence sky-rocketed, of course.

'What I admired about Rusedski was the way he responded. He refused to be disenchanted, he'd taken the stick for his performance, he'd endured all the ribbing and he was willing to come back for more. He turned what might have been a nightmare for him into a plus. We went our separate ways, but I always knew he would go on to greater things. The same was true of Henman, who I had first clapped eyes on as a twelve-year-old and couldn't understand why nobody else could see in him what I saw.

'It might have been because he was knee-high to a grasshopper, he could hardly see over the net and there wasn't much of him physique wise. But he had something about him, something that the LTA didn't have the talent in their ranks to see. I felt he would be a top 100 player at least, if handled properly.'

Henman, now twenty-one years of age, ended 1995 ranked 99 in the world from 161 at the start. The following year saw a remarkable rise of over seventy places and a Wimbledon to treasure. Yevgeny Kafelnikov had just won the French Open to announce his promotion into the upper echelons of the game; indeed it had always been thought that it was just a matter of time before this blond Russian earned a title commensurate with his talents.

When Henman drew Kafelnikov in the first round of Wimbledon, not much hard cash went on his chances – even if the champion at Roland Garros was plagued by an injury which required a heavy blue strapping on his thigh. The dashing Englishman went into the Centre Court free of expectation. It was to be the match which made him.

Henman, taking the bull by the horns, raced into a two sets to love lead, but was pegged back to two sets all by the relentless accuracy of Kafelnikov who had been stung by Henman's start. The Russian had match points in the fifth, but Henman saved them both with aces. It was death or glory stuff. It was to be glory – Henman winning in five, with the crowd on Centre taken to a level of rapture the like of which they hadn't experienced for many years.

Kafelnikov recalled, 'Tim was so eager in front of a big crowd, but I was back in the match and I should have been the winner. He took me by surprise, he went for all of his shots and so many of them came off and I couldn't respond. The crowd carried him. After that, I think he believed he could beat any of the top guys and it is the main reason, I think, why he is where he is today.'

Henman went on to the quarter-finals before losing to Richard Krajicek, and to the last sixteen of the US Open, where he was beaten by Stefan Edberg. His peak achievement that year was to reach the final of the men's doubles at the Atlanta Olympics with Neil Broad – a right hander born in Cape Town and educated at Texas Christian University, who had decided to take British nationality in 1991. The fact that Broad was a doubles rather than a singles specialist, having reached ninth in the world in the doubles rankings in 1990, meant there was none of the furore at his move from South Africa that had been generated by Rusedski's transition.

Henman and Broad were beaten in the Olympic final by the Woodies (the Australians, Mark Woodforde and Todd Woodbridge). Olympic medals were becoming a rarity for Britain so the arguments over professionals playing in an event which was once the distinct preserve of the amateur were conveniently brushed aside – a couple of silver gongs, wherever they came from, would do just fine.

In May 1996 Rusedski switched coaches again. This time, a call from his agent John Mayotte, brother of former pro Tim, suggested Brian Teacher, on the recommendation of another tour pro turned coach, Brad Gilbert. Teacher, the Australian Open champion in 1980, was an imposing Californian with a determined attitude he kept hidden beneath the distinctive laid-back approach of West Coast USA.

The blind date – Teacher and Rusedski first met at St Poelten, Austria – did the trick. Teacher was appointed. 'I'd seen him play a couple of times in the past, but not too recently,' Teacher said to me at the time. 'His father sent me some videos and they impressed me. It was a learning experience for me as well as him. I always thought he had the potential of a Grand Slam finalist, maybe even winning one, one day.' Teacher took him close, mighty close.

When he first saw Rusedski from coach's corner, Teacher couldn't believe how twitchy the twenty-two-year-old was. 'I saw him chewing on his towel as he walked back from a change over, and I wondered what I'd let myself in for,' said Teacher to me in 1998. 'Every two seconds, he'd take a towel from the ballboy to wipe his face, but I don't think he ever wiped any sweat away. I mean this guy was a nervous wreck.

'And there was a lot to do with his technique. He wasn't very good at covering the net, he had hands like stone. I had to help him develop a "feel". Most of the time, he didn't even attempt to make the first volley. His mindset was that if he didn't make his first serve, that was kind of it. He had a great serve, too, no doubt of that, and he used to swat the odd forehand but there were plenty of flaws in his game.

'He was desperate to improve, he never stopped wanting to learn, he took what I said to heart and he did improve. I tried to make him more relaxed, we did a lot of breathing and stretching exercises. I tried to make him stay cool, not to get so overwrought about things. We got a good momentum going.'

So much was expected of the British pair at the 1997 Wimbledon that their quarter-final defeats, Rusedski in four sets to Frenchman Cedric Pioline and Henman's to the retiring Michael Stich, were hard for the Brits to take. The Rubicon would not be crossed, for another year at least. What was worse, the new No.1 Court, Wimbledon's pride and joy, was hardly bulging at the seams for either man's defeat. With more ordinary folk there screaming them on, it might have been different, but tennis championships these days are more about corporate hospitality than making sure the genuine fan is allowed any privileges. You only have to look at the design of the new Arthur Ashe Stadium court at Flushing Meadows in New York with its plethora of VIP boxes on the eye-level concourse, to be assured of that.

The attraction of champagne and four courses in the Debenture Holders' lounge at Wimbledon was a far greater pull than that of a chance to see two British men making the semi-finals. Rusedski was out by the middle of the main course; Henman, even after a delay for rain, was washed away with the cognac dregs.

Henman talked of following the best tennis of his career, against Krajicek in the fourth round, with the worst. It was noted that if Henman had won, he would have had an excellent chance against Pioline in the semis and that would have meant a Wimbledon final. Rusedski said he didn't feel 'the full package yet' adding: 'Over the past year I've made steps forward showing that he (Henman) isn't the only player over here. There are two of us.'

The All England Club issued a statement expressing 'disappointment' at the number of unoccupied seats on No.1 court. They cited the early start at 11a.m. and pointed out that not everyone lives within easy reach of Wimbledon. What they should have added was that if two British quarter-finalists on the same day could not fill a stadium on a summer's afternoon in England, perhaps they should be looking a great deal more closely at who they let in and who they kept out.

Behind the scenes, all was not sweetness and light between Rusedski and his coach. In the year since they had started working together, Rusedski had risen from the mid-seventies in the rankings to the threshold of a breakthrough which could do wonderful things for his career, in both prestige and financial terms. All the time Teacher was attempting to improve Rusedski – and succeeding, without a doubt – he was working on a weekly retainer, and felt it would be more appropriate to come to an arrangement whereby he earned bonuses, which might properly reflect his pupil's rise up the rankings.

'I suppose I was naïve,' said Teacher. 'I was eager to go out there and coach, because I hadn't been around for three or four years and this chance presented itself. There was a lot of raw talent in Greg so, if I focused my energies and got some good results with him, here was a chance to prove myself. I have to say that he rose above my expectations quicker than I imagined. I didn't appreciate that he might be where he was, after a year together.'

Rusedski was being touted as a possible Wimbledon champion before the 1997 tournament. Why not? He had all the ingredients to succeed on grass, but his dispute with his coach over bonuses could not have come at a worse time. Teacher believed he wasn't earning enough, and Rusedski's agent at the time, John Mayotte, agreed. Teacher had been trying to get something down on paper. 'We thought we had the semblance of an agreement, John Mayotte called us together and said 'Greg and Brian, this is what we've decided. It was a piddly little bonus, nothing great. Greg said "OK fine."

Mayotte confirmed there was a meeting and an agreement. Teacher says he invoiced Tom Rusedski after the Championships, only to be told that his son hadn't agreed to anything. 'I didn't want to work with them any more from that moment on,' Teacher said in an interview with me late in 1998. Mayotte, who had tried to broker the deal, also left the Rusedski camp.

Rusedski saw the decision to part with Teacher in motivational rather than economic terms. 'Brian had taken me as far as he could,' he said. 'I needed someone new, I had to keep developing. Tony (Pickard) knows what it takes to get there, to the top and I need that if I'm going to make No.1. It's harsh, but nothing is forever, you can't afford to be sentimental. This is a very competitive business and you only have a short time to try to get to the top. No one remembers what you could or should have become, only your achievements.'

After Rusedski's resonant performance in the 1997 US Open, he returned home to play the Samsung Open in Bournemouth. Within a week, it was learned that Teacher was no longer his coach – hardly a bolt from the blue given their public falling out. Richard Lewis at the LTA had been aware of the deepening problems. He saw the falling out as part of a bigger picture. 'When Brian Teacher first came on to the scene, Greg had gone through quite a bit of a dip and he was back around the No.70 mark,' he said. 'The Rusedski finances weren't all that healthy either, I know that for a fact because I was involved in many discussions with his agent at that time, John Mayotte.

'Greg wasn't on his uppers or eating at McDonald's every night – nothing like that – but he needed financial support from the LTA. We knew he had plenty of potential still. I recall Billy Knight saying from the very first that he was a top-thirty player at least, when not many others shared that opinion. He was definitely worth the investment, he needed help and it was right that we should provide it. And what was right for Greg was also right for Tim, so we did the same deal with him, helping with expenses and costs, that kind of thing.

'Our deal was with Greg, and it was up to Greg alone to make his arrangements with Brian. There were some financial disagreements and I met with Brian a couple of times, as well as with Mayotte. They had different views, which was only to be expected. Our deal was very clearly with the player. We paid a contribution towards him hiring a coach, exactly the same basis as we used with Tim. It was like with like, it had to be that way.

'We have young players like Martin Lee, Miles Maclagan and Arvind Parmar who want to make the breakthrough in the professional game. We can provide them with a coach and, from time to time, we will help them with their expenses. In time, we expect that they will be cut free from the LTA's umbilical cord and become financially independent, good players, top players, who won't need to have money spent on them, and we can re-invest it in younger players. As players get into their early twenties, we take the view they should no longer be regarded as promising youngsters.'

Rusedski and Henman had long since burst out of that bracket. But at the same time as Rusedski was receiving a few more pounds to help him subsidize payments for his coach, so Henman was moving to cut himself free from the clutches of the LTA. Lewis says: 'Around that time, Tim was going through the process of weaning himself off the LTA. His situation had been different from Greg's because David Felgate was an employee at the time, but Tim and he had grown into a one-on-one relationship and Tim wanted him to become his full-time coach. Tim had also started to hit the serious money and said he would pay David himself.

'Ian (Peacock) wanted to prolong David's service for the LTA, to keep both him and Tim under our financial umbrella, to offer them some sort of protection if things didn't go well, but neither Tim nor David was happy with that. Once Tim had grown financially independent, he wanted to be fully independent of the LTA, allowing us to invest the money we'd put into him, elsewhere. He could also be independent of voice of the LTA as well. He and David were free now to be positive about the LTA, but we couldn't question their right to be negative as well if they wanted to be.'

The LTA wasn't exactly doing handstands when the Rusedski–Teacher situation came to light, but there was nothing they could do to prevent it. Nor would they interfere. 'The day a player like Tim or Greg became subservient to the LTA is the day they lost the plot,' said Lewis. 'I've had a few heart-to-hearts, especially with David Felgate on a number of things. They know where I stand. Greg, too, has a very good relationship with the LTA, but he's got all the advice he needs. He doesn't want, or need, me pestering him every week.'

The week of the Bournemouth championship in September, 1997, Lewis took what he described as an 'emergency' phone call in the car park of the West Hampshire Club from Mayotte, about the Teacher situation. 'It was a bizarre conversation,' Lewis recalled. 'We were talking about Britain's No.1, one of the world's top players, his coach was departing after an appearance in a Grand Slam final, Mayotte was wading through financial arrangements, and whether I would support what he was doing. I said, of course I would. And this was after I'd helped him do a deal in the period between Wimbledon and US Open to keep Brian and Greg together.'

But the Teacher–Rusedski partnership gradually fell apart, though Rusedski insisted that as Teacher was 'at the end of his contract' there was nothing wrong with letting him go. 'I was on a weekly salary,' Teacher told me. 'Before the US Open in 1997, I told Greg that I was going to be working with a junior girl from Santa Monica but under no circumstances was I going to take away any of his time to work with her. When I wasn't watching his matches, scouting the opposition, coaching him, I would be working with this girl and he said it would be fine. After the Open he was withholding my weekly salary because I was supposed to split it with the junior girl.'

Even Henman felt moved to speak out on the sacked coach's behalf. 'I feel extremely sympathetic to Brian Teacher,' he said a week after the news broke. 'It's the prerogative of every player to choose his coach, but Brian must still be very hurt. Maybe it's because I've been with my coach David Felgate for such a long time but how must Brian have felt after guiding a guy from No.84 to No.10 and then, just a few days after helping him to a Grand Slam final, getting the sack?

'Without doubt, if any players in the locker room ask my advice about who would make them a good coach, I would not have any hesitation in recommending Brian Teacher.'

On what premise, or past experience of Tracher's teachings, Henman didn't elucidate, but the message was clear enough and its intrusive nature more than played into the hands of those keen to develop the intensity of the battle between the two players. Henman was then having to defend himself. After losing in the second round in New York, he was thought to have made a diplomatic error by deciding to skip the clay courts of Bournemouth and fly off instead to Tashkent to compete in the President's Cup. Rusedski returned to Britain to much acclaim and decided he should immediately go down to the south coast, though his record on clay was pretty abysmal.

Who had made the right choice? Well, Rusedski was the darling of the people, and he milked that for all it was worth. A gushing full page interview in the *Daily Telegraph* with feature writer Sue Mott argued that Henman's decision to 'controversially leave the country to improve his hard court form in Uzbekistan' meant he had been utterly overtaken in the public's affection by the new No.1 Brit playing to the masses in Bournemouth.

The suggestion was that Rusedski was both admired for being a winner because he was playing at home and 'where was Henman when his country needed him to support a British tournament?'

Well, Henman won in Tashkent, to gain his second ATP Tour title, while Rusedski lost in the second round of the Samsung Open and probably wished he'd taken the week off after all that had been taken out of him by the dramas in New York City. Anyway, Greg was happy to play along with the fact that he was now accepted by the people.

'I chose to be British,' he said. 'I've had dual citizenship all my life. My mother's English, my girlfriend's English. This is where home is for me. I initially chose to be English because it's great for me both personally and tennis wise. With Tim coming up, it couldn't be better timing. The two of us have a real rivalry. Everything is really, really, great. There's nothing negative about it. Fair enough, when I first came over here, people said I was trying too hard. Then I lost my first two matches and they said: "He really is British, he's a true Brit." '

The flames of the rivalry were being fanned again, but on the fundamental question of what kind of influence the rivalry between Henman and Rusedski has on them as players, and on British tennis, the LTA's Richard Lewis had absolutely no doubts. 'Greg and Tim have done nothing but bring positive vibes to the sport,' he said. 'The rivalry is healthy, it's something we have to be grateful for, but we mustn't ever fall into the trap of taking the two of them for granted.

'At the start of 1998, we had two players in the top twenty, and it would be so easy to get used to that. Of course, we want them to get higher and higher, it would be great if they could both reach the top ten. Look at the five years before Tim came along and Greg arrived, and it would have been a dream to say that in 1998, at one stage, we'd have had two men in the top ten players in the world. If I had even suggested such a thing might happen, I'd have been told to come back to the real world.'

Rusedski and Henman provided hope where before there had only been despair. As 1997 drew to a close, British tennis had a healthy veneer. Beneath the surface, though, not all was well. Rusedski's success as Sports Personality of the Year meant he was a great favourite with the public, but the other British players weren't exactly prepared to sing his praises and there were times when he didn't endear himself to the proprietors of the game.

John Beddington, acting as tournament director for the Honda Challenge, part of the ATP Seniors Tour, the end-of-the-year bash at the Royal Albert Hall, attempted to organize a doubles event which would offer the current-highest ranked British players the opportunity to indulge in a little fun, though they could take it seriously if they wanted. There was money in it, of course. Rusedski signed a contract agreeing to play, but withdrew at the last minute citing injury. He was able to work out with his new coach, Tony Pickard in an effort to build up his strength and morale for the rigorous year ahead – having to defend his status as the sixth best player in the world.

Beddington was also angry because he had invited along a sponsor who he believed was willing to invest a handy sum of money – six figures had been mentioned – in Rusedski, in return for a handshake, a bit of hobnobbing with potential clients and an indication of interest in future ventures together. Beddington said to me in the summer of 1998: 'I called Greg to ask if he could make an appearance for the sponsor but he said he couldn't, as he was going to the theatre that evening with the president of the LTA, Sir Geoffrey Cass.

'Which is why, when he was made the Sports Personality of the Year, I felt distinctly queasy. I didn't enjoy watching it at all. I don't feel that he's British, though technically, in tennis terms he is. And he's got a British passport, I suppose. Yes, he's popular, but I don't feel comfortable with it.

And he still hadn't been forgiven in Canada either. Louis Cayer, the country's Davis Cup captain, summed up the maple leaf mood. 'Greg was the player we had been waiting for for so long, and it's still a hard knock to have to take that he left us,' he said. 'Time has made things a little easier, and I was pleased for Greg and for his father when he did so well at the US Open. But to me, and many others in my country, he will go down as the first Canadian Grand Slam finalist, and not the first Briton for how ever long.'

Henman had one simple message as the old year closed: 'Look out Greg, I've had enough. I'm after you.'

4 The Desert Song and an Aussie Lament

The choice of long-time Tim Henman suitor Tony Pickard to coach Greg Rusedski had gone down like a lead balloon with David Felgate. The two weren't exactly on each other's Christmas card list. For a start, Felgate knew Pickard had been in contact with Henman and his family several times before, he knew that Pickard had wanted to work with his man and that it was a pretty fair bet that he still harboured those ambitions. Pickard sensed a level of animosity from the Henman camp towards him he couldn't understand.

It was a fascinatingly personal backdrop to what had become a hugely significant rivalry. A high-profile English coach was now working with the British No.1 player while Felgate – who didn't have anywhere near Pickard's experience, but was building a considerable reputation among his peers – was steering Henman's course. The coaches seemed to be just as interested in watching for signs of potential fall-out in the other's working relationship as they were in examining ways of keeping their own player one, or more, steps ahead.

Pickard had angered Felgate by expressing the opinion that he knew the faults in Henman's game and would have loved the chance to put them right. We all knew it was never going to happen unless Henman had a dramatic reversal of the conviction that Felgate was the one and only coach for him.

Nothing served to rile Felgate more than the thought of Pickard

making assertions from the outside, given his reasoning that Pickard
was jealous of his association with Henman. Maybe, it was a sign of an
insecurity which the press would pick up on as Henman staggered
through the first couple of months of 1998.

But, given the fact that he was a coach with an eye for an opportunity and who had turned potential into gold before, should anyone
have been surprised that Pickard wanted to see if he couldn't polish the
still rough-edged diamond which was Henman? Pickard had been on
Henman's trail since he first started to show genuine potential from the
Slater School days. He had hardly kept it a secret that he saw immense
promise, Wimbledon-championship promise in the boy. Greg had the
serve, but Henman had the nerve or so the theory went. With a little
more fine tuning, a clearer knowledge of what winning took, more
constructive game plans, a better coach, so Pickard's theory went, he
could win the big one. No doubt. And, it wouldn't have done too much
damage to Pickard's profile either. There was nothing wrong with a
coach wanting to coach a player he thought would help promote his
own cause.

But the more people pressed from the outside, the more Henman
became attached to Felgate: he liked having him around; they trusted
each other implicitly; but maybe that had something to do with the
player's growing belief that he knew where his career was heading. He
thought increasingly for himself and didn't need someone outside his
close-knit security squad telling him what he should be doing.

David Lloyd's opinion on the player–coach relationship was
instructive. 'I think players need a stable figure, someone they can
get on with, they can go out and talk to in the evenings, who will be
as much a friend as a coach, or go the other way with a Harry
Hopman [the legendary Australian coach] who put more fear and
work ethic into it,' he said. 'I don't think that David Felgate is built
like that, he wasn't good enough as a player, so he had to be a friend.
Tony's the same, he's more of a father figure. They aren't like Tiriac
was with Becker, or Bergelin with Borg: "if you argue with me, son,
whack." '

The relationship Pickard had enjoyed with Sweden's Stefan Edberg
down the years was fantastically successful on the tennis court – over
$20 million in prize money, reaching No.1 in the world, with forty-one
career singles titles, eighteen doubles crowns, two Wimbledons, two
US Opens, two Australians and countless heroic performances for
Sweden in the Davis Cup – but they formed a bond off the court which
was more father and son than teacher and pupil. The two of them were

made for each other. Stefan looked up to Tony; Tony had a captive audience in Stefan. The chemistry was perfect.

Rusedski was an altogether more complex kettle of fish. Pickard, the theory went, must have known what he was letting himself in for, but hoped he would be able to re-kindle with Rusedski what he'd had with Edberg and, for a time, with Petr Korda. The tail end of 1997 saw an improvement in Rusedski and Pickard was at his shoulder. He won the Swiss Open in Basel, reached the final in Vienna – where he beat Henman in the semi-final – the semis in Stockholm and the quarters at Bercy, the Paris Indoor championships. He became the first 'Brit' to qualify for the ATP Tour world championships in Hanover, though he had to withdraw with a hamstring injury after losing two matches. In the calendar year, he had earned a career-high $1,515,473. The days of re-mortgaging their property in Canada were a long way behind the Rusedski family.

The Rusedski serve was an essential prerequisite of his ability to stand up to the best players on the Tour – without it, he would have been pretty much a run-of-the-mill main Tour player. 'He just happened to have the talent to generate an enormous amount of pace,' said an enthused Pickard. 'He has a wonderful rhythm and when everything gels, it's fantastic to behold. I don't think anybody taught it to him. The rhythm, the swing, the hand-eye co-ordination, are all there in one package.'

Pickard knew he didn't have to work on it at all. It was the weapon that had broken down the doors into the world's top five and could possibly blast everyone out of the way to the extent that Greg, with Pickard as his guide, could reach the levels that Stefan Edberg had attained.

'Stefan was the perfect example of good placement of the serve because he didn't have the biggest (serve) in the world,' Pickard said. 'But it was where he put the ball, how much he made opponents move, which was the important factor. If you serve within a yard of where the opponent is standing, it will come back at you faster than it left.

'There were those who could serve over 100 mph with wooden rackets but when I look at the game now, the way it has progressed with better training methods, more professionalism that's made players better and stronger, there will still be the one who comes out of the pack and does something special and that player in 1997 was Greg Rusedski.'

When Pickard first saw Rusedski's proposed itinerary for the year, he tore it up and threw it into the nearest wastepaper basket. Pickard believed too many of Rusedski's past injuries had been caused by criss-crossing the globe like a love-sick Canadian goose, if he'd pardon the analogy. Rusedski had recovered from the hamstring strain that dogged his progress in late 1997 and he had demonstrated to Pickard that he was in perfect shape for the New Year, to the extent that he had put on seven pounds to counter those who argued he didn't have enough bulk to pull his weight as a top ten player. It was time to start playing.

Tennis had taken some strange leaps and bounds since turning the professional corner in 1968, but playing the sport in the desert – what with all that dratted sand getting in your shoes – was one of the oddest. But the Qatar Mobil Open, with its thirty-two-man field, offered $1 million in prize money, so why not fly to the Middle East and hope you were out of the blocks with a rush?

The British press were in attendance so the fall-out from the Sports Personality Award and the controversial Henman first-person newspaper piece was certain to be lingering; indeed the article was thrust into Rusedski's face on the flight to Doha by Petr Korda. 'Seen this Greg?' he asked. 'I read it, I asked Tim about it and he said he was embarrassed at the way it came out,' said Greg. 'There were no hard feelings.'

But, clearly, the two players had a point to prove to each other and everyone else. Rusedski was a Grand Slam runner-up, a top-ten player, and was armed with a coach in whom he had absolute belief. Henman had not been entirely satisfied with 1997, but he was fully recovered from an elbow injury which had dogged his hopes of progress and was certain there was a lot more to come. After all, his world ranking had shown a perpetual year-on-year improvement, so why shouldn't he be confident of maintaining the upward curve?

Everyone had their own viewpoint. Gerry Williams, Sky Television's tennis anchorman and a tennis journalist for more years than he cared to remember, said to me, 'I have known over the years how difficult it is for highly competitive, successful players to be the best of mates,' he said. 'Very few ever seem to manage that. The Swedes did it because of their nature, the Spaniards appear to have it at the moment, they get on famously, but take the Australians – there seemed to be a definite Rafter–Philippoussis situation developing.'

Indeed, Pat Rafter and Mark Philippoussis had formed a successful doubles pairing in 1997, winning at Queens, making the semi-finals in successive Grand Slams at Wimbledon and the US Open. The partnership seemed to have so much going for it, but when it split, neither player seemed to know precisely why they had fallen out with the other.

'We just lost a bit of friendship there, something was lacking,' said Rafter. 'I said to him "Listen, if you're not my friend, if you're not going to be great mates, I don't want to play doubles with you." That's why I play doubles, I play with friends. I don't play because I want the money, but because I want to enjoy it. I don't know why it happened, it just sort of slipped away.

'I'm not regretful for it, he was a mate, if he goes away, I've got plenty of other friends that I hang out with. It's a shame, but I felt more ashamed for his sake, he's definitely changed.'

'It's just not reasonable to ask Tim and Greg to be chums, it needs a degree of realism,' explained Gerry Williams. 'I remember that Jim Courier and Pete Sampras were inseparable as juniors, but look at them now, constantly sniping at each other.' After Sampras was physically sick on Stadium Court in the 1996 US Open quarter-final against Alex Corretja of Spain, he came back from two sets down to win in five, a performance which went down as one of the most courageous of its type. Courier intimated that he felt Sampras had faked throwing up.

Sampras's retort was brief and to the point: 'I think he's pissed that I beat him every time. I don't do gamesmanship. I don't pretend I'm tired and all of a sudden, I have a burst of energy. I know Jim's said that. It's sour grapes.' And these two had been a lot buddier than Henman and Rusedski were ever likely to be.

'I suppose,' said Williams, 'that if Tim and Greg did suddenly become bosom buddies, it wouldn't be any good for them, because they wouldn't want the big prize – the No.1 ranking in the world – enough. But it doesn't surprise me that there is an uneasy relationship.

'I think my eyes were really opened at a tournament late last year where Greg and Tim were there with their coaches, with a small but informed posse of tennis writers present, and it seemed to me that the atmosphere was being made more difficult because of the intensity of the attention. The press seemed to be more supportive of Tim than of Greg. I got the impression, too, that neither of the coaches helped the situation. Tony Pickard obviously had bruises, there was a history there with the LTA and I don't believe there was an awful lot of goodness there between him and them. If I was Tony, I'd probably feel the same. I'm not sure he'd have been bursting with energy to maintain Greg's relationship with the LTA, though originally, when Greg came over to England, the LTA were thrilled with their collaboration.'

Williams confessed that he was an ardent Rusedski supporter, saying, 'He is a smashing bloke. What bothers me most is that he and Tim are such nice people, and I just believe that the situation they find themselves in, their rivalry if you like, hasn't been very well handled. David Felgate, for instance, is "in yer face", he's very ambitious and I like him for that. But maybe he has been a little intemperate with the way he's handled the whole situation. Having said that, it hasn't been easy for him, nor can the somewhat strange situation of his wife working for IMG and being Tim's agent at the same time.'

The results of Henman and Rusedski on the outdoor hard courts of Doha in the opening week of the New Year were acceptable enough; both players won a couple of rounds before Tim fell to Petr Korda in three ruggedly fought sets and Greg lost to Fabrice Santoro, one of the most bemusing players on the circuit, also in three. Time to make desert tracks. Australia beckoned. The tests – and the problems – were about to come thick and fast.

One year earlier, Tim Henman had won the first ATP Tour title of his career in January 1997, at the Sydney International – the Australian version of Britain's Queen's Club tournament. With that victory, he soared fifteen places in the rankings, to No.14. Inside a month, he had reached his first tournament final, in Doha, had broken into the top twenty, and won a star-studded World Series tournament. 'Now I have to set my standards higher,' he said. And he did. A lot higher.

Sydney 1998 should have been just as positive. Instead it was the first evidence of Henman's worrying tendency to falter with the finishing tape in sight. He reached the final once more, his conquests all rich in nature. Mark Woodforde, such a distinguished doubles player, Spain's Albert Portas, Sweden's Thomas Enqvist on a wild, windy day when he played at a sustained level of excellence few had seen before and, in the semi-final, Patrick Rafter, the US Open champion, all succumbed to a level of remorselessness from Henman which took even seasoned watchers by surprise. The 7–6, 7–5 victory over Rafter, given the xenophobic nature of the crowd's support, should have given Henman all the mental strength he needed for the year ahead.

Though Slovakia's Karol Kucera was a formidable opponent, Henman was much fancied. The final – well, after the first four games, anyway – saw the Englishman disintegrate to an effect which would trouble him for months to come. Such were Kucera's nerves, he could hardly get the ball back into play in those opening four games, but from there, the Englishman was to lose eight games out of nine, a period in which he smashed his racket in a fit of pique. When he was trumpeted to make his most significant breakthrough – winning a title is one thing, successfully defending it something else – Henman inexplicably froze. He lost the final 7–5, 6–4 and knew he had let himself down badly. Felgate, watching from the side of the court, couldn't understand it. 'I had wanted to make him more aggressive in his game and a little more consistent,' he said. 'And Tim had been brilliant up until the final, he handled the Rafter match perfectly. Then, he had a mental aberration. It left some scars, I know that. And the Aussie Open didn't help.'

From Sydney, with the losing finalist's instead of the winner's cheque, to Melbourne Park, an outstanding architectural testament to Australia's desire not to be left behind in Grand Slam terms. Indeed, the retractable roof on its magnificent Centre Court was an innovation that left the rest stuttering in amazement. Australia, in staging terms, had come of age and like New York's old Forest Hills grass courts, Kooyong was but a distant memory. Grass was now pretty much Wimbledon's alone.

If Wimbledon always seemed to be held in the wettest two weeks of the English summer, then the Australian Open was normally staged in the midst of a heatwave. The conditions, both overhead and underfoot on the Rebound Ace surface, tested human endurance to the limits.

Rusedski had by-passed the Sydney tournament, preferring to practise on the Aussie Open courts. A first-round draw against novice American David Witt did not appear too full of demons. Henman was bracketed with left-hander Jerome Golmard, from France, ranked 101, whom he had brushed aside in straight sets at Wimbledon the previous summer. Not much trouble there, if the record book was to be believed.

But Golmard proved to be a formidable, frustrating opponent, who would not be shaken aside, whatever Henman did. The Frenchman won the first set, Henman levelled in a tie-break, Golmard stretched him again to win the third, Henman responded dynamically to take the fourth. The final set drifted on, full of anxiety, neither man able to impose significant superiority until Golmard found the touches of inspiration to outlast his opponent 11–9. After four-and-a-half hours under a ferociously burning sun, Henman had been exposed. 'It wasn't that he didn't try,' said Felgate, 'but when he lost, the effect was tremendous.'

In his press conference afterwards, Henman attempted to dismiss its impact by suggesting it had been a terrible performance and that, on any other day of the year, he would have beaten the Frenchman. The words were on the locker-room grapevine within minutes and Henman was thought to have displayed an unnecessary conceit. In defeat, you should be humble and the British player hadn't treated his victor with enough respect. Golmard deserved better, for there were few incidents of lower-ranked players having outlasted someone of Henman's reputation 11–9 in the fifth set of a Grand Slam.

Felgate defended his charge. 'Tim was very damning of himself. He said "I should beat this guy, let's not beat about the bush." Some people thought he was way too open. You don't seem to be able to win in this game. Tim had screwed up, there wasn't anything to be conceited about. He was simply honest, and I don't see anything wrong with that. There are times when there's nothing to say and people want to make more of it than there actually is.' But the fall-out would cling to Henman like a shirt drenched with sweat from the Melbourne sunshine.

Rusedski began without undue concern, defeating Witt in straight sets and then another American, Jonathan Stark, retired, trailing 1–0 in the third set, having lost the first two. Rusedski's third-round opponent was altogether more daunting, the 1997 Wimbledon semi-finalist and regular Aussie good guy, Todd Woodbridge. The crowd was only marginally less hostile to Rusedski than one in Montreal might have been. Pickard said that he had given his player the keys to a better game. 'Now he has to put them in the lock.' Tennis writer Ronald Atkin mused afterwards: 'Rusedski couldn't even find the door, never mind the lock.'

Rusedski lost 7–6, 6–4, 6–2, his serve nullified by the smartness and alacrity of Woodbridge's returns of serve – an art he had honed in so many doubles successes across the years. It didn't help the Rusedski patience threshold that he was foot-faulted six times by the same earnest line-judge. 'When you hit an ace at deuce and 4–4 in the second set and the guy calls a foot-fault after the ball's flown past Todd, it's a bit hard to swallow,' he commented.

Woodbridge won ten of eleven games from 3–1 in the second set and the match was lost. Rusedski came tamely into the press conference, offered few excuses, smiled limply and departed. It was hardly the same emotion-ravaged Greg the tennis writers remembered from the US Open.

Rusedski then stunned the BBC crew in Melbourne by refusing their request for an interview after his defeat to Woodbridge. The thought crossed all of our minds and it troubled Pickard: this was hardly the way to treat the organization which had presented him with their Sports Personality of the Year Award little more than a month earlier.

The Australian Open didn't really catch alight in the men's championships in 1998. World No.1 Pete Sampras, wondering if he should have travelled down under at all as he was fatigued, went out in the quarter-finals to Karel Kucera, the victor over Henman in the final at Sydney. Ultimately, the climax was to pit two first-time Grand Slam finalists, Petr Korda of the Czech Republic, whose career had once been turned round by Pickard, and Marcelo Rios, a young Chilean with attitude who had burst on to the scene, a delight to those who yearned for a return to the Beastie Boy dramatics of McEnroe and Connors. Those who celebrated his rise to prominence were disappointed with Rios' performance in the final. The South American froze utterly, looking as though he was spent, physically and mentally, and allowed Korda to surge through for a notable triumph, emphasized by his unique bicycle-kicking celebration of victory.

5 Split Personalities

Split, Croatia, a beautiful city which had been despoiled in recent years by the bitter Balkan conflict, was back on the ATP Tour calendar. Goran Ivanisevic, born and raised a proud Croatian, was never more thrilled. Henman and Rusedski, however, didn't exactly arrive back in Europe in similar, upbeat circumstances.

Henman was still troubled by his collapse against Kucera in Sydney and the personal despair he felt at his defeat to Golmard in Melbourne. This was the start of arguably the lowest period of his career. He took a wild card into Split and immediately wished that he was somewhere else. A three-set defeat to German Rainer Schuttler in the first round, having won the second 6–1 before losing his way again, and it was Australia re-visited. The funk deepened.

Rusedski, meanwhile, was showing signs of getting back into his US Open stride. With several redoubtable flashes of the left-handed blade, he had cut through his first three opponents and now faced, in the semi-final, the mountainous figure of Switzerland's Marc Rosset, who was to figure in one of tennis's most emotional stories later in the year at the US Open. It would not be a match for the purist, more a bludgeoning, carpet-scarring contest between two players who offered little in the way of fantasy tennis.

It was wham-bam-thank-you-ma'am stuff, which Rusedski survived in three sets to make his way into the final, to face the local favourite, Ivanisevic. This was a match he would have had to have been superhuman to win – against a Croat, *the* Croat, on home soil.

Rusedski did well to hold his own, hanging in there for two tie-breaks. One or two of the line calls at critical moments were of the home town variety, but he couldn't deny Goran. Ivanisevic won 7–6, 7–6, to take his first title since he had beaten Rusedski in five sets in Vienna the previous October when Greg was just setting out with Pickard. Four months on from that defeat, Rusedski was back on an upward spiral again, and would head to Antwerp the following week as sharp as he'd been since New York.

Sunday 8 February was finals day in Split and talk of splits was spreading. Conspicuously. When the *Sunday Express* landed on the front mat of the Felgates' home in Barnes, south-west London that morning David and Jan were gobsmacked. A three-page spread, coated in funereal black, was headlined 'The Trouble With Tim'. There could be no more vivid a demonstration of how Henman's form was being perceived back home.

What's more, the article had been penned by Henman's best friend in the press, the ebullient *Express* correspondent Barry Flatman. Henman had a lucrative contract with the *Express* for his exclusive views on the game and Flatman was the conduit. Here was the classic situation where the writer was trapped in the middle – he didn't want to destroy the friendship with the prized contact which generated the agreement in the first place, but the newspaper paid his wages and wouldn't be happy with a soft soap job. Flatman had to tell it as it was, even if it meant the journalistic equivalent of walking a tightrope.

In the piece, Felgate was quoted as saying: 'I honestly think that for the first time in his life, Tim is encountering nerves. For two years at Wimbledon he appeared the iceman with the way he saved those match points against Kafelnikov in 1996 then went on to beat the man who was the reigning French Open champion. A year later, he was two sets up against Richard Krajicek when it got dark and he calmly went out the next day and finished the job. This year's Sydney final against Kucera was probably too simple to start with against a player he'd beaten easily on a couple of recent occasions.

'Tim did not pay enough mental attention and the next thing he knew, the guy was back in the match. The events of the next couple of weeks, with Kucera beating Sampras in the Australian Open, proved that he wasn't a bad player. Losing to Golmard in Melbourne was his worst performance for a long time and sportsmen have bad days, but there's no excuse.

'Against Rainer Schuttler in Split, everything seemed to be coming back. Tim had a good week in London practising with Edberg and Rusedski [given the court availability at Queen's, that was inevitable if a little uncomfortable] and after winning the second set 6–1 against Schuttler, he looked in control, but he was so determined to win and end this run, he tightened up. You could say he choked, but we sat down, analysed what went wrong and established that he still has a strong inner belief in his ability.'

Flatman went on to examine the growing 'Felgate Must Go' lobby, regurgitating, a touch harshly, the coach's own playing record – he had reached 250 in the world rankings a decade ago and made only one appearance in Wimbledon's main draw when he lost to world No.1 Ivan Lendl on the old No.1 court in 1988. Felgate's response [and you didn't have to read too hard between the lines to discover who was being portrayed as 'The Trouble with Tim'] was to draw upon a footballing analogy.

'Was Ron Atkinson one of the great players?' he asked. 'How many league titles did Bobby Moore or Bobby Charlton win as managers? But I suppose I can take a positive from the situation because it shows how far British tennis has come in the last couple of years. Not too long ago, it was only English football managers who ended up in the rifle sights. Now it's tennis coaches as well, which shows things are moving forward and I'd like to think I've done my bit to improve our lot when you consider that a few years ago, we didn't have a player in the top 100.'

Felgate knew who the snipers were, and they knew that he knew who they were. There was plenty of jealousy abounding, because those who believed they were superior in quality to Felgate, wanted a part of Tim and Tim had shown no other inclination but to carry on with a trusted friend of six years.

'Tim went from No.29 in the world at the end of 1996 to No.19 a year later and that included three months off for his elbow operation,' Felgate told me. 'If there comes a time when his ranking has gone down and he's played terribly through the year, there might be some justification to look for a change.

'I would be the first to walk away. I wouldn't want to hang around if I felt I was holding Tim back. In many ways, Greg's tremendous success of last year, reaching the US Open final and getting as high in the world as No.4 has blinded people about Tim and I suppose there were expectations of him going to the same level straightaway.

'A coach isn't just a coach, sometimes he's a friend, sometimes a father or a big brother figure. He does have to hand out the praise when things go well and the bollockings when they go badly. He's a dining partner, a travel manager, a practice court fixer, a ball carrier. You are a shoulder to cry on in the absolute sense. I suppose a coach is part of a team, but I refuse to use the word "we" when Tim has done well because he is the one who walks out and plays the points.'

But the insinuation that Felgate was in some way holding Henman back, hurt his professional pride. He let Flatman know his views privately. He wasn't happy, but he understood that a journalist had a job to do. 'Barry was trying to answer those who were questioning me,' he said. 'I was worried more about the effect it would have on Tim. If people think I'm no good, it doesn't matter, but it would be dangerous if, through things being said about me, Tim was getting screwed up. I couldn't let that happen to him.'

Felgate was also bothered by suggestions that the relationship between he, his wife Jan, Tim's agent, and the player himself – a situation unique in tennis – made everything appear a little too cosy. 'I had to put up with a lot,' said Felgate. 'IMG have never, ever tried to dictate to Tim who he should or shouldn't work with. They only get involved in his scheduling, in sponsorship things he has to do. Jan will come home and say "we think Tim needs to do this" and I'll tell her if it's right for Tim at that time, or if it has to be changed. We talk about it and work it out.'

Jan Felgate was also hurt by the insinuations. 'I just thought "why do we need this?" ' she said. 'The headline implied it was all David's fault. I work for a major company, everybody reads the newspapers and for the next few days, people were sticking their heads around the corner of my office, asking if David was all right, how was he coping. I ended up defending him again and again.'

The next few weeks were going to make Flatman's article appear as though it were culled from the pages of *Old Moore's Almanac*. From Split, Henman flew to Dubai where, you've guessed it, he lost in the first round to Boris Becker, 6–0 in the second set, then on to Antwerp, in Belgium, where he suffered another unpalatable reverse, beaten by Sweden's Magnus Norman in straight sets. Could the situation possibly get any worse?

Certainly, it could. With an interesting sense of timing, Rusedski was beginning to resemble the fighter from Flushing Meadow, circa 1997. He toughed out a couple of three-set victories in the opening rounds of the European Community championship, against the Moroccan Hicham Arazi and then won 18–16 in the final set tie-break over Guillaume Raoux of France. After that enthralling victory Dutch journalist Franz van der Staay, in the usual stage-managed press conference, asked Rusedski about Henman's refusal to play in the World Team Cup competition the week before the French Open. Rusedski lost his cool.

The gist of his argument was that Henman had dithered and dallied about informing anyone of his schedule for the spring of 1998 and then sprang his intention not to play in Dusseldorf on Rusedski when it was too late for him to make alternative arrangements.

What was all the more incredible, from Rusedski's viewpoint, was that Britain had actually *qualified* for a tennis championship and was now turning down the chance to play. Most players found the playing conditions in Dusseldorf, and the fact that there were no computer ranking points to lose, as the perfect way to prepare for a Slam.

Henman insisted that when he relayed the message to Greg in the locker room at Queen's, 'He certainly didn't give me the impression of being unduly upset. He said he could understand my reasoning for not playing Dusseldorf that particular week.'

Henman's view of the meeting did not exactly correspond with Rusedski's – a situation which once again gave rise to the feeling that there was more to this rivalry than which player had that week's superior ranking. 'I had to chase Tim to find out,' Rusedski insisted in a *Tennis World* article that month. 'I asked him three times for his decision, first before we went to Australia, then when we were in Australia when he was still giving me the impression he probably would play and then finally when he saw me at Queen's after the press release had been issued.

'I just wish he'd come up to me and told me right away, as soon as he had made his decision. It [Dusseldorf] is the perfect way to prepare for the French. You play three matches in six days with coaches allowed to sit on the court. After all, neither of us are great clay court players. We need all the help we can get.

'In 1996, Tim and David were pleading for us to be given the wild card into Dusseldorf and wanted me to play in at least one extra tournament in the qualifying period in the hope that my ranking would climb closer to his. Now, we've qualified on merit, but Tim has decided not to play.'

Was this not a case of the biter bit? 'I've just got to get on with my game and let him [Henman] concentrate on what he wants to do,' said Rusedski. 'That's his prerogative, but I still think it's a shame. It may be that we'll never have two players with rankings high enough for us to qualify again. And this is clearly a case of the top player not making the final decision.' A comment crystal clear in its emphasis and meaning.

This was one of the first occasions since Rusedski appeared on the scene and locked horns with Henman in the Duel for the Crown, that more people sided with him than with Tim. It was all the more astonishing given that the World Team Cup event was sanctioned by the ATP, the Players' Union – an association in which Henman and Felgate were playing increasingly influential roles. That aside, most of the leading players in recent times, Pete Sampras, Boris Becker and Stefan Edberg among them, had praised the atmosphere in Dusseldorf and its value to them in terms of preparation for Roland Garros.

Felgate defended Henman's decision. 'Last year, the World Team Cup would have fitted perfectly into Tim's schedule,' he said, 'but I think this year it is better for him to have a solid four weeks on clay and then have a week off before the French Open. It wasn't until after he lost the doubles in Melbourne that the decision was taken.' Which does seem a strange moment to make a choice about a tournament some five months ahead.

'The main reason Tim had said earlier that he would play was to avoid the criticism he thought there would be about him not playing. But that's not the way to look at things. He must do what he thinks is best for his tennis.' In essence, then, the choice had boiled down to a what's-best-for-me motive, but what could anyone else expect in a sport governed by the pursuit of self-centred ideals?

The end of May seemed a long way removed from the matches of February but back on court, in the Antwerp semis, Rusedski brushed the improving Kucera aside, which meant he had to face Rosset for the second time in three weeks, and this time in the final. No one was surprised when the first set went to a tie-break, won by Rusedski. Rosset pulled level, but when Rusedski broke for a 2–0 lead in the third, there was to be no looking back. He served twenty-three aces in the final alone, taking his total for the week to a blurring seventy-nine, and completed a 7–6, 3–6, 6–1, 6–4 victory in two hours and twenty-six minutes. It was to be the final occasion Antwerp would figure on the ATP calendar but no, Rusedski was told, he couldn't keep the $1 million diamond-studded racket which was kept in a Belgian vault for 364 days of the year.

On the flight home, in readiness for the Guardian Direct Cup, a new British tournament which began on the following morning in Battersea Park, coach Pickard remarked to Rusedski that he would be about to face one of the most difficult weeks of his life, what with the increased expectation from a British audience. 'Don't worry, Tony,' Rusedski insisted. 'I can handle it.'

A three-set defeat in his opening match to the German Marc-Kevin Goellner, suggested that Greg might have been a tad too optimistic. Worse, he had had two match points on one of the fastest court surfaces of the year, and then completely faded away. Pickard's warning was right after all. Battersea had long been known as a home for lost dogs and here was Rusedski out of the event, tail between his legs. 'Having had two great weeks before, it was always important to get over that first match, to start another roll,' he said. 'I just couldn't manage it, which was bitterly disappointing.'

The public who pitched up in the Battersea tent, had wanted to see Tim and Greg go the whole way, but they were both out by the middle of the week. Henman, at least, got through a couple of rounds against fifth seed, Richard Krajicek, in a stiff three setter, 6–7, 7–6, 7–5 and German qualifier Rainer Schuttler in another three, before losing to the eventual champion Yevgeny Kafelnikov. But maybe, just maybe, that horrid winter was out of his system.

He was perky enough on the following Monday to play centre-forward – and score with a magnificent headed goal no less – for an LTA football team against the *Express*, managed by Barry Flatman. I was the referee and though Tommy Hindley, the ever-persistent official photographer, asked me to red card Henman so he could get a saleable snap, I couldn't bring myself to do it. What for? He did nothing but run rings around the opposition all morning. Something of a new feeling for him.

6 Paradise Lost, Paradise Regained

Having spent my own honeymoon at the Grand Champions Resort in Indian Wells, I can vouch for its glorious recuperative powers. Charlie Pasarell had unearthed a jewel deep in the Californian desert. The top floor rooms of the Signature hotel overlook two superlative golf courses, and the head bartender down at poolside makes the best strawberry daquiris in the world.

Greg Rusedski and Tim Henman landed here in early March, in need of something more than a stiff drink, to prevent what had been built up as a year of plenty for them becoming one of serious anticlimax. Rusedski was in stronger order, no doubt of that. His quarter-final defeat in Rotterdam to Richard Krajicek was nothing to be ashamed of, indeed he had extended the 1996 Wimbledon champion to three sets before being vanquished.

A couple of calls to Pickard's Nottingham home (the coach watched the matches, and they talked tactics almost daily) had put his mind at rest. The Californian air – where temperatures touched 100 degrees but there was barely a speck of humidity – was just what he needed. The tournament itself was the first of the ATP Tour's Mercedes Super Nine series, the finest that men's tennis could offer outside the four Slams.

Granted a bye into the second round, Rusedski met the American Vince Spadea and if he wanted a tougher baptism on the hard courts, he could not have found one. Only after three more demanding sets did

Rusedski triumph, 4–6, 6–3, 6–4. He knew it could easily have gone either way; Spadea was a young, durable foe with the local crowd on his side so Rusedski had to dig deep, but he emerged with a victory and an increasing contentment with every facet of his game.

Carlos Moya, who was to win a major within two months, was beaten in straight sets, Sweden's Thomas Enqvist in three, and then the old warhorse himself, Thomas Muster of Austria, succumbed to the power Rusedski was generating from all quarters. One of his serves was clocked at 149 m.p.h., the fastest of all time. (He'd actually served at 145 m.p.h., to break the previous record, in the Enqvist match.) Muster threw up his arms, pleading for mercy from the fire-crackers.

'A lot of people said that things like the fastest serve are irrelevant to tennis, but I wanted this record,' Rusedski said. 'I'm proud of the achievement.' The American fans, who love a showman, whooped it up. But Greg knew he would need several of those left-handed humdingers and an awful lot more, as the final would pit him against the man in the most terrifying form in the game, Marcelo Rios.

The prospect of reaching No.3 in the world was the carrot for Rusedski, a step closer to the ultimate ambition that had seemed so far off in those days when his family would scrape the money together to send him to Beijing for a challenger. Could their lad make it all the way to the top? Against anyone else, he had a real chance, but Rios was a complicated kettle of fish.

The final became a fascinating contest that pitted the uncomplicated power of the British left-hander against the stunning, lacerating accuracy off the ground of the Chilean leftie. Strange as it may seem, no left-hander relishes facing another, and Rusedski's record against them wasn't good. Rusedski had two break points in the opening game, but as soon as Rios had survived those, he broke his opponent to love, zeroing in on the inconsistent Rusedski backhand.

Rios won that opening set, but the second threatened to become one of the year's classics. The tie-break at its conclusion was talked about in the same terms as the 1980 gem between Borg and McEnroe at Wimbledon. Rusedski saved two set points with courageous volleying winners, Rios had three more, also denied him and then, on the thirty-second point of the longest tie-break of the year, Rusedski's forehand volley winner drew the match level. The sun beat down, but neither man flinched. The third set was also decided on a tie-break, Rios winning 7–4. For all the effort Rusedski put into to trying to retrieve the final, Rios completed a 6–3, 6–7, 7–6, 6–4 victory to become the

Newsweek Champions Cup holder. No.1 in the world would not go to Rusedski, but to Rios.

Henman's time in desert California was nowhere near as appetizing. He came to the event in a trough, both spiritually and with his game – something needed a kick-start. His fifth first-round defeat of the year, 6–3, 6–4 to Wayne Black of Zimbabwe, meant he had won only two matches in two months, both of those in a tent in Battersea Park. In the midst of his defeat to Black came a rare violation of the ATP's code of conduct, for unsportsmanlike conduct, after the umpire ruled that what Henman thought was an ace, had been a 'let'. The reaction was one of disbelief, then anger, then despair. Things were getting to Tim. A drama was fast developing into a crisis.

Across America's three time zones, to Florida. Key Biscayne is a spit of land whose umbilical cord with the American mainland and Miami comes via the Rickenbacker Causeway. For eleven years, the Lipton Championship in late March had viewed itself as the 'fifth' major championship, not bad considering the site of the event was once a garbage dump.

For Henman, the Lipton championship was about to have a crucial bearing on the rest of his year, maybe the rest of his career – who knows? Those five first-round defeats in seven tournaments since Sydney had left him in a state of shock, and the doubts were circling just as the Florida birds used to pick over bits of rubbish on the site in its formative days. Reflecting on his defeat at Indian Wells to Black, a player ranked sixty places beneath him that particular week, Henman said: 'It was a pretty stupid player who lost that match,' he said. 'I played to my weaknesses that day.' Apparently, weaknesses were everywhere.

Julian Muscat, the new tennis correspondent of *The Times*, already had misgivings and was willing to put his name to them. 'Henman can be something of a soft touch,' he wrote before the Lipton event. 'For every leading player who touts his potential, two from the basement would relish his name in the draw. Twice in as many months he has been felled by opponents ranked outside the top 100. Yet, over the past fifteen months, his record against players in the top ten shows seven victories and five defeats. But, it is increasingly evident that Henman is compromised by mental frailties.

'His tactics against Golmard in Australia were wayward in the extreme. That defeat signalled the onset of his fall from grace. His confidence took a pummelling. Efforts at revival by his coach, David Felgate, have yielded precious little, prompting widespread (though we weren't told from exactly where) calls for his dismissal. Felgate makes a stationary target. Inexperienced at this level, he is said to be too easy on his charge. A more dispassionate relationship with a new coach may deliver a clearer insight.

'Felgate could certainly be more ruthless, although whether Henman would respond to such treatment remains open to doubt. Only when Henman loses faith in his coach should he consider an alternative.

The Felgates were the target again and if the tabloids were the hammer, the broadsheets could wield a nasty stiletto to the shoulder blades if they so wished. Muscat proffered the opinion that while it was 'convenient' to make coach Felgate the scapegoat, Henman was 'primarily responsible' for his present slump. 'He has appeared powerless to think for himself once a match is in progress. This inability to adapt is a fundamental flaw, one only he can resolve. The dashing young risk-taker who ousted Yevgeny Kafelnikov at Wimbledon two years ago, has only sporadically reclaimed those heights. He has left an adoring public exasperated by his reverses. He may ultimately be remembered as he is now: capable of beating the best before losing to the worst twenty-four hours later. Alternatively, he could be in the throes of a basic tennis education, as implied by Kafelnikov last month. The Russian said that Henman would develop a killer instinct with greater experience in tight situations. He would simply learn how to play the right shot at the right time.'

The final line of Muscat's article was right to the point. 'These are dangerous roads Henman is travelling,' he wrote. 'Any failure to address this profligacy will add substance to the notion that he simply doesn't have what it takes. Henman was not born with the killer instinct. If he does not develop one soon, he appears destined to underachieve.'

Henman's coach wouldn't have couched it in such melodramatic terms, but Felgate knew that his man wasn't getting anywhere near the best from himself. 'It was difficult because you feel for the person as much as the tennis player, but I've always been a believer that if you keep working you get your rewards,' he said to me reflecting on events. 'After the fourth first-round defeat, it was difficult to make myself keep saying "Come on, back on the practice court, it's no good sitting in your room." It's finding the balance to try to convince Tim that he will come out the other side.

'There were periods when the confidence was gone, practice was shocking in the way he was hitting the ball. It was nothing like the guy I knew. With Tim, the press were as bad as they had ever been. They've got a job to do, we all know that, they're entitled to write what they want to write, but some of it was sensationalism, and way too early. They were going after a top sportsman in this country when he had just suffered the first slump in his career.

'His ranking had always consistently gone up, it was still going up and then he suffered some first-round losses. He was battling with his form, he was battling the media. He just wanted to get on with things. Yes, it was a bad period. To me, it was the classic build-them-up-to-knock-them-down syndrome, so beloved of our sports writers. You hear about it, you hope it doesn't exist, you don't want to be too cynical and then you start to find out that it's true because it happens to you, or someone very close to you.

'I didn't think there was anything wrong with the criticism of Tim's game; the press were entitled to express opinions on his wasted opportunities, but when it started to get personal, that wasn't right. There were articles citing his girlfriend, my wife, me, our relationship, it was so unnecessary.'

Watching developments from afar, Richard Lewis didn't want to interfere, but he hoped the phone might ring so he could offer Team Henman a few supportive words. 'It's not my job to phone them once a week or anything like that, it's to be slightly at a distance but to know them all well enough to understand and appreciate what's going on,' Lewis said. 'If I ever thought the relationship was wrong, or Tim was being held back, I am close enough to both of them to be able to say it. And, what's just as important, they know I would say it.

'I'm confident enough to be able to say things to them, because they know I'm looking at it from a positive aspect. And I know they'll be straight with me. I've talked to David numerous times, when they were on their big high in 1996, especially, I thought it was right and proper to talk to him a lot about the lows. That may sound odd, but David is no fool. I said to him "right now, things are good and it's time we talk about when things might be really bad."

'Every player, every athlete, has highs and lows in his career. I would like to think that some of the things we talked about in 1996 helped them through the troubled times in the early part of 1998. Most importantly, they had to keep their heads and remain confident in what they were doing. I knew they would, because they're both extremely sensible people. They've got their heads screwed on right.'

Lewis was right. Unbeknown to those penning premature obituaries in the British papers, questioning the very authenticity of Henman's tennis, the player knew he wasn't washed up by any means and meant to prove it. Felgate sensed a renewed determination. 'He wasn't going to shy away, he was going to put himself right on the line. And he delivered.'

The surface at Key Biscayne – true, bouncing hard courts – suited all kinds of tennis, but the inherent stroke maker, the serve-volleyer, the technically sound, had a chance against the run-them-down-all-day merchants. Given a bye through the first round, Henman was still straining in the first set against South African Grant Stafford, but he raced through the second to win the match that might have meant more to him than any other in the year. A light had appeared.

After that victory, Henman began to play with an assurance he hadn't shown since he played Rafter in Sydney three months earlier. All the old verve was coming back and he defeated Carlos Moya, Petr Korda (the reigning Australian Open champion) and Gustavo Kuerten (the reigning French champion) in straight sets in compelling succession. If it were in his nature, Henman could have raised two fingers to the press benches. Hardly the form of a 'soft touch'.

Considering all that had gone before, the heartache, the self-examination, the doubts and the depression, his performance in the semi-final against Marcelo Rios was not unexpected. The third-round defeat of Pete Sampras to South African Wayne Ferreira meant that the Chilean was in the running to become the No.1 player in the world – only the fourteenth in the men's game since the inauguration of the computer ranking system. Who else could breast the tape? Why, none other than Petr Korda, Partrick Rafter and, yes, Greg Rusedski.

It would require an uncommon sequence of results – even winning the championship alone might not have been enough for a Brit to be No.1 – but the minute Rusedski beat Switzerland's Marc Rosset 6–1, 7–6 to reach the last sixteen, he had a slight chance. His pulse began to quicken. And could Pickard deliver his second No.1 player after Edberg, within six months of taking charge? It was too much to ask, surely.

Rusedski accrued nineteen aces on his way to his third victory over Rosset in a couple of months. 'It will be good for the game if there is a new No.1,' was his opinion, one not necessarily shared by those who didn't think anyone but Sampras deserved such a coveted accolade. 'Boris Becker made it for only ten days, but everyone remembers him as No.1 in the world.'

No sooner had he started to harbour such upbeat thoughts, than a shuddering straight-sets defeat to Sweden's Thomas Enqvist drew a discreet veil over such flights of fancy. Pickard knew he still had a lot of work to do.

Henman had carried his game defiantly through to the last four, but Rios was something different, the hottest player in the world, to be faced on a desperately hot day. Henman's tactics were to try to dominate the net as best as he could, but he knew that, like himself, Rios had not dropped a set. Indeed, he had barely been extended and Enqvist had retired from the quarter-final in the second set, so he was fresher as well.

Rios won the first set against Henman for the loss of two games, but the British player stuck to his guns, broke his man and brought the game back to one set all. But Henman had been spent in taking just one set from Rios and was stamped all over by the end, losing the third set to love. The vindication, even in defeat, was his and his alone, though Felgate had plenty of pride.

'Tim had been to semi-finals and beaten big guys before, but the manner of how it happened in Florida, beating Moya, Korda and Kuerten, before losing to Rios, said something for Tim,' said the coach. 'He had been through so much stuff and his game was coming back. Had he held in the first game of the third set against Rios, I still think the outcome could have been different. He got blown away in the end, but he had the No.1 player in the world going for a while.

'Vindication for me? I don't think I will be vindicated until Tim does something very big. The question will keep coming up. All it does is harden you, I'm aware of it all, I joke with the press guys and if someone writes something I particularly don't like, I'll go after them. Initially what was written about me and Tim hurt, now it just makes me angry.

'I know if Tim doesn't do it, they'll go for me. If he does it, they'll say he was a talented player anyway. What track record did Bob Brett have as a player before he took over as Boris Becker's coach, who had Tony Pickard coached before Stefan Edberg? I wasn't a great player, nobody needs to tell me that, but I was on the tour, I knew what it was all about.

'That's the problem with so-called experts. When I started with Tim six years ago, I don't remember them all saying "Oh, David Felgate shouldn't be coaching Tim Henman because he's going to be the next major tennis-playing star in the country, he's going to make top twenty, he's fantastic, he should be in somebody else's hands, Felgate's not good enough, he'll just screw him up." Not one journalist knew anything about him, hardly anyone in the game had heard of him.

'All I remember hearing about Tim was "nice hands, bit thin, too lightweight". Billy Knight had the courage to put him on a team, and put me with that team. I didn't think Tim was top twenty, nowhere near it, I was just out there with the boys, doing my job. In the last couple of years, everyone has become an expert on Tim Henman – "here's this great talent, he would have made it anyway, this Felgate is so lucky to be coaching this guy". It gets my goat. Where were they four years before? Nowhere.'

7 Feet of Clay

Enshrined on the stone walls of the idyllic Monte Carlo Country Club are the names of those whose endeavours are the stuff of Mediterranean legend. Anthony Wilding, the red-blooded New Zealander who left a trail of broken hearts wherever he travelled, won the Monte Carlo singles championship four consecutive times from 1910 before the First World War cost him his life in the trenches in Belgium; England's Bunny Austin, beaten finalist in 1930, won in 1933 and 1934; Lennart Bergelin (who became Bjorn Borg's coach in his Wimbledon glory years) beat Budge Patty 8–6 in the fifth in 1947; Drobny and Sedgman, Nicola Pietrangeli three times, Ilie Nastase three times as well. Those must have been wondrous occasions.

The British successes in the first 100 years of the Monte Carlo Open were few and far between. You had to crane your neck and blink in the spring sunshine to pick out the significant ones. 'Look up there,' said the tournament's official historian, Michel Sutter, 'there's the 1973 Wimbledon semi-finalist Roger Taylor winning the doubles with the American Marty Riessen in 1970.' Er, that's it.

Walking past this compendium of champions with their names chiselled into stone for perpetuity and up the steps of the marvellous Country Club came the same old bright-eyed, bushy-tailed Greg Rusedski. This was the last week in April but, officially the start of a season on the red clay which, he hoped, would widen both those eyes and his playing horizons.

As he sauntered across to sit on the dusty steps of the club, Rusedski contemplated a world order in which he had risen to No.5 and where the prospects of ascending even higher were extremely bright. Ahead of him were Pete Sampras, Petr Korda, Marcelo Rios and Patrick Rafter. Sampras had never been able to truly come to grips with the unique demands of clay court tennis. Korda was still a patchy player, one able to mix great matches with dross in equal measure, Rios's elbow injury, exacerbated in the Davis Cup tie against Argentina the week after Lipton had meant he wouldn't be defending his title on the shores of the Mediterranean. Rafter wasn't in the main draw either.

Rusedski was refreshingly upbeat, considering his lack of form on the surface. 'There is only one way to achieve my goal (to be No.1 in the world) and that's to work hard, listen to what Tony says and put those words into practice,' he said. 'He doesn't have me out on the court any longer than he needs to; we do the practice properly. I'm not a clay court player extraordinaire, I know that and he knows it, we're just working on the right ideas. I've got to try.

'I find this an exciting challenge. I've been in a clay court final in America but that is a world away from the kind of surfaces we have here in Europe. I need to try prove those players wrong who say I can't succeed on this surface. There will be some tough matches out there, sure, but that's what I thrive on. Rafter reached the semi-finals of the French by serving and volleying, which proves to me that you don't have to have only one kind of game to succeed. I look at this as improving myself, it's a learning experience and, hopefully, it will be a winning experience as well.'

The next couple of days, indeed the next few weeks, were going to make those hopes appear dreadfully shallow. But Pickard was brimming, too. We sat on a park bench amid the splendour of the sponsor's area as the Principality's rich and famous strolled elegantly by, and he spelled out how he saw his charge progressing. 'When we started working together, Greg was totally honest with me. It was a brave decision to part company with someone [Brian Teacher] when he's taken you to the final of a Slam, but obviously he felt very strongly that he needed a change in his career.

'Since we've been together, he tells me that things are so totally different to the way they were and, as it so happens, since we've started working, he's won two tournaments and been in the final of three others. He'd gone from No.11 to No.4 in the world and now he's No.5, a position he's managed to sustain for a while, which is pretty good going.

'When he phoned me the first time, I didn't know him at all, it was a call right out of the blue. We sat down, we talked and the first thing that struck me was how unbelievably ambitious he was and our time together has shown that he was very dedicated to what he wanted to do. His work rate has been second to none, it really has. He listens and he takes it all on board. Also I believe he appreciates the input I give him, because he knows it's working and helping him.

'Of course, with Stefan, it was different. He was sixteen when we first met and I was very lucky because here was a young kid who needed moulding – and we built our relationship on complete trust, loyalty and a belief in one another. With Greg, he has trusted me with the information about his game and all the ancillary things.' That was not to last, as Wimbledon would prove.

'He believes that my input is right for him and in turn, it's proved through our results that it's been working. The clay is an essential part of that education, he needs it in his vocabulary. Experience on this is vital for him. Stefan had a good record on the clay as a junior, he was so much better than anyone else and that was OK, basically he held his own on the stuff and he reached the final of the French in 1989, sticking to the game plan that he would attack the net as often as he could.

'Greg's game is basically serve and volley but over the last six months we've added a lot more to him. There's a bit more consistency off the ground, which is a progression from what Brian was doing with him. Brian did a lot of positive things with Greg's technique, but we've taken it up a couple of notches from there.

'What is vital in tennis is to take care of the assets and build around them. He's a better player now than he was in 1997, there are no two ways about that. He's much better off the ground than he was six months ago, but what is almost more important is that he believes that he's better off the ground.

'He is also very ambitious, desperately ambitious. It's not an arrogance thing – the two are very different. Arrogance is blind, and the other players out there will seek out the arrogant person, jump on them and push them back down the stairs. But there's nothing wrong with being ambitious.

'Greg hits the ball through the middle of you. It is an enormous benefit for him, but we have worked on getting it quicker, to give him more time to get to the net, to punch and crunch away those volleys.

'Before, he was getting there a little bit late, and was having to push the volley rather than hitting it. We have worked on that – as well as other aspects of his game. When people ask what we've done together,

I say that we've worked on everything, those things he talked about, things I've seen, it's been done as a partnership.

'There are a lot of guys out there who win on this stuff and nothing else. For me, it means having the mental strength to control your emotions, the way you play on this stuff is like setting a concrete foundation on which you can build the rest of your game. On all the other surfaces but grass, the ball comes to you perfectly, which plays to Greg's strengths. This one is the real tester. A lot of this game is between the ears. We've spent a couple of days here working hard; it's a period of time I've spent talking, explaining to a player what he can expect. I think Greg has taken it all on board.'

The only way for his association with Rusedski to work long term, Pickard believed, was for him to tell the player what to do and for the player to respond. That was the way it had been with Edberg and Korda. He felt he had Rusedski where he wanted him – only to find out later in the year that he didn't have him where he wanted him at all.

'He expects that from me,' Pickard said in April 1998. 'He'll soon know when I'm satisfied and he'll know when I'm not. If he's away and I can't get to a tournament, we'll speak on the phone. I don't have to be right on the spot to know what's happening. Let's be honest, there is a great chance out there for Greg. There's a different mentality in the game today than there was in the days of McEnroe, Lendl, Wilander, Becker or Edberg. I'm not sure I can whisk off the difference in a sentence or two. To me, there's an air of satisfaction out there now, which wasn't there before. The older guys were always looking for more, wanting more. There's almost an air of "OK, it didn't happen for me this week, there's always a next time, a new tournament, another city." Too many of them are too easily satisfied.'

For Rusedski himself, the advantages of the partnership were beginning to bear fruit. 'Stefan won six Grand Slam titles, he spent two years at the top and he was in the top five for ten straight years,' he said. 'I saw the track record of his partnership with Tony, plus I wanted to work with someone at home, so I wouldn't be away so much. I'm fortunate to have Tony because I know he's one of those who will tell it as it is.

'We sat down and had a chat about what my goals were, what I wanted to accomplish. He was surprised at my decision to part company with Brian and wanted to know why I wanted to change; and I told him truthfully.'

The rest of us were going to have to do a bit more digging.

'We've won two big indoor tournaments together and I've been to my first Super Nine final. I needed someone who would tell me the truth because if I want to maximize my career, that's what I need. The thing with Tony is I don't have to guess at what he wants, I know it will work, because the proof is in the pudding – look at Edberg and Korda. I hope the clay is going to be a learning and a winning experience. I want to turn my clay court reputation around.'

The draw at Monte Carlo offered Rusedski promise. His first-round opponent, on the fantastic Court Central, was Boris Becker, a new Boris, one who described himself as more of a coach than a player, who had settled well into life away from the big picture, who was manager of the German Davis Cup team, who was a spokesman and trail-blazer for Mercedes Benz, who was about to launch his own Management Agency. Becker was No.66 in the world, Rusedski No.5.

When Rusedski sped into a 3–0 lead, the ball was spinning in so many varied directions from Becker's racket, it looked as though he would soon be back in the Mercedes tent, dispensing goodwill and the silver tray replete with the finest caviar. The air was filled with Boris' screams, and they weren't cries of exultation. Then Becker held for the first time, broke back for 4–3, and then broke again to lead 5–4. He suddenly appeared serene and it was Rusedski who was rushing, playing with an edgy uncertainty. The set was pocketed with a beautiful forehand volley winner, like so many glorious interceptions from Becker's racket in the past.

The second contained a single break, in the Brit's favour, Becker double faulting at 15–40, changing his racket, and beginning to get down on himself again. But, in the third set, Becker demonstrated a burgeoning liking for Rusedski's backhand, never his stronger suit. When Rusedski lost his serve in the sixth game, both of the critical errors coming from the backhand wing, it wasn't a surprise. What had been all the way through a 6–4, 3–6, 6–3 defeat, was Rusedski's marked reluctance to come into the net. Becker didn't take long to focus on the point in his interview. 'I was stunned for the first fifteen minutes, paralysed at the back of the court, but he was staying back. That gave me a new dimension. If he wants to have a serious chance on this surface, he has to come in all the time – there's no way around it. Even on my second serve, he didn't chip and come in. To say I was surprised at the way the match went is an understatement.'

The 'coach' had made his point. It wasn't so much that Rusedski had lost to a player who had never won a clay court tournament in his entire, remarkable career, but to one who was only performing in occasional cameos. He was philosophical, but brief. 'I had 101 chances and made zero, he had a few and made them all,' he said. 'It would have been nice to have had another match here, but I said that it would be a learning experience. I've got to learn to hit that topspin backhand more, I think I should be able to come over the ball, but I just kept the ball in play today, I didn't take the initiative. You have got to take the positive out of things, even those mistakes I was making over and over again today. To lose a match like this doesn't mean it's going to be bad for a year. My first goal is to win my first match this season, then progress from there.

'I had a good opportunity to do that this week, hopefully next week in Munich it will come. I need to get on a roll. Boris is always difficult to play, he's hitting a lot of tennis balls, even if he isn't playing in so many tournaments these days.'

And with that, he was gone, tail slightly between his legs. Soon to be followed by Henman, beaten 6–2, 6–3 by Galo Blanco of Spain and similarly bewitched. If Blanco didn't possess the armaments to blow Henman off the court, he had the nous, the ability to switch from power to precision, to outwit his opponent. 'Where does Tim go from now?' Pickard asked me immediately after Tim's departure. 'He is tired and he's in a hole, how does he get himself out of it? He and his coach are learning.' And you felt like saying right back to him: 'So are Greg and his.'

Henman's cry was the familiar one – this is the Spaniard's territory, they are brought up to spend hours sliding and top-spinning their way to success. It was anathema to the English – odd how all the values we had learned to appreciate from watching two weeks of tennis on grass were absolutely reversed in the weeks that led from Monte Carlo, to Hamburg, to Rome and, climactically, to Paris for the French Open.

This was not serve, volley, 15–0 tennis; it was the tennis of the fencer, of the slingshot against an opponent with a stave and net, it meant dragging your opponent in, forcing him back, extending every sinew and muscle in the pursuit of success. Occasionally getting bloody in the process.

Larry Stefanki, the American who had taken on the difficult task of coaching Rios and trying to get inside the Chilean's complex mind, said he couldn't understand why his fellow countrymen – and the Brits for that matter – didn't take the clay court season more seriously. 'The reluctance of people to spend a few weeks in Europe on clay is a mystery to me,' he said. 'To win at Roland Garros, you must assimilate yourself totally to Europe, its culture, its food, its way of life.'

Henman, to be fair to him, had just returned from Tokyo (where he should have won the tournament, but lost to Jan-Michael Gambill of the USA with the field wide open) on the eleven-hour red-eye, and had committed himself to the clay, for six weeks without a break. His first-round defeat to the Spaniard was not wholly unexpected, even given the discrepancy in their rankings. 'He is just about the most difficult opponent I could have found,' Henman said. 'I've got to learn different styles of game if I'm ever going to be up there with the best. I need to be more patient. He was playing the ball so deep, with loads of top spin.

'There were times today when I really did realize how big a learning process it is going to be. There's no point setting targets. These weeks are an unknown quantity for me. My expectations are relatively low. The most important thing for me is to improve as a player.'

That night he had a special celebration to attend, the players' gala at the Monte Carlo Sporting Club, where Prince Rainier, his heir Prince Albert, and tennis mixed openly. Henman attended the party ostensibly to receive an award to celebrate his first ATP Tour singles championship, the 1997 New South Wales Open.

Tim, David and Jan Felgate didn't stay until the end of the cabaret, making off to the Beach Plaza hotel next door for an early night. The next steps of the campaign had to be discussed. There were Tim's commitments for the rest of the summer, six weeks to Wimbledon and plenty of decisions to be made. Who would they grant interviews to, who would they turn down? Which of his sponsors could they accommodate? Would Tim finally agree to go on *TFI Friday* with Chris Evans? The answer, for the umpteenth time, was thanks, but no thanks.

It all seemed so far in the distance, but the minutiae had to be taken care of now rather than be allowed to gather moss until Tim arrived back in England. The three of them did their best to get everything sorted. For now, Munich was the next stop. And if Monaco was hardly a resounding success for the Brits, it was a positive pain in the butt for the Yanks.

Pete Sampras dismissed Andre Agassi in two thrilling sets, suggesting that he had finally comes to terms with clay, only to come back the next day, and be made to look like a fly that had strayed too near a spider's web. Sampras was to be completely obliterated by the moon-balling, double-fisted-on-both-flanks Frenchman Fabrice Santoro.

Two of the finest players in the world both gave press conferences in a state of wide-eyed shock. Where had we heard quotes like these before from Agassi? 'I should have pulled the trigger a little earlier, at crucial times against Pete, I didn't step it up,' he said. 'To beat Pete, you have to be aggressive. My confidence could be better. I've been thinking one game at a time, to try to get better tomorrow. I'm continually looking to improve. I have had a solid few months, and I'm trying to bring that thinking into these matches. I know it's coming around and it's important to keep that belief. For me it's not a case of what my ranking is [it was No.20 as we spoke] it's what I'm feeling.' So how fragile had the Agassi confidence become, after he had slipped from the top ten to beneath 120? Many wondered if he had lost his appetite altogether. 'Sure, my confidence went away quickly last year, but you've got to work to stop the bleeding.'

The French Open was the one Grand Slam, as it was with Sampras, to have eluded Agassi. 'If you get a look-in at these titles, they are beautiful things, but you can't really begin to talk about them until you are down to the last weekend. The French would be an awesome accomplishment for me. What I can say is that I'm having the best time of my career right now.' It was hard for us to see how.

It was no surprise that the Monte Carlo title went to the 1997 Australian Open runner-up Carlos Moya, one of the armada of Spaniards on the tour, all of whom had rankings in and around the top twenty, who all possessed the same style, and, more or less the same personality. Nice guys to a man, but not in a manner that the British press found particularly headline-grabbing.

From Monaco with its Mercedes parked in every other garage and on every other meter, to the BMW Open in Munich. Rusedski received a bye through to the second round where he would face hometowner Oliver Gross, a twenty-five-year-old who had spent most of his career on the Challenger circuit. The Challengers are the next rung immediately beneath the full tour, a tour within a tour, where points gained mean an entry into higher echelons, but where the life – on and off planes into God-forsaken hotels on God-forsaken points of the compass with no-one watching – can be gruelling. It's a circuit frequented by the young trying to make their way up, or those who can't get into the major tournaments because of their world ranking.

Gross had reached his highest ranking of No.60 in May 1995, but had done nothing of genuine note in his career and was trying to get his act together down at No.121. If all of this suggested Rusedski, No.5 in the world remember, might be able to kick-start his clay-court season, a 6–4, 6–0 defeat put paid to such fanciful notions. It was written of his performance that seldom can he have made so much involuntary use of the racket frame. So true.

'This is one of those matches you have to try to forget as soon as possible,' he said, before he came out with the immortal line: 'Some say grass is for cows, I guess clay is for making bricks.' It was he who was dropping them.

By contrast, Henman's work looked to be bearing fruit. He could have gone home to London after Monaco but had stayed on four further days in the principality to practise four hours a day on the clay. He would not be shaken from his commitment to working this damn surface out. The German Jens Knippschild was a player he knew pretty well, his third round defeat at Queen's in 1997, having been a particularly painful memory, for the German was a doughty rather than spectacularly difficult competitor. Henman's hours on the practice court, and his increasingly confident manner, paid off with a 6–4, 4–6, 6–1 victory and even a straight sets defeat to the Swede Tomas Nydahl in the second round could not blunt his enthusiasm. 'I don't expect my best results to come on clay,' he said, 'but I think the work I'm putting in now is an investment which should take my game further on all surfaces.'

Hamburg, the site of the German Open, was not exactly welcoming. I was stupid enough to leave my overcoat at home and the weather for the first week of May was a bitter change from the shirt sleeves and shorts of Monaco. Rusedski was drawn in the first round against the Spaniard Emilio Alvarez, a match which was to be extended through a couple of dismal days and which was a succinct summation of Greg's dislike of the clay. For the tournament's second seed, a match out in the boon docks on a grey, miserable Tuesday morning was not the welcome he had expected from the Germans. But they had obviously seen his clay-court record and guessed – accurately as it turned out – he wouldn't be around the event too long.

Alvarez wasn't exactly household opposition and the match drew a single-figure crowd. The Spaniard was bedecked in a natty ensemble of black shirt and shorts, topped off with what looked like a pink handkerchief tied, in piratical fashion, around his head. One wondered if he'd come to play tennis, or sharpen the groundsman's shears.

To add to the distracting garb of his opponent, just alongside Court Six was one of those fairground attractions into which Germans slugged tennis balls as hard as they could. All in all this was about as far removed from the mainstream as it was possible to be. Not even every man jack of the small group of British tennis writers present could be lured from the abundant German hospitality to watch one of two men they had been despatched to the event to write about.

In this brass monkey weather, Rusedski produced tennis of a variety which could – politely – be described as rusty. The elements and a desperately slow court negated his powerful serve, and the capricious, cutting winds served to confuse both men off the ground. There was not a threat of a service break until Alvarez, pouncing on Rusedski's increasing uncertainty, had four set points at 6–5, all saved in a variety of fashions – with one volley played from beneath the tape forcing Alvarez to flail a backhand pass wide, the best of all. Rusedski smoothed his way through the tie-break, but then, incredibly, went into freefall and lost the second set 6–0, collecting a mere six points.

Rusedski's match was stopped for rain and then bad light with the British player leading 3–2, 15–30 on the Alvarez serve. The next morning, in frustratingly similar conditions, Rusedski took a 4–2 lead and managed – just – to hold his game together through the four break points the Spaniard had when his opponent served for the match at 5–3. Rusedski had sneaked his first-ever victory on European clay. Pickard hailed it as a breakthrough triumph. The press corps ho-hummed.

While Rusedski was having his travails outside, those with Centre Court tickets were treated to tennis beneath the roof which had cost the German Federation some £15 million to erect. It meant tennis early in the mornings and late at night. Very late. At 9.30p.m. on Wednesday, Henman's second-round match against Moroccan Hicham Arazi was called. The roof may have kept out the rain, but it couldn't prevent the cold seeping through into your bones. A second sweater was the very least required to ward off hypothermia. Vapour trails filled the air. And what sort of sad person was it who would want to watch a tennis match in Germany between a Brit and a Moroccan which might well last until 11p.m.? Obviously, a few of those who had spent most of the day sipping the local brew couldn't raise themselves from their seats to go home.

Before he'd had time to blink, Henman was 4–0 down to a player with a wonderful leftie flourish, a rapier-like use of the racket reminiscent of Henri Leconte in his pomp. Arazi was stunning; Henman, who wasn't playing badly at all, was in danger of disappearing beneath a blizzard of winners. The ship steadied when Henman recovered for 4–3, the serve beginning to make its mark, the overheads put away with increasing aplomb, but when he broke a string on set point at 3–5, the British player's momentum was irretrievably interrupted.

In the second set, Henman's impatience resurfaced. A single service break to grant Arazi a 3–1 lead was handed to the Moroccan when, attempting anything he could to break up his opponent's rhythm, Henman failed with an audacious backhand drop shot from the baseline. Arazi served out for a 6–3, 6–3 victory, completed just before 10.45p.m. There would be no time for a press conference, and the bleary-eyed among us weren't too unhappy at that prospect. The next day, Tim was bright-eyed and bushy-tailed again, playing a knockabout doubles in partnership with Rios, losing to the Australians Andrew Florent and Joshua Eagle before returning to the sanctuary of the players' lounge to consider the first third of his year.

'I believe the way I played in Key Biscayne was the turning point of my year,' he said. 'Suddenly, there was a purpose back in my tennis again which I had lost before that tournament. Those were the best matches, in terms of quality, I had played in my career. Coming into that event on the back of so many first-round defeats, I was struggling, a mental thing more than anything.

'It's been a learning process for me and I still believe I have another two years – maybe longer – before my game comes together. That's the exciting thing for me, I really believe I have so much more improving to do. I've been No.14 in the world, and there's a lot I can do better. I've always set my standards for the top and there's no way No.14 is good enough. There will be no resting on my laurels. I have a fairly good idea what's being said about me, but whatever is written, whether good or bad, it has no bearing on the way I feel. To be honest, I don't care what people think. My game is coming on leaps and bounds. Whatever is said about me, my coach, anything, it's what I want that matters, isn't it?' There was no arguing with the lad.

Rusedski was the second seed in Hamburg but, once more, the sport had not taken a player's past reputation on the surface into account when deciding the seedings. Rusedski had to make do with a stage far beneath his billing, a match on the No.2 court against Goran Ivanisevic, to whom he had lost in each of their previous seven meetings. Every time he had played Greg, Goran had got out of bed on the right side.

A single service break concluded the first set, but Rusedski's capitulation in the second, when he twice had points for a 3–0 lead, was little short of total. He hurled his racket at a fence, grabbed it and thumped it down on his bag, from whence it bounced into the umpire's chair. A pity he hadn't saved such physical resource to fight his opponent. On the first match point Rusedski netted a tame backhand service return, to a less than Goranesque second serve – and the British press, normally inquisitive to the point of frenzy – couldn't even be bothered to ask to speak to him.

Was there a more sparkling antidote to a week amidst the ordered regimentality of Germany (you *knew* when the spectators were going to clap) than the Italian Open in Rome (where you let your hair down and lived a little. Dangerously if possible). We couldn't wait to get there.

The Foro Italico has long been a glorious place to watch tennis although the sport was often little more than a fascinating distraction. Maybe the atmosphere wasn't quite as crazy as in years gone by, when the players shared the delights of their lives with the press on the Via Veneto, and the personalities on the court weren't in the same luxurious supply, but there was still a passionate vibrancy about the arena.

Once the sport was done for the day, as a springtime dusk settled over the Eternal City, the lucky amongst us made our way to Sabatini di Testavere for the finest in Italian cuisine, in the hope that the maitre d' could find you a table outside where, if you shooed away the persistent trinket sellers, you could sit, sipping the finest Chianti and watch the lovers of the world go by. It was one of those weeks where being a tennis writer had a distinct advantage over the hotel-room practice-court routine of the tennis player.

Tim and Greg had little opportunity to indulge in any such aesthetic luxuries, not this week anyway. The business of winning tennis matches on clay had already driven them to distraction. It wasn't to become any easier here than it had been in Monaco, Munich or Hamburg.

Rusedski, seeded fifth, was beaten in his opening round by the competent but hardly frightening Czech Bohdan Ulihrach. His performance was described as 'like that of a man trying to unravel the complex dynamism of blow football in a wind tunnel'. In truth, Rusedski hadn't been in the best mindset for the championship, his awful clay court form aside. He had been having doubts about his Wilson rackets for several months and, although the company had come up with a succession of different models, Rusedski felt uncomfortable with all of them. It was beginning to affect his morale, to the extent that he was considering a change which wouldn't have gone down too well with a substantial endorser at such a critical stage in his career, even if the contract was coming up for renewal in the autumn.

Then, just before the German Open, Wilson produced a racket

Top: The bandanna which caused the Canadians such offense – Greg's Centre Court debut, Wimbledon, 1995.
PROFESSIONAL SPORT

Right: Rusedski waves to the French crowd after the greatest triumph of his career: his first Super Nine title, in Bercy.
PROFESSIONAL SPORT

Below: John McEnroe, the most gifted analyst in tennis, who has controversial views on both players, acknowledges the crowds at Wimbledon. PROFESSIONAL SPORT

Top: The inseperable friends, Tim Henman and his coach. PROFESSIONAL SPORT

Below: David Felgate – 'When Tim finishes, I don't think I'll have any more left to give.' ACTION IMAGES

Below: Tim Henman with the trophy for winning the singles title in Basle, when he beat Andre Agassi in the final.

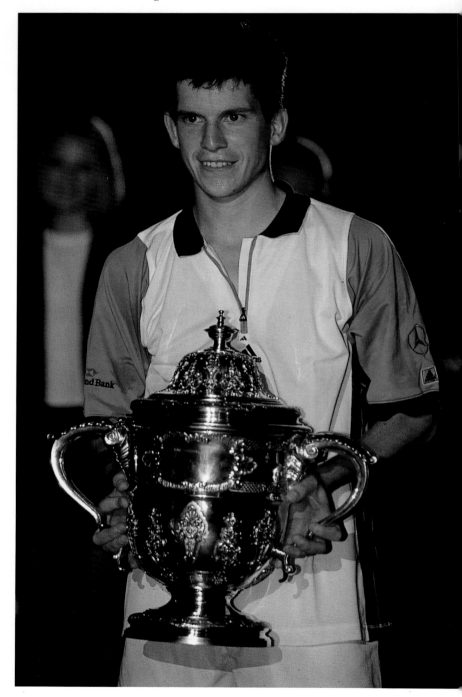

Top: Friends in high places – Tim and Pete Sampras play doubles at Queen's club. They lost in the first round.

Below: Freeze-framed – Tim Henman moves to the net to pick off a volley.

Top: Rusedski with his former coach Brian Teacher.
PROFESSIONAL SPORT

Left: Greg and Lucy Connor – the English girl he fell in love with and will marry in 2000.
PROFESSIONAL SPORT

Top: Lucy Heald, Tim's girlfriend, watches from the Centre Court players' box at Wimbledon with fitness trainer Tim Newenham on her right. PROFESSIONAL SPORT

Below: Jane and Tony Henman, a study in stoic support. PROFESSIONAL SPORT

Top: An ecstatic salute to his coach after he plays a winner.
PROFESSIONAL SPORT

Left: In full flow – the Henman forehand in all its glory.
PROFESSIONAL SPORT

which Rusedski was absolutely satisfied with. Although Pickard had felt more optimistic about his form in Hamburg than most of us watching him, and was talking Greg up – I had no doubt that the coach's views were designed for the player's ears rather than convincing anyone else – he knew that it was no good if Rusedski was not confident with his racket. All the two of them had worked upon would count for nothing if Greg believed he couldn't keep the ball in play.

When Rusedski arrived in Rome, armed with the satisfactory model, he scheduled a practice session with the Moroccan Arazi, the man who had beaten Henman in Hamburg, at a local sports club on the outskirts of the city. Unknown to either player, the ATP Tour had organized a charity event at the same location, at the same time as their practice and the courts were surrounded by autograph hunters when they arrived. Rusedski was steaming, furious. So much so he showed no interest in the practice, and promptly declared that he didn't want to have anything to do with the racket he had described as perfect for him a week earlier.

Lucy Connor's sister was asked to fly out to Rome before the Italian championships with a supply of the old Wilsons Rusedski hadn't been happy with for ages. Not surprisingly, his game was easily picked apart. 'The French is the one that counts,' was Rusedski's retort after his defeat to Ulihrach. 'I will do a lot of fitness work, to get my standard up, to get strong. In practice, it has been fabulous, in terms of my strategy, technique, everything. Now, it's turning it into matches on clay but when I needed to raise a level today, I couldn't do it.'

Henman went one better, indeed his first-round victory over Santoro of France was comprehensive to say the least. There hadn't been many 6–1, 6–0 victories in his career on any surface – but on clay? Those at home must have thought it a misprint. Nothing should be taken away from any victory, but Santoro had reached the quarter-finals of Monte Carlo – where he defeated former French champion Sergei Bruguera and then hammered Pete Sampras – and the same stage in Hamburg, with eight uncompromising sets in four matches, before he succumbed to Albert Costa. To say that the Frenchman was drained, both physically and mentally, was an understatement.

In this game, though, you felt sorry for nobody else's physical state. Getting yourself right was the priority. Henman's victory took him into a second-round meeting with top seed Rios – their first since the semi-finals at Key Biscayne – a player with whom he was building a decent kinship. They had been clowning around in the players' lounge at Hamburg, they had clowned around on the doubles court, but now it was the real thing again. And, on a clay court, the Chilean was undoubtedly the most formidable foe in the world.

There would have to have been at least a 50 per cent improvement in Henman's appreciation of clay court tennis to keep Rios's interest on a sweltering Roman afternoon. It was hard to believe, given their appearance, that the Englishman was a year older; after all, Henman was fresh-faced, whereas Rios wore a scowl, Henman was leggy and athletic while Rios loped around baggy-shorted, and thick-set, the antithesis of an accomplished athlete. (Indeed, at the French Open, when caught on TV peeling off his shirt, the female coterie among the American tennis writers made caustic comments on the Chilean's bulging love handles.)

Never mind that he didn't look the part, Rios was a stunning tennis-playing specimen. As he skipped into his ground strokes, so he had the ability to despatch the ball with a fascinating variety of winning angles. Henman was easily lured in and then picked off, winning only four points on his own serve in the second set as he went down 6–3, 6–1. Rios was complimentary of Henman's progress. 'He has a game on clay if he wants to do it, but today this is my surface,' he said. 'I don't think Tim has a bad game from the baseline, but he stays there too long and he gave me the rhythm I needed today.'

The vanquished Brit remained upbeat. 'It's stating the obvious to say he dominated me, especially in the second set. If I was to have any chance I had to get off to a fast start, but a player of his calibre doesn't let you dictate. You take his strength off the ground for granted, but his serve is as good as anyone's on this surface. I feel I'm moving better around the ball, constructing the points better too. My improvement curve has been pretty steep but to be beating Rios after four weeks without more than a couple of victories would have been asking a lot. I've lost in the first round of the French in the past two years and I'm at least expecting more of myself than that. If I get a good draw, I expect good things of myself.'

Into the back of the interview room, unseen by the press, had sneaked Sampras, who had become a close friend, a confidant and an occasional doubles partner to Henman. 'I'd like to stress how important it is to keep my practice going on the doubles court,' said Henman and those seated in front of him wondered why he had brought the subject around to doubles, considering he hardly played it on tour. 'I think I can improve in the next game and I'm sure my partner is feeling the same way.'

How will your doubles partner do in the French Open, he was

asked. 'Tough question. For sure, he's got a pretty good chance.'
Question: You play doubles with very good players, do you choose
well, or are you a nice person? 'Tell them nothing,' laughed Sampras,
causing the press to swivel their heads on recognition of his voice. 'I
choose well,' answered Henman.

8 Oh to be in Paris

If Glenn Hoddle had said the equivalent about his England football team with the World Cup looming, he might have been accused of high treason against his own sport, marched into the street and flogged. But David Lloyd, the British Davis Cup captain, had never minced his words. 'These clay court guys will eat Tim and Greg alive,' he said, and there weren't many who disagreed with him. There was a long way to go before we could start considering seriously the presence of a British male in the final at Roland Garros.

What seemed a better bet was Rusedski and Henman checking out of their five-star accommodation in Paris before they'd been in the city long enough to put one lot of laundry through. 'I've watched Tim and Greg on clay and I don't think they've learned enough yet, they think too much about things, they don't gamble,' Lloyd said.

'Take players like Adriano Panatta and Yannick Noah who won the title, McEnroe and Edberg who got to the final. They didn't wait on the baseline to hit enormous great topspin groundstrokes and get themselves involved in tremendous rallies hoping to wear the opponent down. They couldn't do it, they knew that the Spaniards or the South Americans would take them apart.

'Tim and Greg have to be aggressive; not to serve and volley on every point, but be ready to attack. There's no possible way they can win matches in Paris if they don't play that way and they have to prepare themselves to play like that. Greg, especially, has a fantastic sliced backhand, it's a great weapon to bring himself to the net behind.

Tim's got the ability to play any game he wants to. He just has to make better use of his chances.'

No one could possibly win the French Open by having a good day and then sneak through a couple of rounds, the championship simply wasn't made that way. Every single point had to be earned and five sets on clay was a monstrous physical endurance which demanded the use of every muscle and sinew, and all a person's spirit. It broke more people than it made.

The first day had, by virtue of a string of notable collapses down the years, become the day to wave British interest *au revoir*. The distant past had been different, with Sue Barker winning the title, despite losing a set to love to Renata Tomanova in the 1976 final and Jo Durie making it to the last four seven years later. The men's performances had been little short of grotesque – a procession of defeated players lamenting the fact that no one laid clay courts in England any more, neatly side-stepping the thought that they could always have spent a few months in Europe getting used to the idea of red dirt on their socks. No, rather not, thank you.

It was a short-sighted, damaging attitude, reflected in the arrival of five British men for the 1998 qualifying programme. They all lost in straight sets and headed straight back to England to play in a National Club League for the chance to pick up a few thousand quid in prize money.

So, there were two names in the main draw, Henman and Rusedski. Neither had a match to savour, but then playing a match on clay had, by virtue of their recent experiences, become a prospect not dissimilar to Chinese water torture.

Henman drew Sargis Sargsian, a swarthy Armenian who had lost eight first-round matches so far in the year, but who would have fancied his prospects against an Englishman on clay. He wasn't on until the middle of the afternoon. The first match on Court Three astride the Avenue de la Porte D'Auteuil, where those walking the street could peer through the mesh and catch a glimpse of the tennis for free, featured the championship's fourth seed, Rusedski, against Belgian Johan van Herck. The Belgian journalists didn't exactly greet the prospect with enthusiasm.

Tom Rusedski was seated next to Tony Pickard as Greg broke to lead 4–2 in the opening set, finishing with a majestic forehand down the line. Van Herck was nothing to write home about, but this was Rusedski on clay. Nothing was certain. Even three stunning first serves in the next game did not prevent van Herck, returning with an increasing certainty, from breaking back. Rusedski looked to the faces in the crowd, and they must have been as expressionless as his tennis was to become. The Belgian broke the next Rusedski service game to 15 and then cemented that lead by breaking the only time in the second. 6–4, 6–4. No way back.

The first game of the third, on Rusedski's serve, lasted about as long as many grass court matches. Van Herck had eight break points, Rusedski three chances to hold, before a forehand crosscourt winner sped from the Belgian's racket with the Brit, his implement flailing, unable to intercept.

At that moment, Bill Norris, the ATP trainer, was summoned, and started to massage the Rusedski neck muscles. There was little freer movement as the third set gathered momentum. Van Herck finished a 6–4, 6–4, 6–4 winner, leaving the British No.1 to reflect on a single victory in five weeks on clay. What Tom Rusedski whispered to Tony Pickard as they left the court was indecipherable. But those who saw them in the lobby of the players' hotel later in the evening were able to reach only one conclusion. If the partnership stayed together during the summer, it would be a miracle.

Rusedski's press conference was the usual mixture of banality and half-smiles. The lady from the *New York Times* whistled 'Rule Britannia' as we were summoned to the inquest. 'What a sad day for Great Britain,' Robin Finn reflected, as the glum-faced Brits attempted to play along with her sarcasm.

'I just have to work on my game some more,' said Rusedski. 'At least I go out there and try to play my best on the clay. A lot of the Spanish players don't even bother trying to play on grass. I'm just going to have to learn from this year. I've been practising well, but I haven't been able to take that next step forward. If I can do that I'll be absolutely fine. It's the boring old saying "it's a learning curve" which you guys print in the papers far too often in the clay court season. Maybe you can print next year that we have a winning formula.' We doubted it.

The irony was not lost on Rusedski that, the very morning of another shattering reverse, he had risen to No.4 in the world rankings and here he was, the first seed out of the French before a glass of Brouilly had been taken. 'What can you say, a good day for Mr van Herck today. I'm sure he's pleased. I made somebody happy today. He played well, deserved to win.' *Au revoir*, Greg.

And yes, van Herck, ranked No.96 in the world, was feeling exceptionally good. It was his day in the headlines and, funny, I couldn't remember seeing him play again the entire year. Good feelings were not the exclusive province of van Herck, though. A little later this manic Monday, a certain Sargis Sargsian would discover that it was a great day to be facing the Brits. Tim Henman was out on Court No.7, against the Armenian, hoping to hide the extent of the injury to his back that he had strained going for a routine backhand in Sunday afternoon practice against former French champion Yevgeny Kafelnikov.

Trainer Bill Norris was summoned. He tried to manipulate Henman's lower body to alleviate the pain from his back but this wasn't something that could be cured in three minutes, and, anyway, Wimbledon was on the horizon. No point wrecking your body. After Henman's serve had been broken to trail 5–2, he came to the net to shake hands. Match over. The Brits were done and dusted.

'I had felt better this morning,' Henman said, 'but between practice and the match it got stiffer and stiffer. I wanted to see if it would loosen up but it went from bad to worse. This makes me feel pretty sick because I know I've been improving on the clay. I didn't want these six weeks to go to waste, but there's nothing I can do about it now.'

'Tim and Greg go out to grass' said the *Daily Mail*. 'All over by tea for Henman and Rusedski in France,' said the *Guardian*. 'Greg and Tim flop out before tea time,' commented the *Daily Mirror*. The man from the *Mirror*, Kevin Garside, and his oppo from the *Sun*, Mark Irwin, were going home the next day, their purpose for being at Roland Garros having departed the championship. Even the Press Association – once the last organization to pack their bags at any sporting event – called their man home. How times had changed. The rest of us stayed in town. There was still a championship to cover.

Most international attention had turned to the eighteen-year-old Russian Marat Safin, who, aged fourteen, had been plucked from Moscow and sent, thanks to the generosity of a Swiss Bank whose name he couldn't remember, to the Spanish city of Valencia, where he trained long hours on the clay courts, developing his technique and match toughness. If I had been working for the LTA I would have demanded to know the name of the bank, Safin's coach, the whereabouts of the club and immediately paid some of the millions they made from Wimbledon for half a dozen of the best British juniors to go and spend some quality time down there.

Safin was a marvel to behold. He won two five-set matches in succession – and not against any old opponents. Andre Agassi stared down the Safin gun barrel once too often, and then the defending champion Gustavo Kuerten was also despatched in the most mesmerizing match of the fortnight.

It was only when the French crowd roused and raised Cedric Pioline in the quarter-finals that Safin was beaten, once again in five sets. But he had sealed his fame this fortnight and, when asked if he would accept a wild card into Wimbledon, said he would prefer to go to Roehampton and qualify.

We couldn't believe it, so he was asked again. No, he didn't want a wild card, he insisted. It sounded quaint at the time though and he was only eighteen years old, and learning the game. Safin would ultimately take the free entry – Go Direct to the All England Club, pass the gateman and collect lots of money – where he promptly lost in the first round.

The final at Roland Garros was between two members of the resurgent Spanish battalion, Carlos Moya, who had won Monte Carlo, and the engaging Alex Corretja. It wasn't a stunning climax, but matches between close friends – Moya and Corretja dined out together during the tournament and were even pictured sipping from the same Peach Melba on the Champs-Elysées – aren't often classics.

The two of them appeared spent by the rigours of the fortnight. Indeed, after Moya's 6–3, 7–5, 6–3 victory, the abiding memory of the Sunday was of dear old Don Budge, who won the first Grand Slam of the four major tennis championships sixty years earlier, having to be helped on to the Court Central to take part in a ceremony which was completely overshadowed by Pele juggling a football around. Oh yes, another sporting event was about to hit town.

9 The Pressure Begins to Show

Alone, heavily traumatized gentleman in a kilt was spotted in the doorway of a restaurant on the Champs-Elysées on the second Thursday of the French Open. It was the first physical sign that football was taking over and that the tennis fan had better start to make tracks before he was trampled beneath the stampede about to descend on the French nation.

Scotland were playing world champions Brazil in Saint Denis, on the northern outskirts of the capital in the opening match of the 1998 World Cup Finals. On Wednesday 10 June there can hardly have been a person on the planet who didn't have an inkling that something big was about to happen.

The England to which a crestfallen Rusedski and Henman had returned was at fever pitch, debating ad nauseam the decision of coach Glenn Hoddle to omit Paul Gascoigne from his final squad of twenty-two – though how anyone so palpably unfit and lacking condition, whom senior players had tried to sober up two nights before the squad was announced, could have been selected for such a prestigious championship, was beyond rational debate.

Hardly anyone in the media had dared to suggest that Hoddle would do what he did, which made Gascoigne's omission all the more startling. Manchester United manager Alex Ferguson, writing in his column in the *Sunday Times*, put into words what all sensible people in the nation had long been saying: 'The sheer stupidity and arrogance of Gascoigne's behaviour made me shudder, it suggested he thought he was untouchable, which is a ridiculous delusion. Hoddle deserves all the credit for having the courage to do the right thing in the interests of his team.'

What football had reaped, so it would sow. Later in the year would come the news that Gascoigne had checked himself into a drying-out clinic. His demise was further compelling evidence of the demands that a nation placed upon its sporting heroes. Professional athletes weren't allowed to step out of line for a minute, so surely would the wrath of the tabloids descend upon them. It wasn't easy to live up to grand, often unreachable expectations, as Gascoigne demonstrated.

Tennis, thank God, bred a different kind of person but then it was an altogether different sport, one in which pandering to team-mates, showing off for the lads, going out and getting drunk, wasn't an option. The fascination of tennis remained that it was private torture played out to a public gallery. Henman and Rusedski, who thrived on the intensity of the battle, realized that their moment in the sun – though preferably out of it in its newspaper context – was nigh.

In the eternal changing of the sporting seasons, it was time for tennis to matter in Britain again but this was one of those years in a four-year cycle where even Wimbledon, its party piece, had to settle for second billing. From the wall-to-wall coverage on the back and front pages of the national press, it was clear that nothing else mattered bar World Cup '98. The greatest football show on earth was centre stage, three-quarters of the nation checked their fridges were fully stocked with beer, circled the matches they'd watch and prepared their excuses for a few days away from the office. The nation's solicitors readied themselves for an influx of divorce papers.

Henman and Rusedski were fortunate that their exploits in Paris were buried in the small print away from the avalanche of column inches on the football, which meant they were able to return to the grass with barely a single, intrusive camera lens pointed in their direction.

Grass might have been becoming an anachronism in tennis terms, but it was considered Britain's surface – though a British male hadn't won on it at Wimbledon since Fred Perry more than sixty years earlier – and with the attention turning to thoughts of who might do what, both this year and in the future, the Lawn Tennis Association was eager to hitch itself to the momentum generated by the personality and performances of its leading lights.

Another new initiative called Play Tennis 98 was to be launched with the backing of famous faces from the world of showbiz – Sir Cliff Richard was there, as always, along with Angus Deayton and Zoë Ball. The opening in a park in Lambeth, south London was attended by the Sports Minister Tony Banks, never a politician knowingly to side-step a photo opportunity or avoid a microphone. New Labour, he said, was thrilled to be backing a scheme to get more kids playing and would do whatever it could to promote tennis.

The Prime Minister himself had wanted to get involved and a phone call was placed through to the LTA a month earlier, asking if Britain's No.1 tennis player wouldn't mind knocking a few balls around with Britain's No.1 politician. The LTA slavered at the prospect. Public relations didn't come much better than this. They contacted Rusedski to ask him if he could spare some time for the PM. The reply shocked them.

Tony Blair would have to be disappointed. Greg had made it clear that he wanted to appear in the World Team Cup in Dusseldorf that week and although Henman, remember, had aggravated him by turning down the chance to play, Rusedski needed to practise, Pickard wanted him to practise, and that's where he would be. Practising on a clay court. It was what was best for him. The LTA had to return No.10's call and apologize.

The ATP Tour had swung into its month-long grass overdrive and the first port of call was the Stella Artois tennis championship, held at the Queen's Club in Barons Court since 1979, not so much a tennis tournament more a pseudo-aristocratic party where, if you could be tempted away from the sponsor's tent for a while, you might just see a tennis ball being socked back and forth.

After Paris – where you could go to lunch with a bottle of Brouilly and know that they'd still be in the same set when you reached the dregs – came the biff-bang frenzy of grass court tennis. It was the most jarring of all the tennis culture shocks.

Henman and Rusedski had been back in England for ten days, largely undistracted. That was until Henman turned up to practise on the indoor courts at Queen's and was taken aback when he saw Greg's father Tom there, taking copious notes, digesting every move he was making. When it was his own son's turn to practise, Tom Rusedski reached for his video camera. He knew, Greg knew, this was their moment. Nothing could be left to chance.

Tony Pickard warned me that this wasn't a good time to try to talk to Rusedski's father. 'I wouldn't approach him right now, the water's very choppy at the moment,' said the coach. 'When Papa is around, Greg's a different guy. It doesn't make my life easy.' Was this not an indication that the relationship between father and coach might also be rocky? Rusedski, the player, did not need choppy waters with Wimbledon on the horizon.

The outlook was cloudy in more ways than one. The opening day, as with most first days back in the mother country, was wet and bleak. You awoke to clouds and went to bed with clouds. The gaggle of teenage girls sitting in the main stands made Rusedski blush and proffer a little wave as they screamed their delight at having spotted him. A few more tried to force their attentions on to one of the outside courts where Henman was helping to launch Robinson's Aces, a scheme designed to persuade more five-to-twelve year olds to pick up a racket.

Chris Clarke, of Robinson's parent company Britvic, summed up Henman's appeal. 'The success of Tim Henman has brought a much better image to the sport, we know that Tim will be an excellent ambassador for the Robinson's name; he is an ideal role model for all youngsters. Tennis is on the up and up and we have to capitalize on that now and encourage more kids to play the game, and to be involved in this sport rather than others in their teenage years.'

That was for the future. For those in the media not consumed by the drinking and womanizing habits of English football players, Wimbledon was on the horizon and, suddenly, Tim was public property again. When he was breaking through into the public consciousness and his inside-leg measurement was all the rage, Henman railed against such intrusion. One interview in particular, with a feature writer from the *Guardian* in 1997 enraged him.

The headline 'Anyone for tennis?' was hardly original. Its tone was overtly condescending. 'Hooray Henman, tiger Tim, inspirer of Henmania – hoards of screaming girls who paint their face T-I-M – is a sensible boy. His accent is neutrally southern, ex-public school infected, with the trans-Atlantic "liddle" and "gotta" of the international sports star.

'Henman is routinely described in interviews as "a nice chap" – more of a Steve Davis than an Alex Higgins, an Alan Shearer, not a George Best. I wonder if he'd trade in the nice chap thing if it meant he'd win Wimbledon. "Oh yeah, I'd much rather be a champion," he replies. "Because there's going to be times when I piss people off here and there. But, at the end of the day, if I'm going to be the best at what I do, I think that's definitely worthwhile." '

The whole tone of the piece was that here was another routine, boring sportsman. Henman was livid when he read it and asked Jan Felgate not to arrange such interviews for him again. He didn't think his private life should be stripped bare and splashed across the papers. And he didn't see the point of being made to look uninteresting. Nothing should deflect him from the task at hand – but he had to be open to some interviews, for he knew that a British tennis hope at Wimbledon time couldn't avoid being in the papers.

In a back room at Queen's Club a year on from the *Guardian* piece, Henman was extremely personable as a journalist from the *Daily Star* tried to get him to talk about his image. 'David Seaman says he's going to marry his girlfriend after the World Cup, Tim.' A leading question if ever there was one. 'If that happens to me, I'll be telling you first,' said Henman.

'Would you have picked Gazza?'

'I was happy to leave that decision to Glenn Hoddle.'

'Will you be drinking alcohol before matches at Wimbledon?'

'No, not really.'

'Robinson's Barley water I suppose?'

'Yes.'

'Are you Mr Nice Guy, or as Adidas are trying to portray you, Mr Nasty?' I asked him. Adidas, Henman's clothing sponsor, had released a TV commercial showing a brooding Henman taking up the challenge that 'No Englishman will ever win the Australian Open, no Englishman will ever win the French Open (a safe bet), and no Englishman will ever win Wimbledon.' With one unleashing of his serve, Henman brought the walls of doubt crumbling down. 'I don't have any problems with the advertisement about me,' he said. 'It's up to other people how your image is portrayed, it's not something I pay a great deal of attention to. It's your job to write what you want about me. Sometimes I'm nice, sometimes I'm nasty. There's always going to be a following in the press, it's not as if you go unnoticed for eleven months. But for one month, it's chaos. The press becomes more intrusive, it's inevitable. It goes with the territory.'

'Do you want to be liked?'

'No. Sometimes people write nice things about me, sometimes they don't. There's nothing I can do. I'm out there to be a tennis player, hopefully a good one and if people don't like it, there's nothing I can do about it. If all my family and friends started disliking me maybe I'd have to start thinking about whether I was doing things right. That *would* be a problem. I think I'm a fairly consistent person, I still dot my "i"s and cross my "t"s. There are some people in the world who change to accommodate what they might want others to think about them, but that isn't in my make up. What you see is what you get.

'The press will always try to dig out something and I don't have a problem with it. There are times when you can't actually give the right answer to a question, you know that and they know it. I have a pretty good relationship with many of the press and I hope it stays that way.'

Which was just as well because Queen's wasn't going to be a particularly amusing week for anybody. The sky remained, for the most part, a forbidding grey. In fact, on the Wednesday it was reckoned to be the coldest June day in London for twenty years. Frostbite threatened. Greg Rusedski might have wished he'd succumbed to that before his fateful Friday afternoon.

Rusedski, seeded two behind Pete Sampras and with a bye into the second round, had beaten French left-hander, Jerome Golmard, Henman's Aussie nemesis, in three sets. It was not a resoundingly convincing win, but a win nonetheless, and those hadn't been easy to come by for quite a few weeks. The grass felt good beneath his feet.

Henman had comfortably avenged his Paris setback by defeating Sargsian in straight sets for the loss of seven games and wanted to get going again as soon as possible. Inevitably, the weather intervened, to such an extent that, by Friday, the scheduled quarter-final day, the tournament was a full round behind. Clive Bernstein, the referee, was polite to everyone, players, fans and press alike as has been his wont over the years, but this was a terrible frustration – one he shared but could do nothing to ease. Wimbledon, the real reason we were here, was bearing down fast and no-one could get any grass court experience.

It brought back into the tennis discussion the sheer nonsense of a mere two weeks separating the end of the French Open and the beginning of Wimbledon. There was no doubt that maintaining such a schedule was damaging to Wimbledon's reputation. There were hardly two less compatible surfaces in tennis than clay and grass; and grass was becoming more and more of an anomaly in international tennis. If it was to preserve its relevance, then a lot of thought had to be given to extending the period players had to get used to it.

The British press might scathingly dismiss those players who by-passed the grass courts of the All England Club – Thomas Muster had become a perennial non-performer and the Spaniards only tinkered with the event – but which other sport would grant its top performers barely a couple of weeks to prepare for the ultimate championship in the world?

The ITF, the ATP, the Women's Tennis Association and the four Grand Slam chairmen themselves had long failed to grasp this nettle and make the decision which would benefit everyone concerned, the tournaments the players, the media, the spectators, everyone. John McEnroe argued that if there weren't at least three weeks between Roland Garros and Wimbledon pretty soon, grass would not long remain a viable tennis surface.

A week like the one endured at Queen's highlighted the sense in McEnroe's argument, as it meant that most players' practice time was going to be limited to eight days at best. Skipping in and out of showers, watching groundsmen demonstrate how quickly they could get the covers on, might have become the frustrating norm for an English summer, but it was to tennis' discredit that this situation had been allowed to drag on, without sensible resolution.

Glory be, the Friday of Queen's offered a sunnier window of opportunity and for once, the London Weather Centre was spot on with its forecast of brighter spells and fewer showery interventions. Sampras played Mark Woodforde first on Centre Court and, mimicking his recent performances, was undone by a thirty-three-year-old Australian whose game was a throwback to more genteel times. Not for the ginger Woodie the biff-bang of so much of today's game. He is a mellow individual, with a wonderful leftie serve and a fine touch at the net. Indeed, one of his half-volley lobs from the baseline which left the Wimbledon champion stranded would have been the talk of the day, but for what would become the moment the world fell in on Greg Rusedski.

It might have been different had the order of play committee at Queen's not had to pander to its corporate client list. The committee knew that the big bucks boys would be guzzling until early afternoon – there were deals to be done, hands to be shaken, contracts to be signed – so the schedule was for Henman to play Goran Ivanisevic on Centre at 2p.m.; with Rusedski starting against Laurence Tieleman, ranked 253 in the world, at the same time on No.1. If they both won their matches, the two of them would meet later that day and that was perfect timing for the executive clientele.

Suddenly, a tournament that had struggled all week for a trace of a mention, would be the focal point of a nation's sporting attention. Henman and Rusedski had only met twice as professionals on the Tour but never in England, and never this close to Wimbledon. Even the World Cup might be consigned to beneath the fold.

Still, there were dark murmurings among the press about the fact that the third-round matches were to be played simultaneously. The ingenious among the Brits found the answer – they would stand on the balcony just to the left of the 'Royal Box' at Queen's where, if they craned their necks, they could watch both matches, or the top half of four torsos.

I decided that Rusedski was bound to win against a player whose ranking was vastly inferior, so I settled into the front row on Centre to concentrate on Henman versus Ivanisevic, the twice former Wimbledon finalist, a player with a remarkable first serve, a fiery personality and a crushing downer on himself. Henman, settling to his challenge with perspicacity, broke the first Ivanisevic service game to love, led 3–1, held for 4–1 and all seemed to be hunky-dory. Then, Chris Bailey, once Britain's No.3 and the brave Brit in that unforgettable battle with Ivanisevic on Centre Court in 1993, leant across from a couple of rows back. 'Neil, something's happened on No.1, Greg's hurt. He's pulled out.' It was to be the injury, which made the story, which made the year.

There was a major kerfuffle on the balcony, the press boys were desperate because they couldn't actually see what was going on – Rusedski had gone down out of their view but they'd all heard the scream. In his Radio Five Live commentary booth above Centre Court, from where he could only see the heads on No.1, BBC radio tennis correspondent Iain Carter was baffled as to why the score stubbornly refused to move from 2–2, 30–30. His television colleague, David Mercer, came rushing in with the news that would wipe the World Cup off the top of the sports news for one day, at least.

Rusedski, moving from the baseline to play one of those crosscourt backhand put-aways that are the staple of a highly confident player on grass, had slid forward, only for his left ankle to crumple beneath him, taking the entire weight of his body. Rusedski's 'howl of pain' as Pickard was to describe it later, indicated that the injury was potentially serious.

The tournament doctor, a dapper gentleman called Johnny Gaynor, was summoned to a press conference and gave the sort of performance you would expect from a doctor faced with a room full of people trying to find out what was wrong with his patient. His face gave nothing away, nor did his answers. 'Wait until 6.30p.m. when we'll have a better diagnosis,' he said. That was getting too close to deadlines for comfort – what if there was nothing more to tell later on? The press were getting anxious.

Rusedski's father Tom was in a similar state as he accompanied his son to the hospital. According to Pickard, Tom Rusedski had been like a 'cat on a hot tin roof' while awaiting the prognosis on his son's injury. This was the year when the dream had a great chance of being fulfilled and here it was, in tatters. Greg came out on crutches smiling that trademark smile, beaming like a Cheshire cat and we marvelled at his ability to laugh in the face of adversity.

Just before 7p.m. came the news from Cromwell Hospital, west London, that Greg had severely sprained his left ankle, that he had damaged one of the three ligaments on the outside of that ankle and that, according to Dr Gaynor, his chances of playing at Wimbledon, which began ten days hence, were 'less than 50-50'. The doctor was to be proved exactly right.

So, the prospect of Tim Henman meeting Greg Rusedski in the Queen's quarter-finals had been denied us by the fickle finger, or ankle, of fate. Henman conceded that he had been building himself up to face Rusedski and to make a statement in his backyard about which of them was the best player in Britain on the Friday, just eleven days before Wimbledon. Instead, he was to be faced by Laurence Tieleman, a journeyman professional who lived in London himself, but who could walk down the street without a single soul knowing he was a tennis player. Henman had played a full match against Ivanisevic while Tieleman had completed only four games against Rusedski when he was handed the match on a technicality, but that shouldn't have mattered much.

What happened later that afternoon was typical Tim. He was sweeping Tieleman aside as the difference in their rankings suggested he should when, to everyone's horror, he took his foot off the gas at a set and 5–2 up. Here was our boy, on the threshold of victory, his first ATP title on home soil in sight, when concentration ought to have been paramount. At this potentially defining moment, Henman was aware of some disconcerting movement on the side of the court.

TV people had moved down from the rooftop perch with a cameraman and sound boom operator in tow. The three of them exchanged whispers and fidgeted about, getting their equipment ready for the interview with the winner which would fit neatly into their schedules. The tournament press staff, armed with their walkie-talkies, began to emerge from the twilight zone beneath ground, to find out how much time Henman would want after the match before coming in for his obligatory press conference.

Henman saw them out of the corner of his eye and made a gesture asking for quiet. His focus, believe it or not, was to be irrevocably

broken. Some might say it is incredible that such relatively inconsequential movements could cause such alarm, but ask the professionals
and they will tell you that anything out of the norm can distract – a
ballboy in the wrong place, the sun glinting from a watch face, and, for
certain, people walking around when they should be standing still.

It didn't help Henman either that those swimming up to their neck
in Pimms were admonishing him for not getting the match over quickly
enough so they could stagger off and watch the World Cup. The more
exaggerated his swing at the ball, the worse his shot-making became.
The bad choices began to take over to such an extent that he couldn't
get himself back into focus. He went from bad to worse and eventually
lost the match 2–6, 7–6 (11–9 in the tie-break), 6–4. It was a terrible
reverse with Wimbledon pending. Or so the professionally objective
amongst us would have thought. Felgate didn't see it that way.

'It's not an occasion for hard words,' the coach insisted after a
night of reflection – though those who felt he was too soft believed
that a well-aimed Reebok might have been better than an arm around
the shoulder. 'Tim played a good match [against Ivanisevic] during
the day which was the aim, and he certainly put himself in a position
at 6–2, 5–2 to beat Tieleman, but once he was on the back foot, he
couldn't dig himself out of the situation.' There were unrestrained
sighs and looks of disbelief among the press, and Felgate became
increasingly tetchy with the lines of questioning. Indeed, Henman
himself eavesdropped one long, rambling diatribe from a journalist
and mockingly remarked from behind the assembled group: 'Great
question.'

The coach, watching Henman disappear with a flurry of notebooks
in his wake, returned to his theme. 'If he was playing badly and not
trying then I'd be entitled to have a go, but I'm not worried at all. He
knows he's had opportunities this year and they are something that he
has to grasp and handle better than he has done. Queen's is important,
of course, but it is only a World Series tournament; Wimbledon is the
big picture as far as we're concerned. How Tim will play there is
another issue entirely. He will get himself up for that, these lapses
won't happen. There have been times when I've torn a strip off him but
this wasn't one of them. He knows he has to put it right.'

Pressed into a corner of the squash court that doubled for the press
room at Queen's, Henman was as defensive as his coach had been. 'I
know as well as anyone that I had a great opportunity to win this tournament. Having match points doesn't make it any easier, and that's why
I have to move on, to put it to the back of my mind.

'Yes, for a split second it did cross my mind that I would probably be playing Greg in the next round, I wasn't aware of what had happened to him. I suppose it just wasn't meant to be. Of course it hurts, I'm still reflecting on it now. When you have to turn up to a tournament the day after you've lost in the singles [Henman was in the doubles with Sampras, though they were to be thrashed by the Indian pair, Leander Paes and Mahesh Bhupathi on Saturday morning], it's the last place you want to be, especially when you see other guys getting ready for matches you know you ought to be getting ready for.'

He continued his theme the next afternoon. 'I would have loved to be playing singles today and Sunday, but my main objective here, having come home from Paris with an injured back, was to come through unscathed. We've seen what's happened to Greg and the courts weren't even slippery today. In the doubles, I was thinking about Greg, it was there in the back of my mind each time I moved towards that tramline, it makes you realize how much can happen to your career in a split second. I've had experiences like it before myself. I suspect he has played that backhand hundreds of thousands of times, and that's the way it goes sometimes. The last thing I wanted to do here was pick up a silly injury running for a drop shot on a wet court. I think that's why both Pete [Sampras] and I were pretty cautious today.'

As Henman cogitated on a championship lost, Tieleman reached the final. There, in a final pairing no one could have prophesied, he lost to the less-than instantly recognizable Australian left-hander Scott Draper, a twenty-four-year-old from Brisbane. A championship whose roll of honour included Connors, McEnroe, Becker and Lendl would add the name Draper to the list.

10 The Championships

If Greg Rusedski's tennis world was crumbling beneath him, Tim Henman's mood wasn't exactly ecstatic as Wimbledon approached. There were too many demands on his time, he didn't want to keep hanging around signing more autographs than he should. The greatest moment of his sporting career was for the taking and he knew it. Nothing should be allowed to get in his way. Even his favoured sponsors. When he said there were fifteen minutes for a picture opportunity, he meant he'd prefer ten.

Even the *Express*, which had signed him exclusively for quite a princely sum, could not persuade him to pose for a picture outside the gates of the All England Club.

'In the past, he probably would have done the picture, but he didn't want to,' said Jan Felgate. 'There was nothing wrong with that. It showed how much he was prepared to give at a crucial moment in his life. I have never heard a sponsor say they were disappointed with Tim, it has never happened. He's never going to give less than he thinks is right. But he has become more selective too.' And, of course, the pressure was growing. Trust the paper that supports 'our boys' to come up with a negative story to bring Tim down to earth.

Beneath the headline HENMEANIE, the *Sun* said that Henman had refused to play tennis four days before Wimbledon against a three-year-old wonder-kid because of his fear of injury. The newspaper had arranged for Thomas Lester of Peterborough to meet Henman at Roehampton, expecting to get a nice front-page picture of the lad knocking up with his hero. But Henman refused, allegedly saying he didn't want to get hurt. He did stop for a picture later, posing with Thomas on his shoulders, but the *Sun* still made its point. Tim had to live with it. It was just as well they buried the offending article deep in the paper. The World Cup was still all over everywhere else.

So to business. The press gathered in what would become the busiest – and certainly the most expensive – eatery in Wimbledon the following fortnight, the Press Restaurant.

The All England Club was bristling with activity a week before the first ball was served. Purple and green predominated, the lawn mowers were humming, there was clatter and chatter everywhere. The Old Lady of Tennis was looking at herself in the mirror and could be well pleased with what she saw as the courts had never looked better.

The Tuesday before the Championships was the day of the draw. Alan Mills, the tournament referee, and John James, secretary of the Lawn Tennis Association, were dab hands at making a complex process seem so straightforward. Unlike the Football Association, whose crass indulgence of the cameras had turned the FA Cup draw into a made-for-TV pantomime, there was no need for amateur dramatics at Wimbledon. The only time the process of calm was shattered was when the redoubtable John Oakley of the Press Association would interrupt Mills and James, so he could keep pace when names which needed the aid of a spell-checker, like Barabanschikova, Ghiradi-Rubbi, Squillari, Knippschild, Sanguinetti and Pescosolido were drawn from the velvet bag. (When Miss Schwarz drew Miss De Swardt, Oakers cackled away merrily.)

The seeds were traditionally drawn first and Rusedski, as the No.4, found himself placed in the bottom half, in the quarter where Frenchman Cedric Pioline, the previous year's semi-finalist, was a prominent figure, though Goran Ivanisevic, plucked from No.25 in the world to be seeded 14, was Rusedski's designated opponent in the last sixteen.

This was a tough assignment for anyone, anywhere in the world, but this was also an opponent who had twice reached the Wimbledon final and had never lost to Rusedski. It was no draw for a one-legged man.

Tim Henman was seeded 12 and drawn to face Rafter, the US Open champion, in the fourth round, with a potential semi-final against Sampras, if he could improve upon his previous two Wimbledons and survive beyond the last eight. Tim was talking confidently – but even if he managed to qualify for the semis for the first time ... Sampras? The British press, somewhat chastened by the draw, nonetheless dashed for the phones.

Henman's first-round opponent was the Czech, Jiri Novak, who, it was discovered, was playing in a Challenger event in Zagreb, on clay, the week of the draw. Novak went on to win the event, and a message came through to the referee's office at Wimbledon that he couldn't get out of Croatia until 8.30a.m. on the Monday morning. When the Order of Play was announced, Henman v. Novak was third on Court One – Air Croatia willing. Rusedski wasn't scheduled to play until Tuesday. On the day of the draw, he was still rated less than 50-50 to be fit.

The voice of Chris Gorringe, the chief executive of the All England Club reverberated across the grounds on Monday 24 June. 'Ladies and Gentlemen, may I have your attention please, may I have your attention please,' he intoned. 'Welcome to the first day of the 1998 Championships. Would you please make sure you don't leave any personal items behind if you leave your seat or they may be removed, and please, would you turn off your mobile phones when you're near the courts. I hope you have a very pleasant day here at Wimbledon.' It was a sure sign that it was about to rain by the bucketload.

Wimbledon remains the grandest championship of the lot, retaining a mystique to which the others could only aspire. The French has lots more chic and plentiful foie gras de canard, the Australian Open has responded to developments in technology, New York is a wonderful city in which to spend a fortnight, but Wimbledon is *the* two weeks of the year if tennis is your drug.

Defending champion Pete Sampras would open proceedings on the first Monday, on Centre Court, at 2pm precisely, as tradition dictated. The four times champion had no doubt where his priority lay. There were those who felt that maybe Sampras was running out of time as No.1, that the bucket which was once brimful of motivation had sprung a leak.

The French had passed him by for another year, he had struggled with his form for most of the year, but Wimbledon resuscitated him. 'A lot of the guys look upon it as the biggest championship we have,' he said. 'I enjoyed watching it as a kid, I used to get up in the morning in Florida and tune in live. There was something about the echo of the ball on the grass. It was kinda unique. As much as I'm an American, there was never quite that feel about the US Open. Wimbledon just has an aura you don't feel anywhere else in the year. A lot of people are interested in tennis, the whole world watches when you play Wimbledon.'

Sampras was in a constant battle against those who felt that though he was No.1 by right, he was not the truly decorated leader the game required. There is no more personable man in the tennis, but Sampras is also essentially private. He walked across the baseline with his shoulders hunched, he didn't look the public straight in the eye, and this made them suspicious.

Yet, his record at the All England Club bore critical scrutiny. Four wins in the past five years, he was right up there. A victory this year and he would equal the five titles of Sweden's Bjorn Borg in the late 1970s, and of Britain's Laurie Doherty at the turn of the century. 'On clay you might get away with things but on grass [he snapped his finger], it's gone. There are double faults, bad points, bad luck, you can't afford to let them linger, to affect you because in a couple of minutes on grass, a set can disappear.

He went on, 'I still have the desire. I want to be the best player I can be, I want to be able to live with myself when my career is done and know that I've given everything my best shot. I'm not saying I'm going to win every week, I still have my bad days, but I'm going to prepare the same way I have for the past six years. I look on the next six as those I need to take advantage of while I'm young and healthy. I don't want to have any regrets when I'm done playing.'

John McEnroe and Pat Cash knew what it was like to enjoy the crowning glory on Centre Court. McEnroe won the title three times in four years between 1981 and 1984; Cash did not drop a set in the final three rounds of the 1987 championship, smashing Ivan Lendl into submission in the final and setting a trend with his instinctive, emotional dash into the arms of his family and friends in the Players' Box. It was a gesture never to seem so spontaneously joyful again.

Neither McEnroe nor Cash needed to curry favour. Their views were forthright and sincere, very often right, occasionally wrong, always spellbinding. McEnroe was in unequivocal mood: 'To my mind, Tim Henman has taken a couple of steps back over the past two years. I think it has been difficult for him to maintain his level of play and confidence, maybe because of the expectation he's placed upon himself. He has an excellent game, and all the attributes, but I don't think he's ready for this championship yet. Rusedski is a quirky guy who clearly has a grass court game, and there's a hint of brashness about him. It's important to have that. I hope his injury doesn't affect him too much because he has a belief in himself that he'll win something and we need more people in the sport willing to put themselves on the line like that.'

Cash was equally forthright. 'All Tim needs is a bit of animal aggression, he needs to hate to lose. You've heard this before, I know, but he's too nice. If he *really* gets determined, if he hates everything and everybody for two weeks, he will win the championship. It's as simple as that. I know that Greg has the weapons to beat the big guys, especially that left-handed serve which is a wicked strength to have on a grass court, but I wonder if he can return as consistently as you need to to win Wimbledon.

'The attention is evenly shared now with Rusedski and it's been tough for Tim to be able to deal with that. There might be some jealousy, but I think if you took the best bits of Tim and the best bits of Greg and put them together, you'd have one helluva tennis player. I would take Tim's flair and give it to Greg, and Greg's guts and determination and give them to Tim. They have to learn from one another.'

In the week before Wimbledon, the British press traditionally decamped at Eastbourne, for the Direct Line Ladies Championships at Devonshire Park. There was no better place to suck in the sea air, clear the mind and knuckle down to the Wimbledon supplements which were the bane of all of our Aprils, Mays and early Junes. So many words to churn out, so little time, all of us hoping we had a better interview, stat, picture or surprise than anyone else. This year, sad to say, the tennis being played outside the doors of the Press Centre in Eastbourne was almost incidental.

Finally, on Saturday morning, forty-eight hours before Wimbledon began, Tony Pickard admitted to me that he had been trying to make contact with Rusedski since the middle of the week, but he hadn't been able to. So, it transpired, the coach couldn't tell us whether the player would be fit or not. He simply made it clear that Rusedski should inform Wimbledon before the start of play, as a courtesy to his fellow competitors and the event itself, of his progress.

His management company, unless they were stalling or deliberately laying false trails, didn't know of Rusedski's whereabouts either. A one-line statement put out by ProServ to say that Rusedski would be fit hardly quelled the tennis writers' displeasure. The press felt they were being treated with contempt. But maybe ProServ, like the rest of us, had no inkling of the turmoil behind the scenes which was to spill out in such mesmerizing fashion five days later. The press was stuck – it couldn't say Rusedski would be there, it couldn't say he wouldn't.

The first day dawned, reasonably warm and fresh. England were playing Romania in the second of their World Cup group matches that night, so it dismayed us all when Monday's Order of Play came through and Tim Henman was third match on Court One. The explanation was reasonable, that his opponent was flying in from Eastern Europe that morning, he probably wouldn't reach the grounds until midday, and it would be unfair to expect him to play anything other than last match.

Thus we had to wait for Andre Agassi to defeat Spain's Alex Calatrava in straight sets and Monica Seles to put Maria Sanchez Lorenzo to one side, before Henman could even step onto court. This was the second year of the new, rotunda Court One, as distinct from the old No.1 court, which had once symbolized so much of the Championships' intimacy. That structure had been razed to the ground, to be replaced by the new model in another corner of the grounds, one yet to enjoy a similar place in Wimbledon's affections. The players weren't that keen on it either. A lot of them came into press conferences bemoaning the eccentricity of its bounce, of how different it was from what they had been used to.

Eventually Henman strode into this arena, hardly bothering to glance up to the crowd. This was business. A couple of females wolf-whistled. His eyes never left the floor. Novak looked a powerful opponent, a twenty-three-year-old built like a sturdy willow, tall, lean and clean cut. He had been to No.30 in the world, but surely such a transition from clay to grass with hardly the benefit of a practice set would prove too much – jet-lag notwithstanding. The local hero would prevail, and we could all get back into the Press Restaurant well in time for the 8.00p.m. England v. Romania kick-off.

Henman broke to lead 3–1, pressing confidently. But, in the seventh game, he became a bit too casual and pushed a forehand volley wide on break point down. 4–3. Henman extended the twelfth game to three deuces, but couldn't deny Novak his right to a tie-break. One Novak double fault was the crucial difference. Advantage Timbo.

The second set was another slog. A shaft of sunlight – the first of the afternoon – broke across court as Henman put away a delightful cross-court backhand volley from over his left shoulder to break for 6–5, and serve out for the set. The TVs beckoned, even more when Henman again pounced first in the third set to break serve to lead 2–1. Novak, though, broke back immediately. The crowd groaned.

The set stayed with serve until the twelfth game when Henman's serve, which had been betraying him for weeks, began to disintegrate again. He double faulted to 15–30, a net cord wrong-footed him to give Novak two sets points at 15–40 and when Henman put a fore-hand half-volley over the baseline, it was two sets to one. 'Come on, hurry up, we want to go home and watch the match,' a voice shouted. Henman looked agitated. He had two break points in Novak's first service game in the fourth set, but a wrong-footing forehand left him on his knees and a netted backhand service return allowed Novak to hold. There were five more break points in the third game, but Novak held once more.

The Czech was surviving, just, so it was remarkable when Henman's serve crumbled first. He double faulted twice in the tenth game and then allowed a backhand service return to drop inside the line when he could easily have put it away with a backhand volley of his own. Two sets all. We were going to miss the kick-off after all.

People were beginning to filter away now, beginning to think the unthinkable, that Henman would lose. The English press boys on deadline were watching from the TV monitors at their desks. In the press box on Court One, I was alone. David Lloyd remarked on it. Where was everyone? I was halfway through the explanation but Lloyd turned away, concentrating again on the kid he had known since the age of ten who was in deep trouble.

Then, in the fifth game of the final set, Henman's fierce backhand drive took him to break point, and he managed to make it, his first success in nineteen opportunities. I looked at my watch. It was precisely 8p.m. England were underway. In the seventh game Henman had four more break points, producing his best shot of the match on the fourth – a backhand drive from behind the baseline which flew past Novak at the net and landed right in the corner – to break for a 5–2 lead. After three hours and ten minutes, he concluded proceedings with an unreturnable serve. Why the hell had it taken so long for him to come up with that? 7–6, 7–5, 5–7, 4–6, 6–2 would go down in the record books. It had been a very long day.

'It was a real battle,' said Henman to a sparse press audience later that evening – the seats in front of the TV monitor in the press restau-rant were decidedly more popular. 'I felt I struggled a lot with the court, I remembered losing to Stich on it last year. Then, in the fifth, I allowed my mind to drift back to Melbourne, the first round of a Slam – to the match against Golmard. This match was slipping a lot, but I didn't want to let it happen to me again. Not at Wimbledon.

'But I struggled with my concentration again, I got distracted by the crowd. When they started to shout about the football, it irritated me, I needed to get it out of my mind quicker than I did. This doesn't shake my confidence. I'll focus on the good points and forget the bad ones. I'm through to round two and that's what today was all about.'

Tomorrow was another day. The headlines would be all about England's defeat to Romania anyway. Glenn Hoddle was on the rack. He had left out David Beckham again, preferring Darren Anderton. Le Saux had had a nightmare at left wing-back, David Seaman let Romania's winner through his legs. Tim Henman scraping through in five sets on Wimbledon's first day, merited a downpage piece inside. He was probably grateful.

No one had seen much of Greg Rusedski since he had hobbled from Cromwell Hospital grinning broadly – on crutches on the evening of his fateful fall against Tieleman at Queen's. None of the British press had been able to get a word from him, so we waited anxiously to see his condition as he walked on to Court One on Tuesday afternoon to face Australian qualifier Mark Draper.

What we witnessed took the breath away. Rusedski has a stilted walking motion anyway, right shoulder slightly above left, but the way his left ankle had been protected, the padding, the support, made him appear even more like Lurch from the Addams Family. 'Give us a wave, Greg,' the crowd implored. 'Give us your shirt, Greg.' screamed a female admirer. 'Where have you left your crutch, Greg?' might have been more appropriate, but, whatever his physical state, the No.1 court crowd was decidedly more roused on Tuesday for Rusedski than it had been on Monday for Henman.

But the man couldn't move without an exaggerated stumble. He certainly couldn't run. This was a shambles. Wimbledon was being cheated, there should be calls for a refund. Rusedski's own body language was all wrong, and when Tony Pickard and Steve Green, Rusedski's fitness trainer, took up their seats at the opposite end from Greg's girlfriend Lucy Connor and a couple of her pals, we knew something more than his injury was up.

Rusedski chose to serve, which was gallant enough but exposed his limitations right away. Unless he got a first serve in, he couldn't make anything of a point. He held gamely, but double faulted twice, and sent down one ace. Double faults three and four came in the following service game, but he still held. Five, six and seven followed in the fifth as Pickard held his head in his hands. Eight and nine in the ninth although he held that game too, and then, lo and behold, Draper froze in the tenth game. Rusedski earned three break points, clocked a backhand service return and won the set. This was incredible. The crowd roared their approval, or was it their astonishment?

When double faults ten, eleven and twelve followed in the opening game of the second set and Draper finally had hold on his racket firmly enough to break, Rusedski couldn't respond. He rapidly lost that set 6–2, and was trailing 5–4 in the third when play was abandoned for the evening. He would spend the next few hours agonizing about whether he should return to court the next day.

The official ATP Tour trainers, who usually attended to players during the championships, weren't sure how they should approach Rusedski, as he had his own physiotherapist, the Iranian Reza Daneshmand, in the locker room. Daneshmand taped Rusedski's ankle that evening, he used some ultra sound on a slight groin strain and then massaged his client. Pickard wasn't happy with the procedure, he would have preferred the usual trainers to do their stuff. Rusedski noted Pickard's displeasure with concern, but was reconciled to come back the next day and try again, whatever his coach might have been thinking.

As he left the practice courts on Wednesday morning and was grabbed by the BBC's Garry Richardson for a few words, he said – grin still fixed – that he was going to play, that everything was OK. Within, an hour, Rusedski had taken counsel from 'those I trust' and an official statement from the All England announced he had decided to retire. He had come to the sensible, if belated conclusion that he should prevent his body from taking any further punishment. Mark Draper of Australia had won his first singles match at Wimbledon, but nobody really noticed.

We weren't to know this at the moment of Rusedski's default, but when he returned to the locker room after his meeting with the referee, in accordance with tennis procedure, he found Tony Pickard waiting for him. 'Sit down, son,' the coach said. 'Our relationship is over.'

The official press conferences with Rusedski and Pickard on Wednesday 24 June made for some fascinating discoveries. Here are some extracts:

Q: Greg, does it (the ankle) hurt?

A: No, it seems fine. The injury didn't get any worse than it was yesterday, but I just felt, the state I was playing, it didn't get any better. I was hoping for it to get better today so I could move a little quicker and do better, but unfortunately for me, that didn't happen. Even if I had gotten by my first round match, it's kinda hard to win seven matches that way.

Q: Does it hurt mentally?

A: Yes, obviously it does, because I think my preparation for the championships was perfect. Even though I lost a lot of my matches on clay, my game was getting better, my confidence was coming. But what doesn't kill you, makes you stronger.

Q: Wouldn't it have been wiser not to have gone on court in the first place?

A: Well, I think I had to satisfy myself and give back to the public who supported me and I couldn't have done any damage. I saw the doctors, I saw my physio, I spoke to them. They said I couldn't make it worse. So I decided to give it a go, and I'm pleased I did.

Q: Greg, what was the thinking last week? You seemed to burrow away on your own with Reza and not let anyone know your business and what it was about. What was the thinking, didn't you want your potential opponents to know what the picture was?

A: I think I needed to get away myself and just try to sort out the injury myself and I think by everybody always getting involved and always being there, you know, it doesn't help to get the injury better. If you're always having to answer questions about it, are you going to play, are you going to do this or that, it's not always the best thing for you. You need to have a clear mind, stay focused and try to get ready. My goal was to be ready for the championships and that's what I was hoping for, so I was trying to keep a clear mind and stay positive.

Q: Were you surprised by today's reaction in the media. A lot of people were quite critical, saying you shouldn't have played.

A: I don't read the newspapers, so I don't have any opinions. That's the easiest way, because if I started reading the papers, I don't know if I'd speak to you guys.

Q: Greg, what happened today. You went and hit this morning and the TV people grabbed you and you said you were pretty hopeful and things were looking OK. What happened between then and your decision?

A: I just spoke to my physical trainer, Steve Green, and he felt it wasn't the right decision to make. I listened to what Steve had to say, because if he says that, then I believe it. Plus I spoke to my physio last night, I spoke with my girlfriend, her parents and everything and I just decided at the end, you know, if he felt that strongly about it, I wouldn't do it.

Q: What were your initial thoughts when the injury happened at Queen's?

A: I was positive and optimistic. Everybody else was a little bit glum, shall we say, but I always like to stay positive and believe I can get through anything. I like to prove people wrong and do my best out there. Getting negative doesn't help you recover, does it?

Q: Would you have taken the risk of playing if it hadn't been Wimbledon?

A: I think it's definitely Wimbledon. It only comes around once a year, it's the biggest tournament in the world, it's at home, it's the one the British public comes to support and come to see myself and Tim and all the other British players do well, so I don't want to miss it. I would have been gutted if I hadn't stepped out onto the court at least. Can you imagine sitting there for two weeks and watching Wimbledon go by?

Q: I'm assuming, knowing you, that there were no pain killers, no injections, nothing?

A: No, I don't believe in pain killers or injections, or anything. In the US Open final I was offered something for my throat and I don't believe in taking any of those things, because all it does is hide it and you can't tell what's happening. So, if you want to injure yourself, take those things.

Q: Has all this injured your relationship with Tony as a coach, because, you know, you said yourself you wanted to go away and sort things out for yourself, have your treatment, make your decision?

A: Tony feels that he doesn't want to work with me any more, and that's it. So the relationship is basically done. So that's what his comments were for today, after I decided to pull out. So that's his choice.'

Q [as the press room began to buzz and Rusedski half-rose from his chair at the end of his ten-minute stint]: Do you regret now playing, in relation to the way Tony feels now?

A: No, I don't regret it, because I felt it was something I had to do. I had to go out there and play and I don't regret it in the least. I think I made the right decision for myself, and I was thinking of what I needed to do and the people around me, and I had confidence in my physio and I had confidence in my physical trainer and the people that were around me and if that's the way he feels, that's fine. But I don't think that's the most supportive way to be supportive to a person, or the time to be supportive as well.

Q: That must obviously come as a blow to you, because all along you said what Tony is going to do for your career, and how Tony had worked with Stefan, and everything that's gone before. Did this come as a bolt from the blue for you?

A: I think the timing of it is a little bit suspect. You know, fair enough, he didn't like some of the decisions made with my physio-therapy and the people around me but, you know, just because I get this injury, and it happens to be Wimbledon time, and I decide to give it a go, does not give a person a reason to make that choice, but I guess that just shows a person's true colours.

Q: Greg, do you have any ideas about a replacement coach?

A: I'm not worried about it. The player always makes it. The coach can help, but it's the player at the end of the day.

Exit Rusedski, grin not so prominent, stage left. The only people who could have been happy with his performance were sponsors Nike, for he wore a black beret-like piece of headgear, back to front, with the 'tick' logo prominent and they were to replay the press conference on every television medium across the country that night. Wimbledon normally fights shy of such unadulterated showmanship.

The air was now thick with intrigue. Was Pickard still on the premises, had he gone home? The press boys couldn't have only one side of the story. They needed the erstwhile coach's response. John Parsons of the *Daily Telegraph*, who had become a member of the All England Club a couple of years earlier and therefore had privileges beyond the reach of the rest of the press, was asked to venture inside the corridors of power to seek Pickard out.

If any other country had been wanting to get hold of a coach in similar circumstances it would have been impossible. Being English at Wimbledon definitely had its advantages. Pickard, it was discovered was still there, having afternoon tea. Parsons asked him if he would come into the interview room. Pickard acceded to the request. Half an hour later, in he strode, resplendent in smart suit, club purple and green tie, member's badge prominent on his lapel.

Q: Greg tells us your partnership has been terminated. Can you tell us, did you just sit down and have a chat?

A: Yes, I waited until he'd made the decision that he wasn't going to play but I'd thought long and hard about it over the past two weeks. I sat him down and told him it was over.

Q: Can you expand on your reasons?

A: There was a total breakdown in communication. I mean, for two days, I had no idea where he was and at this level, unless there's complete trust, it stops working. It would be wrong of me to say that we haven't had trust, but over the last ten, maybe twelve days, it seemed to go out of the window.

Q: What was the straw that broke the camel's back?

A: When he stopped listening.

Q: And that was?

A: Well, I think you are a witness, what you saw.

Q: In your words, though.

A: I didn't believe he should have played. There were outside influences telling him he was going to be fit to play. I didn't consider he was – and the other straw that broke the camel's back was that for two days I couldn't find him.

Q: Did you have reservations coming into this, Tony?

A: No, I didn't, I didn't really. I had no reservations at all for nine months. It's been good. We've just come through possibly one of the most traumatic times of his life on the clay and we came through that fine, but for some unknown reasons, suddenly, when we got back here, it was a different ball game.

Q: How did he react when you told him?

A: He didn't say much. He was very quiet. There was no ranting and raving. It was just a sensible conversation.

Q: He could have talked you out of it?

A: I think you know me better than that.

Q: He seemed to hint that you hadn't been very supportive of his decisions and he also said that it shows a person in his true colours. Do you fancy expanding on that?

A: Maybe the young man would be a lot better to say nothing because if I was to elaborate for you, then I think you would all tear him to pieces. So I think it's better that I don't make any comment.

Q: Tony, is it a feeling of sadness, relief or what?

A: In one way, last night nearly killed me, sitting and watching somebody destroying themselves out on the tennis court was almost heart rending. In a way, in one respect, sadness, because I think we'd achieved something better than what he believed he could achieve over that period of time. But then, once the trust goes, then it's not going to work, and I'm big enough to know I don't need to sit on a pot if it isn't going to work.

Q: He said, Tony, that there was never a chance of him doing any further damage to his ankle, that the ligament had repaired and that it was just a question of him getting power back into the leg. Presumably, you didn't see it quite that way?

A: Well, I think the whole world saw it. If it was as simple as that – I mean, last night he ran once and the rest of time he served and walked. These rehabilitations take time.

*

The boys rushed to their PCs. The tournament had not been graced with a single match worth keeping the Press Bar shutters up until 11p.m., and here was a God-sent story. British No.1 player breaks up with coach who he had said would take him to the top.

Greg came on television, talking about wanting to play for his fans. It had been a hard decision to pull himself out but he knew that Britain had been rooting for him and he didn't want to let them down. And now, the self-same fans had only Tim [and Chris Wilkinson and Samantha Smith who were still going] to shout for. 'I sure hope they'll support Tim even more now, but I'm so grateful they were all behind me today.'

The Rusedski story would rumble on and on. When Pickard said he would come into the green-panelled one-on-one interview room a spit and a stride from Centre Court on Friday afternoon, there were still parts of the story left untold, but he was willing to offer a few more insights. He revealed, for instance, that he had telephoned Rusedski the Wednesday before the Championships to tell him he was coming to London for a funeral, so he would pop around to find out how the ankle was healing. He was told by Rusedski not to bother, as he wouldn't be there.

'He said he was going away with Reza,' Pickard said. 'I thought they might be going to a health farm or something, but I went by his flat on Thursday, rang the bell and there was no answer. I tried again, no answer. I phoned continually, no reply. Then, after tearing a strip off certain people close to Greg, I found out where he was and they must have tipped him the wink because he called me on Friday evening, from out of the country. I had made my decision then that whatever happened at Wimbledon, we were finished. I didn't think there was anything evil in what he did, he did it because it was right for him and that's the only way it can be judged.'

What about Rusedski's 'true colours' quote, which could have been construed as an indication that Pickard had never been totally supportive? 'I'm a pro, I'm English and I'm proud to show my colours in whatever way,' was Pickard's unequivocal response. 'You have to realize that we've all been twenty-four. Maybe Greg will realize one day he made a comment that, with more thought, he wouldn't have come out with.

'I behaved in a way I considered to be polite and professional. In my opinion, he wasn't fit to play. I told him not to go out there and be a hero – he would get no points for that. I asked him what he was going to do and he said he was going to give it a go. I was worried for him because he was someone I'd grown reasonably close to. I had to be there on the court, offering support, but what he did was unprofessional.'

There were those in the game who felt Pickard had acted too quickly and, perhaps, too harshly. He acknowledged, in his own words, that a tennis coach was there 'to cut any corners possible for his player to win'. But, this time, he had cut off his nose to spite his face. Rusedski's reaction, after the stunning way in which the news was delivered, was to treat it as just another lesson in life. He still had his goals, and one man's decision to drop him, wasn't going to stop him doing everything he could to achieve them.

No one expressed a great deal of surprise: with two such combustible, strong-willed characters, anything was possible. The LTA's Richard Lewis, for one, had seen the explosion coming. 'My strong impression was that there had been a great deal of tension in the camp a number of weeks before they split up,' he said. 'I would have staked my reputation that it wouldn't last until the end of the year.

'I knew Tom very well, we had been through a lot together involving Greg and I knew Tony, we had been through a lot together as well, for better or worse. Tony first took me abroad in a tennis team when I was seventeen years old, I think I know quite a bit about how he works and when I saw him and Tom Rusedski sitting next to each other during Greg's first match in the French Open, and in the players' hotel later, I knew there was something up. Exactly what, I didn't know then, and still don't.

'Maybe even Tom and Tony didn't know the real reason, but the tensions had been building up. I know Tom will make comments during a match. I sat there with Tom, Helen and Brian Teacher at the US Open last year, Tom would say a few things about Greg which Brian wouldn't react to. But I knew he heard them. That's why I was watching Tom and Tony so closely in Paris. I knew what Tom would be saying and I knew what Tony would be saying back to him.

'I've always found Tom Rusedski to be exceptionally polite, but very straightforward, he speaks his mind and says what he thinks, especially where Greg is concerned. And I get the feeling that Greg can still feel very insecure about himself in certain situations.'

How many official coaches had there been since young Greg first picked up a racket? His dad, *le plus important*, Patric, Schultz, Diepraam, Brooke, Stolle, Teacher, and now Pickard. He had been dumped by an Englishman, to boot.

To be honest, Pickard didn't seem the least bit concerned that the partnership had ended. He didn't look like a man at the end of his professional tether as he re-joined family and friends sipping the finest champagne on the Member's Lawn on Friday afternoon. To who knew where in the tennis world after that?

Tim Henman didn't have an inkling that Pickard and Rusedski were snapping at each other only a few yards from where he was preparing for his second-round match against David Nainkin, a South African who had survived the rigours of Roehampton and qualified for a spot in the main draw. To a player of Nainkin's ranking and relative inexperience, this was like winning the title itself, so there was no doubt he was match hard, temperamentally sound, and would prove to be a limpet-like opponent. Centre Court awaited, expectantly, for its first sight of Gentleman Tim this year.

Henman liked order – as much as it was possible during Wimbledon – to prevail. He liked to know where everyone was, so there would no surprises, no shocks. His coterie took their places in the front row of the Players' Box in the same seats, striking the same poses. David Felgate sat in the far right-hand corner, hunched, half-turned away from everyone else, his fingers held prayer-like to his lips, giving nothing away except the odd positive nod when Henman looked his way. To Felgate's left was fitness coach Tim Newenham, a perennially positive influence, a former athlete and bobsleigher who had begun working with the player in 1995 after a spell as the coach to Britain's javelin team, and had done wonders with his level of conditioning.

Tim's girlfriend, surgeon's daughter Lucy Heald, came next, English prettiness personified then his agent Jan Felgate, his mother Jane, who often pressed her hands together as if wiping the sweat from her palms; and finally, on the extreme left, dad Tony, applauding his son's good shots and those of his opponents with no visible hint of favouritism. Tim was comforted by their presence. He felt comforted, too, by the unique surroundings of Centre Court.

Little was known of Nainkin, even the aficionados shook their heads, reached for their media guides and rummaged around for a couple of titbits of information with which to stun their readers. The right-handed South African, ranked 234 in the world, was about to prove as stubborn as his compatriot Hanse Cronje became to

England's cricketers at the Test match venues of the summer.

When Henman served a love game within a couple of minutes, a brisk tone had been set, but Nainkin was sharp, rugged and obviously not prepared to roll over for the local hero. Indeed, he contrived the first break point, in the seventh game, and only forfeited it to an unforced error on the backhand. Henman, thus reprieved, broke in the next game when Nainkin pressed too hard and twice double faulted. An ace on his third set point completed the first set in thirty-four minutes.

The second set was to become one of those rarities on grass, where the server is generally king. Henman broke to lead 3–2, Nainkin retorted to square at 3–3, held for 4–3 and then, in the eighth game, broke Henman for the second time in succession, producing a brilliant running cross-court pass, which even a patriotic crowd vigorously acknowledged. The applause seemed to act as a wake-up call to Henman who responded in the very next game – it was back to 5–4 to the South African.

Henman held Nainkin at bay for one game, but when he was broken for the third time in the set, with a lame double fault, the match was squared at one set all. No one completely engrossed in Henman's travails in the middle of the third set could have known that just at the moment he lost his service once more to trail 4–2, Rusedski was telling the world that he and Tony Pickard were a former item.

Henman recovered to win the set 6–4, a perfect time for the message about Rusedski and Pickard's parting of the ways to be relayed to the front row of the Players' Box. Felgate knew his man was still in a tough match. This guy wouldn't let go. Indeed, Nainkin had to be prised apart, 6–3, 5–7, 6–4, 6–2 – another toughie, another round of careless shots interspersed with moments of brilliance from Henman. All was not yet well.

'He was staying back, hitting his groundstrokes really heavily and returning so well that it came to a stage at the end of the second set that I ran out of ideas as to where to serve,' Henman admitted. 'But I stuck to my guns, and kept battling, I knew his second serve was vulnerable, and though he passed me a lot, I had to keep coming in because that was the right play. In the past, I've been too up and too down but I thought it was my consistency today that brought me through. I feel a lot more confident now.'

Henman knew the question about Rusedski's withdrawal would come up and he answered it as best he could, without sounding as though he was intrigued (though he was) or was interfering (which he wasn't). 'It was a nightmare situation for him to have had the injury in the first place, but I don't think he was ever going to do himself justice out there. I think, overall, your sympathies are with the guy. It's the biggest tournament in the world and he's not 100 per cent fit,' Henman replied.

Then came mention that Rusedski and Pickard had split. What was Henman's reaction? 'It's been an eventful day,' he responded, politically correct as ever. 'I'm a little bit surprised because they seemed to have a good relationship from the day they started working together; Greg was always talking about how much he had learned from Tony and how well things were going. There's always rumours about a coach's relationship with his player, and it just goes to show that I'm very happy the way things work with me, and I like to keep continuity, if that's the right word.'

Sitting at the back of the interview room a faint smile crossed Felgate's lips as Tim discussed the events of the day but Felgate himself would not be drawn to comment. That smile was to be wiped unceremoniously away the following morning when his attention was drawn to a debate that had been aired from Radio Five Live's commentary positions scattered across the grounds of the All England Club.

With loads of air-time to fill as the clouds deposited further droplets across SW19, conversation inevitably turned to where Rusedski's career would go from here. The BBC team were encouraged to chip in their ten penn'orth and Chris Bowers, a freelance tennis writer and broadcaster, offered the opinion that Henman would probably be getting a call pretty soon from Pickard. The call might even be made the other way. He could hardly have expressed an opinion less likely to meet with Felgate's approval.

Maybe it was said just to get people going. It had that effect with Henman's coach. Felgate was apoplectic. Bowers' remarks were like a red rag to a bull with a sore head. He must have known how fed up Henman's coach was with stories about how he was going to lose his man to Pickard and here was the debate being fuelled and given credence on the country's most reputable sports station.

John Inverdale, the host of Radio Five's Wimbledon coverage, asked the rest of his crew whether they saw any prospect that Pickard and Henman might work together, and though most of them thought it utterly unlikely, the fact was the idea had been raised. Felgate decided next morning to visit the BBC Radio studios just to make sure the record was put straight.

The Rusedski affair would not go away. We wouldn't let it. John McEnroe and I sat in the restaurant next to the Wimbledon studios of America's NBC network – McEnroe had become one of the finest analysts in the business and a columnist for the *Sunday Telegraph* – trying to unravel this particularly knotty dilemma. The former world No.1 was his usual restless, sometimes distracted self, but he was keen to talk about his sport, keen to get to the bottom of what had become a strange business.

'Maybe tennis has decided if it can't beat the World Cup it should join it,' he said. 'The coaches are dropping like flies over there in France, but at least they usually make it through a couple of matches. Tony didn't survive one.

'I never had a lot of success personally when someone was travelling with me. I preferred to be with friends, travelling with them, practising with them. My first coach, Tony Palafox, was someone I'd call on the phone, to be able to exchange stuff with him. In this day and age, everyone has a coach. Greg Rusedski has obviously been a difficult one to figure for a long time, which can sometimes work to the player's advantage.'

McEnroe said he was disappointed with Rusedski from the beginning over Brian Teacher, a very close friend of the former Wimbledon champion. 'Brian helped his career, and then he gets short-changed. Whatever the reasons for the parting, I couldn't understand how a guy at that stage, looking at what he'd done for him in the previous year, taking him to No.4 in the world, didn't try to resolve it. Instead of criticizing a coach, you go out and give him another year's contract.'

It riled McEnroe to hear Rusedski questioning Teacher's abilities, both in terms of tactical appreciation, and scouting the weaknesses of the opposition (Tony Pickard was to tell me later in the year that Rusedski liked to have everything written down for him, so that he could study the paper and learn all that he could about an opponent).

McEnroe said, 'Brian hadn't been away from the pro game for that long, he was a lot more in tune with how the current pros played than Tony. None of it makes any sense. When Tony was around with Stefan, he had an influence there, he had about a year with Korda when he improved. But to say Tony knew more about players than Brian wasn't being up front.'

McEnroe wanted the two to compromise – he spoke to both Teacher and Rusedski's agent John Mayotte but he feared that the split was inevitable. 'A player is entitled to do what he wants, don't get me wrong, but how he handles situations like this is the key to how people view him as a person. In my opinion, you have to handle these things with a little dignity and class. If anything, you go the extra mile to make sure the person who has helped you gets what he deserves.

'Obviously Rusedski was the man who had to play, but Brian Teacher was a positive factor. I hoped they could work on their differences, whatever they were. I told Brian I thought he was entitled to what he was asking for, it wasn't something he should have backed down from. You have to stand up for yourself and say "This is what I deserve."

'I know Brian felt he had Greg going the way he wanted him to go. They stayed together between Wimbledon and the US Open, but then Brian gets dropped. It shouldn't have happened.'

If McEnroe had little sympathy with Rusedski over the departure of Brian Teacher, he felt more for him when he was confronted with the prospect of missing Wimbledon through the dreadful ill-luck of his ankle ligament injury. In this case, he believes, a player has to do what a player believes is best for himself.

'Tony was the coach, he's not a physio. Greg obviously thought he could get through two or three rounds at 80 per cent fitness, the fans were behind him, and he must have believed it was possible to improve. It isn't inconceivable that he could get a couple of matches under his belt and get better. This is the biggest championship of the year, for God's sake.

'Ultimately, the coach has to support the player. We all want to be 100 per cent, but how many players here are that? You can go down the list and there will be some kind of ache or pain, it's amazing what a dose of adrenalin will do. It might have been a long shot for Rusedski, but it doesn't mean you break up with your coach. If I had been Rusedski I would have told my coach I was going away to Turkey because I was hoping something miraculous was going to happen. He wanted to be right for Wimbledon, there's nothing wrong with that.

'Things like this happening make me appreciate what I had in my career. The best part of not having a coach is that when you won, everything came your way and when you lost, you had no one to blame but yourself and that's OK, I preferred it that way. I felt more in a comfort zone than having to come through with a team who, ultimately, don't know what you're really thinking and don't know where your head is.

'Succeeding as a coach takes a special person. They have to pick the right time to tell the players things, to let certain situations go in one ear and out the other, and wait for the usual "I can't even hit a fore-hand now, it's all your fault." But there has to be a time, also, when you step from out of the background and tell the player "I don't think you should do that." You need balls to do that. At a certain level, you do get to care about the player as a person – you're spending a lot of time together, travelling the world, you had better get along.

'The only reason I had a coach near the end of my career was that I needed a motivation to practise between events. I worked with Larry Stefanki [who was to be sacked by Rios before the US Open in almost a carbon copy of Teacher's dismissal by Rusedski] for a time, and even my old buddy Peter Fleming [with whom McEnroe won four Wimbledon titles, three at the US Open and countless others], but the relationship we'd had was too cemented and when I needed to be listening to him, that didn't happen.

'Rusedski isn't an easy guy to deal with, it's pretty clear to see. I'm sure that Henman would be the easier guy to coach. And you can bet your derrière that the reason he and Felgate get along so well together is that the coach does all those things I've talked about – listen, know the time to walk and be quiet, know what to say and when – to make the relationship keeping on working.

'I'm also sure that people have been asking whether Henman can go to a different level if he had a Pickard type of guy. But because Henman cares about Felgate, he can use the incentive of people sniping, and continually asking questions, to say "Hey, I can do this *with* him." It's a tough call, but Henman is no fool.

'Rusedski is more quirky. He's more of an American, with this very un-Brit like behaviour. Well, he's Canadian, he's got that bouncy type of character you see more frequently the way they were brought up. But Canada has the same little brother kind of attitude with the US, like Wales has with England, something along those lines. The littler brother is always over-compensating, trying to do things that get noticed.

'Then he comes to England and here's a whole new situation to sort out, it's not his personality. I think he's done quite well with it – I don't think I could ever be a Brit – but this is the first time that things have started to turn the wrong way. I was fascinated with his "true colours" quote, but I think both Rusedski and Pickard showed their true colours.

'How can Pickard go from a genius in Rusedski's eyes to be char-acterized as "Well, it shows what he knows?" When guys get injured they do desperate things. Someone convinces Rusedski he's going to get better and did he really *want* to fly to Turkey? I'm sure it wouldn't have been his first choice. He wants to get treated in London, but he doesn't believe there's anyone here who can treat him, so desperation takes over and he'll do virtually anything to play at Wimbledon.

'This whole thing is bizarre. There are so many competent people in this country, not just involved in tennis but so many other sports. Wasn't there someone here who could have helped him and with all these people around, didn't someone tell him that in eight hours on a plane, your ankles normally swell. This has been an amazing episode, without a doubt.'

With that McEnroe finished off his spaghetti bolognese, pulled his baseball cap down over his greying temples, put on his dark glasses and stepped out into a cool, cloudy London afternoon.

Rusedski was not the only seed to have disappeared without leaving much more than a passing trace. We had wanted so much for Agassi to reproduce the form of 1991, and, despite his own misgivings and the lack of impact in the spring, his return to the love of the game had provided tennis with a sparkle. We all respected him.

His was to be a controversial second-round exit, tragic even, because he was the victim of the kind of decision everyone endures from time to time, but you just didn't expect on Centre Court at Wimbledon. The light was fading on Thursday night when Agassi's opponent, the American-trained, German-born Tommy Haas, smacked an approach shot that was clearly both wide, by a couple of inches, and long.

Experienced umpires and line judges will tell you that, apart from clay where you can actually get out of your seat to check a mark, calling lines on grass is the next easiest. But it didn't help Agassi in this case. No call broke the air. Agassi looked up, pleading with Scottish umpire John Frame, but unless the official believed he had seen a clear fault, and overruled promptly, there was nothing he could do. There was no third umpire to call upon for adjudication. At the end of the next game, the match was called for bad light, and the American had a night to stew over the injustice. He came back the next day, succumbing to Haas 6–4, 1–6, 6–7, 4–6.

The seeds had been crumbling all around. The Russian Yevgeny Kafelnikov, Spaniard Alex Corretja, Sweden's Jonas Bjorkman, the previous year's finalist, Frenchman Cedric Pioline, Slovakian Karol Kucera and Chile's second-seeded Marcelo Rios, were all out before the championship had drawn breath. Rios said that he simply didn't care about Wimbledon, that losing in the first round meant about as much to him as losing in the first round of the Tierra del Fuego Closed. The tournament bade him farewell. But with all these premature departures, the field was spreading itself out wide for someone unheralded to burst through. It couldn't make Rusedski feel any better that Chris Wilkinson had his customary flirtation with the headlines by reaching the third round at Wimbledon for the third time in a career usually spent in pursuit of victories far away from the public's glare.

The other wild-card Brits fell by the wayside fairly cheaply. The twenty-eight-year-old Mark Petchey's defeat to Swede Magnus Gustafsson prompted him to talk about quitting the pro circuit, an attitude that had grown on him a couple of weeks later when he lost in the first round of the Bristol Challenger Trophy to Danny Sapsford. Petchey formalized the announcement in July, hoping to embark either on a coaching career or perhaps an opening in broadcasting with the satellite channel, *Eurosport*. Sending their new reporter to interview Rusedski, the man he argued had helped precipitate the end of his career, would make for fascinating viewing.

Henman's voyage had been choppy, the hull had been holed a couple of times, but the water wasn't yet breaking over the guardrail. His third-round opponent was the Zimbabwean Byron Black, a tough little competitor, who struck the ball powerfully off the ground and, when he roused himself to the net, was an effective volleyer to boot. When dusk fell on the Friday evening Henman was leading 6–4, 3–2 with a service break. Everything seemed hunky-dory. It had certainly been a far more convincing performance than the nerve jangling opening two rounds.

A new day, a new Timbo. Henman served out for the second set without too many travails, though in the tenth game, serving for the set, Henman was trailing 15–30. He punched the air as he sent a forehand cross-court pass deep into the corner, reached set point on a net cord and then produced his finest delivery of the match, a ferocious serve which touched the outer rim of Black's racket as he stretched in vain.

There wasn't that much coming cleanly from Henman's weapon, and when he netted two volleys in the second game of the third set, the Zimbabwean broke for the first time with a double-fisted cross-court service return. Three games later, Henman should have retrieved the match, but he played wayward shots on all three break points. The concentration lapses were all too familiar. An utterly awful mishit from Henman's forehand on the second set point and Black was back in genuine contention.

'He's switched off again,' said Chris Bailey of the BBC, who didn't allow his friendship with Henman get in the way of his increasingly insightful commentaries on the game. 'Tim starts putting in some three-quarter paced serves and then gets stuck in a rut. Black's a bit too sharp for him. I don't like the look of this.'

When Black missed with a backhand service return by the width of a racket string on break point in the opening game of the fourth set, a warning had been posted. Henman ignored it, losing his serve in the fifth game and barely troubling Black until the Zimbabwean had the opportunity to serve for the set. At 30–40, Henman encroached to within a couple of yards of the service box to try to upset Black on his second serve. Henman's backhand return clipped the baseline but Black believed it was long – and players are generally more often right than wrong with their own calls. He pleaded with French umpire Bruno Rebeuh to be strong: 'Don't be scared of the crowd, man, don't be scared.' But the words fell on deaf ears.

Henman had broken back and was on a four-game roll, jumping all over Black in the twelfth game to settle the match 6–4, 6–4, 3–6, 7–5 in two hours and forty-eight minutes, securing a fourth-round meeting with the Australian Patrick Rafter, the US Open champion. What a tasty dish to set before the Centre Court.

Henman could hardly have been accused of exhibitionism during the opening week. Simon Barnes, in *The Times*, described him as 'one of the best ham actors of our time'. Henman loved the stage of Centre Court, but tried his best to hide the fact from those in the audience urging him to do away with the bad guys. There was none of the overt body language of a Becker or a Connors. God forbid, Tim wouldn't want to have grass stains on his gear, and would think no more of punching the air wildly over his head and thrusting out his pelvis as he would granting an interview to *Hello!* magazine.

The first week had been an excruciating mixture of the absurd and the aesthetic. From the trough of despair, when it looked for all the world as if he might be about to lose, Henman went into one of those mind-sets, of controlled frenzy, shall we say, when suddenly the opponent's defences were ripped to pieces. At Wimbledon, he managed to find that zone tennis players dream of stepping into, a period of serenity inside allied to ferocious aggression on the court. The phrase 'fighting shy' best fitted Henman the tennis player. No one fought shy at Wimbledon better than Tim Henman.

The fact was that this year, with the World Cup continuing to entrance and dominate the airwaves and newspages, Wimbledon needed Henman as much as he needed it. Nine of the sixteen seeds had departed the men's singles, and the fourth-round pairings had thrown up some massive who-cares occasions for the British public – the Italian Davide Sanguinetti against Spain's Francisco Clavet for one; and the all-Aussie clash between Jason Stoltenberg and Mark Philippoussis another.

They were to be despatched to the outer limits of the All England Club grounds. Henman would have centre stage for the rest of the championships, which could have been construed as home help, but for those paying £28 each for their Centre Court tickets, the prospect of watching Magnus Larsson against Jan Siemerink while Henman played on Court One would have provoked a riot.

On the second Monday, the match everyone wanted to see was Henman against Rafter – gentleman against heartthrob, Anthony Andrews versus Brad Pitt. Centre Court would play to the home hero, Byron Black certainly thought as much. 'Centre is *the* place to be,' he said, 'it's the television court, the show court, the best court in the world. It is what tennis is all about. When you face someone like Sampras or Henman on there you feel as if you start a break down. And Tim is a lot smarter player than he was last year, so he has another edge.'

Henman knew he would have to be smarter to beat Rafter, though he remembered his victory in Sydney seven months earlier, when the tables were turned and the Aussie crowd were rooting hard against the Pom. Rafter had won a Slam as well, so there was no taking him for granted. He would have the support of those who read *GQ* before *Ace* magazine, who liked their tennis players ruggedly handsome, with long hair tied back in a pony-tail.

'Everyone in life feels a purpose and this is mine,' Henman said, unfazed by the comparisons about whether he or Rafter generated higher levels of testosterone. 'I'm feeling kind of lucky at the moment. The other evening I got back into the locker room in the middle of my match with Black and England were playing Colombia, I saw David Beckham shape up and take that free kick and I knew he was going to score.

'I'm not taking anything for granted against Rafter, I know I have to play my very best tennis to beat him, but I've got this nice relaxed premonition that I'm going to do well. And I'll be out there on court for Tim Henman and nobody else. Anyone who suggests anything else, doesn't understand me, the sport of tennis or what Wimbledon is all about.

'I feel a lot fresher at this stage than I have in the past two years, my tennis has improved with each stage. In terms of the popularity of the opponent, I think only one guy who could burrow deeper into my support than Pat is Andre Agassi. Pat is hugely popular, especially with the female contingent and of course I've heard about him being termed a sex god. Good for him, but I don't lose any sleep about not being spoken of in those terms and if the choice is between being called a sex god and a place in the Wimbledon quarter-finals. I'll take the latter.'

Rafter would know what he was in for when, during the knock-up on Monday afternoon, the crowd cheered every time Henman struck the ball back over the net. The Centre Court was right into this one. Was this the nice, polite objective crowd foreigners expected to find in England? To hell with those niceties. The mood clearly affected the Australian.

In his second service game, he twice lost control of the ball as he bounced it out in front of him as part of his action. And as he built up the service momentum, there was a definite tightening of his grip and a trembling through the right arm. It was a hot day, sure enough, but he seemed to be sweating more than necessary, considering we were only in the fourth game. Maybe, though, we just wanted Henman to win too much and were imagining the extent of Rafter's twitches.

Henman was not expending any unnecessary energy. He began with an ace, dropped only a single point in his first three service games and broke the less than secure Rafter serve in the eighth game with a rasping backhand return down the line. On his first set point, Henman attempted a delicate backhand drop volley which barely reached the net, but he was not alarmed, completing the set in twenty-nine minutes with a powerful serve the Australian could not re-direct back over the net.

Once again, in the second set, first blood went to Henman who broke to lead 3–2, an advantage he was able to hold until he prepared to serve for the set. He reckoned that up until then he had served as well as at any time in his life. Suddenly his arm started to buckle and you wondered if it was a throwback to that prepubescent injury, when he was eleven years old and attending the Slater School, which meant he would never be able to extend his serving arm as fully as he would like.

A double fault on the first point presented Rafter with his most important opening of the match and he jumped all over it with a fore-hand service return blasted back past Henman, who slipped coming in to try to make his volley. 0–30. Another double at 15–30 gave Rafter two break points and he clipped in a precise forehand return on the second, to break back to 5–5. The tie-break dawned.

A couple of superb backhands, one cross court, the next down the line, gave Rafter a 5–2 advantage he was not to squander, settling the sudden-death with another superb backhand service return. What was it about Henman that he contrived to make life so difficult for himself?

And what was it about him that he could change around again, full circle. The third and fourth sets – and thus the match – were won with an effortless ease, yet there was no discernible change in his attitude, his jaw didn't set any harder, he didn't appear to become more aggres-sive, he just got into a relentless groove. Yes, there were glitches, with the odd horrendous double fault and airy service return thrown in, but this was to be England's day, completed with matter-of-fact assured-ness after two hours and thirty-one minutes. Rafter thumped his racket into his bag, then tossed it high into the crowd as though glad to be rid of it, while Henman clapped the strings of his own in his usual self-effacing, thanks-for-coming style.

Rafter confessed, as we had perceived, that he was nervous, more nervous than he should have been for a man who had survived so many tight occasions in his career. 'It was just one of those things, I never felt loose out there,' he said. 'I've played a lot of big matches, Davis Cup, Grand Slams, you'd think I'd be able to deal with it and that's what I'm trying to work out myself, why do I have fear and doubt when I'm playing a fourth-round match at Wimbledon.

'I get those feelings in other places too, but I usually get through them. It's just not enjoyable to go out there with those [negative] thoughts. To win a Slam you have to be in a zone for a couple of weeks, mentally, just in a zone, but you need a couple of big shots also. I think the only person who can win a Slam without playing at his peak is Sampras. Tim can definitely get there, he has a great chance of winning a Slam.'

A British voice piped up. 'Pat, out of Tim and Greg, who would you say is the better player and why?' Rafter: 'That's a tough question, mate. I'll keep my views to myself. Thanks, anyway.'

Henman was through to his third Wimbledon quarter-final in successive years, a notable feat. 'I feel very, very relaxed about the whole situation, in fact I'm surprising myself just how relaxed I do feel,' he said. 'I was very loose in my whole game today and the way I was serving with a good rhythm, that's when you serve your best. And against a guy like Pat, who attacks at every opportunity, your game plan is more or less decided for you. You can play to your instincts.'

On the BBC *Match of the Day* highlights that evening, a croaky-voiced Greg Rusedski proffered the opinion that Henman would certainly beat the Czech Republic's Petr Korda, the third seed, in the quarter-finals on Wednesday. That smile never left his face, whether answering questions or waiting for them to be asked.

The morning of the quarter-final dawned utterly dismal in England. A nation mourned. Not because rain threatened once more but because the World Cup was over as far as much-criticized head coach Glenn Hoddle and his squad were concerned. For the third major football championship in succession, England had been beaten in a penalty shoot-out, but worse, much worse for an increasingly judgemental public, was the behaviour of Manchester United's David Beckham.

Beckham, barged over by the Argentine Diego Simeone in a manner which warranted a red card, flicked out an impetuous right leg, and caught his opponent on the back of the calf. Simeone fell, pole-axed, and Beckham was sent off by the Danish referee. The *Daily Mirror* put Beckham's face in the middle of a paper dartboard and suggested their readers throw their arrows at him.

The poor guy was hounded on to Concorde and sought refuge away from a nation damning him, in the Waldorf Astoria in New York with his fiancée Posh Spice. What would happen to Tim Henman should he venture on to Centre Court and lose to Petr Korda that afternoon? One doubted he would be forced to flee the country.

David Felgate was happy with his man's form, but his mood changed when he digested the morning papers. Looking for a different angle on the match, a couple of the British tennis writers had gone in search of Pickard, who was still on the Wimbledon premises, and was, quite naturally, asked about his two years coaching Korda, a period without conspicuous playing success but which had established a genuine friendship and loyalty between the two.

Though Korda was now being coached by fellow Czech Tomas Petera, he still valued Tony Pickard's advice and had turned it to it once Pickard had parted company with Rusedski. Here was an irony so delicious it couldn't be overlooked – Tony Pickard, the man who had never hidden his admiration for Tim Henman, supervising the hitting sessions of Petr Korda, the man who stood in the way of the dream which had inspired Tim from childhood.

Like all coaches who worked on the professional tour, not only did Pickard have views on the player he worked with but he watched enough tennis week in, week out to identify and categorize strengths and weaknesses of other players. In a world where the difference between so many players is a weak backhand here or a dicey second serve there, it is important to be clued up on as many people as you can be. It was only natural that Pickard would have a view on Henman, he knew the family, he knew Tim, he had wanted to work with him during the time he was blossoming at the Slater School.

Whether Pickard knew how to improve Henman as a tennis player would have to remain his secret. Edberg, Korda and Rusedski had always spoken highly of his tactical nous, of his ability to work on their faults and pinpoint those in the opposition. But we could be absolutely certain of one thing as Henman stood on the threshold of a monumental breakthrough in his career – he would have to do without any assistance from the country's most experienced international coach.

In the newspaper article Pickard was asked how he saw the Henman–Korda quarter-final confrontation panning out. 'I feel I'm in a win-win situation,' he said. 'I have a very high regard for Tim and if he wins I will be delighted to see one of our players make the semi-finals. But if Petr wins I'll be pleased because we're old pals. If Petr wanted to talk to me I would talk, but if Tim wanted to talk to me, I would also be happy to talk.' (It was possible to imagine the blood rising in Felgate's neck as he read this). 'But Petr already has a coach and I would tell Petr to speak to him.' (No mention that Pickard would similarly tell Henman to talk to Felgate).

'There was something wrong with one of Petr's strokes on Sunday so I helped him. But he was playing several rounds away from Tim, so I don't see a conflict. I think it could be a fabulous match because both of them play the game beautifully and the interesting thing is that they both have a tendency to switch off mentally.'

Reading these quotes in his morning paper cannot have delighted Felgate. He was trying to get Henman ready for another huge occasion in his life, and the headlines were all about the former coach of a player who had limped tragically out of the competition. But all the disruption was in the Rusedski camp, whereas Henman couldn't have been happier, nor more confident about his chances. Indeed, his column in the *Express* was beginning to ooze the kind of self-belief we didn't expect from an Englishman at Wimbledon.

Korda, feeling more settled with Pickard to turn to for advice, was nonetheless peeved that his status as a Grand Slam Champion – he had won the Australian Open in January, remember, but had only ever reached the fourth round at Wimbledon – hadn't merited a greater share of appearances on the hallowed Centre. He said he had only played on it once in fifteen years as a professional.

Korda said he would not lie down to Henman just because he had an injury which had required treatment during his fourth-round defeat of Holland's John van Lottum. 'I shall stand out there and fight,' he promised. 'I do not give in.'

Neither would Tim. Within a couple of minutes of the match starting he had achieved a notable first, breaking serve for the first time in a Wimbledon quarter-final. It seemed he had been too uptight to manage it in the past but there was a mood about him on 1 July, this was an uncompromising Henman, a focused Henman – I think he only looked up from his chair once, seeking eye contact with Felgate for confirmation that all was going well. All was.

When he sent down a 114 m.p.h. second serve in the seventh game, it was clear he would not be for the beating by Korda. Henman won the first set with one service break and was similarly effective in the second, when he broke to lead 4–3 in a game in which he was chasing down, racing across and lobbing to such effect that Korda was entranced into double faulting twice.

By the end of the first game of the third set, the match looked over. Korda managed to send down an unreturnable serve on the first break point, but a crunching Henman backhand on his second and the momentum was his. He broke again to lead 4–1 and the only resistance the third seed offered was the first time he really threatened Henman's serve, a game later. But the British player would not give him the break point he really needed and finally took a 5–1 lead after four deuces with a backhand volley winner from the top drawer.

Could it possibly have been much better – a 6–3, 6–4, 6–2 victory completed in an hour and forty-four minutes? A semi-finalist at last, after twenty-five long, bewildering years. And what a semi-final to savour – against the defending champion, Pete Sampras. The American had already told us that he regarded Wimbledon as his sporting Valhalla. It was not difficult to appreciate why. I recalled the late, great Englishman Fred Perry, having seen Sampras for the first time in a former tour event, the Ebel US Pro Indoor championships in

Philadelphia in 1988, telling those of us fortunate enough to be in his company that this boy would win Wimbledon one day. And not just one day, but on a few days.

What would Fred have made of Sampras now? Four victories in five years on the finest stage of all, with a defeat to Richard Krajicek in the 1996 quarter-finals his single blot – meant that this was the player of his generation. McEnroe had described him as the salvation of the men's game in the nineties, someone who had been willing to put himself on the line time and time again while the rest wavered and hesitated. Sampras had had the mental strength – and the game, of course – to want to be the No.1, to get to No.1 and to remain at No.1.

Sampras's route through the event was competent rather than flamboyant – typical Pete. But every time he needed to step up a gear, he did. And now for Henman. It hardly sent him reeling back in his seat when the first question to Sampras after his quarter-final defeat of the imposing Australian Mark Philippoussis didn't even mention anything about the match he'd just completed. Everyone bar the Aussie writers wanted to know how the world's No.1 felt about playing the British No.2 on Centre Court at Wimbledon. Especially as the English nation was still trying to come to terms with the trauma of World Cup exit and needed a little bit of solace.

'I played Tim here many years ago [the second round of 1995 to be precise] and he's obviously a far different player today,' said Sampras. 'I've been in this position before, playing Boris Becker in front of a German full house in the ATP Finals and I know it will be tough. Hopefully by Friday, the mourning for the soccer team will be over. I felt so sorry for that guy [David Batty, who missed the final penalty of the shoot out against Argentina] last night.'

Next question: 'You're very popular here, obviously the defending champion who has won four times, and here comes the home town favourite. How are you going to be able to deal with the crowd and what do you think their reaction will be when you guys are out there?'

Answer: 'I'm expecting them to be rooting for Tim but in a match I played a couple of years ago against Rusedski, when he all of a sudden turned English – sorry, is that good for you guys? I'm trying to help [much mirth in the press interview room]. I'm in trouble now [more laughter]. The crowd was obviously pulling for him. I'm ready for what the crowd will have to throw at me. It's going to be tough.'

Especially as, over the past couple of years, Sampras and Henman had become as close as top-class sport allows two professionals to become. 'I know Tim pretty well, he's a solid guy,' said Sampras. 'I practise with him a bunch but we won't be too close on Friday, that's what it's all about. You have friends on the tour but you leave it once you step on to the court. I'm not taking anything personally, I'll just go out and play the match.'

Sampras *needed* Wimbledon, maybe more than any other year. Questions had begun to be asked about his level of motivation for a sport over which he had been so pre-eminent. Sampras had indicated that he would stick to his recent policy of concentrating on the majors, even to the extent of not making himself available for certain Davis Cup ties. It did not go down too well with the American authorities, but Sampras believed he had paid his dues.

There might have been those who found his style unappealing, many thought him a turn-off, but you couldn't take away from Sampras his eagerness for a sport which had consumed him. 'I suppose I have an edge in the locker room for Wimbledon,' he told me, 'and if that helps me cast an aura of intimidation, then I'll take it.

'Wimbledon is very tough, what with the weather, the rain delays, knowing that the kind of mistake you can get away with on another surface, murders you on grass. For some reason, over the past five years, I've managed to find a way to play well enough to win four of them. It is a feeling "that this is it" for me, this is what I play for – for these matches more than any other in the year. It isn't like a sensation comes over me, more like a familiar feeling, it's about being comfortable. I had a problem in my early years here. I felt a little overwhelmed, the Centre Court especially does that to you. Now I feel good about the place, the scenery, I've grown to love it, I suppose.

'I have never quite had that feeling at the French Open – Wimbledon seems to agree with me. Last year, not being the Wimbledon champion felt strange, but it's a part of sport, I'm not going to win every close match on Centre Court. I accepted my defeat and I moved on. I will go out there against Tim so pumped up, there's something about the place that forces me to be like that. I don't need any more motivation tomorrow, I really don't.'

Henman was quiet confidence personified. His ritual during the championships didn't change. He stayed at his home in Barnes, and usually travelled to the house rented by IMG in the village for his lunch and last-minute contemplation before driving down to the club. He slept well the night before the semi-final, his mood was unaltered, his confidence quotient high.

Neither David nor Jan Felgate had felt that elated during the

Championships this year, a sure sign that the 1998 Tim Henman was a far different player to the one who had excited them royally in 1996 and 1997. It was as if they believed Henman should qualify for semi-finals in Grand Slams. It ought not to be a surprise. This was where he belonged.

Jan Felgate said: 'I asked David on the morning of the semi how he felt and he said "just normal". I spoke to Lucy and asked her how Tim had been in the morning, and the answer was the same. It was a curious situation, we were all much more up for previous years. But it meant, I think, that Tim was really ready to play Sampras. He knew he could win.' Certainly, his column on the morning of the semi-final was akin to an emphatic statement of intent. The headline read 'Simply the Best – But I know I can beat him.'

'Pete Sampras is the greatest player ever to walk out on court,' he wrote. 'However, before Wimbledon started, when I said I could win the title, I knew I'd have to beat the best. I stand by my claim and believe the way I am playing is good enough to beat even someone as good as the world No.1. Of course, Lady Luck has to be sitting in my courtside chair but if I perform as well as I have been doing over the past couple of matches, particularly from the service line, it will take a very good player to stop me.

'No one is assured of playing at their best, particularly if the other goes on the attack from the start and there's no way I'm going to rest on my laurels. I've beaten two Grand Slam champions, Patrick Rafter and Petr Korda, and I'm determined to make it a hat-trick with Sampras. In fact, it's a shame that Carlos Moya isn't still in the competition and in with a chance of getting to the final because I'd love to be the first man to beat all the reigning Grand Slam champions on the way to a title.

'The first time I lost to Sampras was four years ago in Tokyo, when I wasn't in the world's top 200. Then, in 1995, I went down in straight sets at Wimbledon when I was outside the top 100. I have improved considerably since then. There aren't many weaknesses in his game but he can experience lapses. And if I get one or two chances a set, I've got to take them.

'What have I got to lose? I don't feel any pressure and I've nothing to be afraid of. That feeling usually translates into me producing my best tennis. I'll be focused on the job in hand. I think the novelty of me has worn off. Two years ago, people were going to my school and the pubs in the village where I grew up trying to find out things about me. Now there is nothing else to find and my tennis is doing the talking. With any luck there will be plenty to talk about this evening with a British player through to the Wimbledon final for the first time in sixty years.'

Incredibly, they had both lost their last match on grass the same fateful Friday at Queen's, when Rusedski had turned over on his ankle. Mark Woodforde of Australia had defeated Sampras that day, and wondered if he had a couple of hints for Henman. 'I just wanted to keep getting the ball down to Pete's feet and come in a lot, trying to take the net away from him,' said Woodforde. 'If I stayed with him early on, I felt I might have a chance.'

The last time we had seen Sampras and Henman on the same grass court was on the next day at Queen's when they lost a doubles match 6–1, 6–1, and it was so cold and miserable that Sampras asked the umpire if he would send for a couple of cups of hot chocolate so they could warm themselves during the changeovers. A ballgirl dutifully returned ten minutes later with the best Queen's Club crockery. There was not a photographer near the scene – what a pictorial scoop that would have been.

The weather twenty days later was an awful lot more like summer, even an English summer. Sampras v. Henman was the second semi, following Holland's Richard Krajicek, the 1996 champion, against Goran Ivanisevic of Croatia, losing finalist in 1992 and 1995. It was to prove a very long, frustrating wait. Up at IMG's house in Wimbledon, Mr and Mrs Henman were dining with Jan Felgate, when Tony Henman remarked that he and his wife had been looking around the grounds to try to spot Rusedski's family. 'Tony said they thought it was time they introduced themselves, because they had never met. I thought that was a bit of a shame,' said Jan Felgate. The Rusedskis had been back in Canada for almost a week.

Which is about how long the first semi-final seemed to last. As the match promised a third set tie-break, I was on the phone to Pat Cash in his Fulham home discussing an article he was preparing for the *Sunday Telegraph* that weekend when Cashy suddenly realized he was due to be the summarizer on the second semi-final alongside the BBC's senior tennis commentator, John Barrett, who was prowling outside the box wondering where the hell Cash was. Cash dropped the phone, sped to the All England Club, and then had to wait around for two hours while Ivanisevic and Krajicek came to their exhausting conclusion, the Croat winning 15–13 in the final set. 'Thanks a lot, mate,' he said.

When Henman and Sampras were summoned from the men's

locker room – an hour and a half after they were first told to be ready to play – they entered an amphitheatre which, instead of being super-charged for such a match, was on the verge of mental exhaustion, so long and draining had been the previous semi. Indeed, Centre was only two-thirds full when the defending champion and the toast of the Home Counties walked out. The Henman coterie took its seats in the usual order in the Players' Box, looking composed and restrained, as if their boy was about to play in the final of the Oxfordshire men's singles. In the row behind them sat Sampras's coach, Paul Annacone, his fitness trainer Todd Snyder and girlfriend, Kimberley Williams. They, too, were the essence of unassuming confidence.

The first two points were symptomatic of Henman's Wimbledon thus far, a service winner followed by a double fault. Two more service winners followed; Henman was grooved, and he drew Sampras into a forehand service return error for first blood. Sampras held to love, Henman likewise, Sampras held to love again, Henman held to 30 and then, in the sixth game, it was the British player who had the first break point. He had a chance to take a significant lead, too, but netted a relatively straightforward backhand half-volley. That is if anything could possibly be straightforward for a British player against the world No.1 and defending champion in a Wimbledon semi-final.

This was the slight opening Sampras required, and he broke in the next game, courtesy of another of those untimely Henman double faults. When he broke in the ninth game as well, finding an impressive groove on his returns of serve – so often the weapon which ultimately wins Wimbledon – the champion had pocketed the first set. Would this be the comprehensive straight sets defeat most of us had feared for Henman?

When Sampras held his first service game of the second set to love, it seemed like a good moment to sneak away for a moment's relief so you didn't have to miss the ending. But something kept you from leaving your seat. Not only did Henman steady himself, but, to the astonishment of even those in the Union Jack hats, he suddenly stepped up a level, bamboozling Sampras with a couple of rhythm-crushing lobs. 0–30. A delightful backhand pass. 0–40. Sampras responded with an ace but when he pushed a backhand half-volley into the tramlines, Henman had achieved a notable breakthrough.

The pressure undermined Sampras' rhythm. The champion double faulted. Break point. Survived. Henman stayed with him, picking away, moving to another break point with a winning forehand service return and then watching Sampras net a forehand volley. Henman led

4–1 and it was the first time since the Australian Open, in his quarter-final defeat to Slovakia's Karel Kucera, that Sampras had lost his serve twice in a match. In the fashion of a champion, the American did compose himself and break back for 4–2, but Henman dropped only one more point on his serve in the set, completing the game which levelled the match at one set all with a particularly brutal swinging serve into the Sampras body. We were about to witness the finest set of the entire championships.

In the second game, with Henman beginning to get into a pene-trating service groove, one of his most powerful incendiaries broke the strings of the racket Sampras had strung more tightly than just about anyone else in the game. The champion tossed it into the crowd, and someone had a souvenir to cherish. Indeed, Henman held the second and fourth games to love, but the sixth was slightly different, when the British player committed an unforced error on the backhand, pushing it beyond the baseline to surrender a break point. This was a time to test Henman's temperament and he wasn't found wanting, producing a classical low backhand volley winner. The crowd was now beside itself. This was combat of the most passionate, ferocious kind. Between friends.

Something would surely have to give. Henman was consistently losing the opening point on his serve, something which would put an intolerable burden on any player, not least one with so many expecta-tions mounted upon him. He managed to survive to trail 6–5, knowing that if he held in the twelfth game, he had the chance of taking Sampras into a tie-break which, almost certainly, would decide the fate of this semi-final.

Once again, Henman fell behind 0–15 but countered and aced for 30–15. It was at this time, emboldened by his two winning lobs in the third game of the previous set, he tried another on a crucial point, but Sampras leapt backwards and smashed athletically into the open court. A service winner rescued that break point but Henman had to survive another when he netted a low forehand volley from a blistering Sampras service return. That, the Englishman managed when, after an intense rally, Sampras netted a forehand at full stretch.

Henman had a point to take the set into the equivalent of the penalty shoot-out. Where did you pick to serve to Sampras, who was crouching, prowling, in the advantage court? Was it better out wide to the backhand to leave the court open to put away your volley from a splayed return; or down the middle, knowing that the returner had little chance of controlling his response? Henman chose to go down the middle, hit the ball on the sweet spot, a puff of chalk rose, but Sampras, guessing right, conceived a moment which freeze-framed his champion's quality.

With right arm fully extended, the American managed a quite incredible riposte which was back past Henman before his momentum had taken him to the net. Deuce again. And this time Sampras was not to let the position slip, wrong-footing Henman with a cross-court backhand volley for his third set point, and inducing Henman into an error, when he netted a backhand volley. At the Royal Box end, Sampras leapt from the scuffed grass and punched the air as if he had won the championship itself. For it felt as if he had.

Henman had a break point in the first game of the fourth, but a service winner prevailed. It was to be his one chance of effecting a fight back, for Sampras broke in the fourth game, with some brilliant court coverage, ending with a forehand volley winner. From then on, Sampras varied his service action with an absolute mastery of his technique, slowing down second serves to bamboozle his man, punching away winners. Henman hung in, he sent down an ace for his final serve of the match as a defiant gesture, but two of the same from Sampras in the ninth game wrapped up proceedings.

The score was 6–3, 4–6, 7–5, 6–2 in two hours and twenty-two minutes. Henman had been courageous, but, as he said later, courage was nothing if you were a loser. It was hard to feel, on such an occasion, that he had lost anything, but only Henman knew how bitterly upset he was. The rest of us could just guess at his innermost feelings. Sampras knew he had been through one of the toughest matches of his career. He walked into the interview room, sighed and sat down. 'It was very intense, but it has to be that way at this level and at this stage of the tournament,' he said. 'Tim is a very, very solid player and he will, eventually, go on to win this tournament one year. He's twenty-three and he's going to get better and better as the years go on. I felt I was playing Tim and the crowd so, yes, I showed a little more emotion than normal.

'The levels of tennis were very high. As fast as the court is playing, so much is down to reaction. I wasn't surprised at how well he played, because I've been practising with Tim consistently over the past six months and he's good, almost to the point of being a great player. He's capable of playing unbelievable tennis. I don't see many holes in his game, he does everything very well. If there was a difference between us today, it was probably our second serves. But there's very little else between us at this point.'

Which would have been music to anyone's ears but Henman's in the first throes of defeat, when no one wants to hear anything that is said to them, or about them. They say that in football, the worst moment to lose is the semi-final, on the cusp of the greatest moment in your life. Only a chosen few get to play on finals day, and Henman knew he had had his chances.

The dimwit who asked 'Are you very disappointed?' got the answer he should have anticipated: 'Yes.' Henman was asked if there was some satisfaction in being the first person to take a set from Sampras since the previous year's quarter-finals. 'The score is irrelevant,' he retorted. 'It's about winning and losing. I've always believed that I can compete with and beat the very best players and I had a good opportunity against the world No.1 today. I'll learn and I'll get better. The way I've played here makes me very positive and optimistic for the second half of the year.'

As for future Wimbledons? 'I've got plenty more opportunities, I hope I have another seven, eight years left of this championship and I think I'll have a good chance in each of those years. I'll be doing my utmost, continuing to give 100 per cent to my job.'

Henman would not be allowed to escape the feeling that a nation built up – quite unnaturally, given that it was more than 60 years since we'd had a Wimbledon men's singles champion - to expect him to win, should be plunged into mourning because he had somehow let the side down. 'I've said all along that when I'm winning I'm not playing for the nation, so when I lose, I'm not letting anyone else down,' he explained, quite rationally. 'When I'm on court, it's about myself. I win and I lose, it's as simple as that.'

With that, he was gone, out of the front door of the All England club, back up the hill to IMG's house in the village where those trying to offer him condolences were treated to a shrug of the shoulders and as much small talk as he could muster. He wanted to be away from all the fuss, have a quiet dinner with Lucy, David and Jan Felgate, and forget about losing a Wimbledon semi-final because, frankly, it hurt like hell.

If Tim couldn't quite seize the moment, British tennis had to. Not in two generations had the game been blessed with such riches. John Lloyd had been one of the closest to achieving. Arguably, he had as good a game as Henman, but he couldn't help taking one eye off the ball and casting it at the ladies. He admitted that he used to choke at Wimbledon.

'You couldn't package anyone better than Tim from a PR point of view if you tried,' said Lloyd, who had flown in from his home in Los Angeles to commentate for the American cable network, HBO. 'He is the perfect combination – handsome, a lovely manner about him, articulate and stylish. He plays a brand of tennis that's exciting, a nice family background, as true a Brit as you could find.

'I may have had all of those things, too, but he is different to me in that he has a far greater hunger to succeed than I ever had. I was nearly in his position, but I was satisfied too early because I was earning good money – nothing to compare with what is on offer now – but good money for that time.

'I got comfortable. I wasn't as huge a partygoer as some people said but I liked a drink and I liked the ladies and, for a time, practice was something I did because I had to do it rather than wanting to do it. I got to No.20 in the world with a huge chance of a breakthrough but the money started to come in, I was happier doing the extra interviews rather than the extra hours on court. Tim is totally the opposite. Much more single minded.

'I always found it difficult to play my best tennis here, but Tim loves it. I spotted him in the locker room before the Korda match and it seemed as if he was just about to have an hour's practice, but this was a quarter-final he knew he should win because his opponent was a bit dodgy fitness-wise. Bloody hell, in those circumstances I would have been as tight as a duck's arse.

'Tim is a slightly younger version of Sampras to me. His game is the same in many ways – his serve isn't as good, nor his explosiveness – the question is whether he can find that missing five per cent.

'He's got the mind for it and that's huge – in all sports. I don't think there's a comparison between Tim and a lot of other players mentally. I just wish he had that body strength, an extra ten pounds would probably do it. To see him against Sampras was like watching a bantamweight up against a welterweight. But he'll be back and stronger.'

Pete Sampras duly won the Wimbledon title for the fourth time in five years, to place himself in the vanguard of the greats of the game. Few had seriously doubted that he would let Goran Ivanisevic spoil his Championship Sunday. Though we may have differed on the number of sets it would require, Goran's uneven temperament was bound to betray him.

It wasn't a classic final, but it lasted the distance, Sampras having to extricate himself by the skin of his teeth, much as he had done against Henman in the semis. But, when the chips were down, when the cham-

pion was required to produce, so he produced. In truth, Ivanisevic had
a couple of chances with backhand service returns which would have
won the second set and had he brought them off, from two sets to love,
he couldn't possibly have lost. Henman, watching, knew that he had
never lost to Ivanisevic and felt that the Croat would have buckled
under the pressure of Centre Court with a British player in the opposite corner. But, in the end, this was all hypothesis.

Ivansevic lost in five. I have never seen any beaten finalist as discon-
solate as he sat, immovable, at the umpire's chair, towel wrapped
around head, refusing all offers of condolence. Referee Alan Mills had
to prod him on the shoulder when it was time for him to receive his
runners-up plate from the Duchess of Kent.

The photographers wanted their pictures, but Ivanisevic would not
raise his plate above thigh height. He refused to listen to exhortations
for him to smile, he barely acknowledged Sampras. He said he wanted
to kill himself, such are the emotions of the man.

For Sampras, victory equalled vindication. So many had questioned
whether he had any more championships left in him and, while not
having to play at his absolute peak, he had laid that particular indict-
ment to rest. It was doubtful, though, if America would be laying out
the laurel wreaths when Concorde touched down at JFK on the
Monday morning.

The United States had an ambivalence to Sampras it is hard for an
Englishman to understand. Just how much more did the man have to
do? He didn't pout, holler or make the obscene, purile gestures of a
Jimmy Connors, he didn't carry the anti-establishment baggage of
John McEnroe. Neither, though, was Sampras regarded as a sporting
diplomat in the manner of Arthur Ashe.

Here was an outstanding twenty-six-year-old athlete, whom no
one in tennis could touch, having to try to live up to what other people
wanted him to be. He simply wasn't allowed to be himself, a quiet,
reflective, sincere, decent guy, who was an absolute phenomenon on
the tennis court. Oh that Britain had him – we'd show America how
to promote and delight in a sporting superstar.

Sampras had dealt with stresses and strains along the way – the
untimely death from brain cancer in May 1996 of Tim Gullikson, who
had coached him to many of his memorable triumphs, the knocks
about his personality – but kept on trying to win tournaments while
everyone else pursued him with vigour. 'His standards are so high,'
said his current coach Paul Annacone, 'you easily lose sight of his
accomplishments. It is part of the way we watch sports and see our

heroes – it becomes a self-fulfilling prophesy. When he loses, it's like "What's wrong?"

'Players are always looking for a chink in his armour. They wonder, when he doesn't win every tournament, how Pete is feeling, whether he might be vulnerable. They look for signs. They think to themselves "Maybe this is the time." The fifth set at Wimbledon in a final, is the biggest moment of anyone's career and the way he responded against Goran, showing who was in control, said so much about him.

'Pete talks about his professional goals – of course he does. He's the rare athlete who puts just enough pressure on himself to do what he needs to do. It's rarer still that he can get those skills to work. Most athletes do that to the point where they get nervous, get tight and choke. Pete says "I know where I'm going to shine." He doesn't do it with bravado, he knows he'll do it.'

In the back row of the interview room after each of Henman's matches, the LTA's Richard Lewis was to be found in whispered conversation with David Felgate.

'I wanted to make sure David and Tim were happy that every area of their partnership had been covered, and whether there were other areas they hadn't thought of,' Lewis said. 'I wondered how much fresh input they were getting, how many fresh ideas. They had been together for a long time and I wanted them to be careful that no staleness was creeping in. David assured me it wasn't.

'And I'd read all about the relationship with Sampras. I wondered if it was simply a matter of the odd dinner here or there, the round of golf, or if it could be something more that would help Tim in the future. I was reassured that Sampras is at the age and in the stage of his career now where he feels comfortable saying to someone like Tim "Work on that, do you realize that if you do this or that, you can improve, when I'm down the other end of the court, your shots feel like this." It was exciting to know that the world No.1 was talking in these terms about Tim.'

Greg Rusedski, knowing more about these things these days than Lewis, wondered whether the fact that Sampras chose to practise so often with Henman was because he knew he would never lose to him. The more you thought about that prognosis, the more it began to make some sense. A champion saying to a young pretender, that you can look up in awe, but that's where I always want to be. Of course that was it. And why should Greg harbour any grudges because Sampras preferred to practise with Henman? Maybe it gave him more credence as a challenger.

Anyway, as far as Wimbledon 1998 went, Rusedski had had a difficult tournament and Henman knew he had missed a golden opportunity to put all his knowledge of Sampras to good use. But there would be more chances for both of them. They could both summon the vision of their arms cradling the golden cup on final Sunday and know that it wasn't too far-fetched. To the future.

11 After the Lord Mayor's Show

Greg Rusedski might as well have done a runner back to Canada for all the impression he made on the British newspapers in July and much of August. He wanted to start his tennis comeback in the Canadian Open, but the tournament turned down his belated request for a wild card. While it could be argued that Pete Sampras and Andre Agassi had better cases, by dint of ranking and that the tournament always held invitations in reserve for members of the Canadian Davis Cup team, bitterness, obviously, still ran as deep as Lake Ontario.

The news that Rusedski had subsequently withdrawn from the ATP Tour events in Los Angeles and Cincinnati was worth a paragraph or two but the appointment of a Dutchman as his new coach had nowhere near the seismic impact of another Dutchman's appointment, Ruud Gullit's at Newcastle United FC.

Rusedski was desperately in need of some positive public relations. I suggested, both to ProServ, through his advisor, Fran Ridler, and to the LTA, that so badly had Greg come out of the Wimbledon experience in PR terms, that it would do him a tremendous amount of good to sit down with a group of the British media as soon as he could to explain what had gone on before, during and after the Championships.

The idea was rejected by ProServ before, one suspected, Rusedski was even brought into the conversation. Greg, they informed me a trifle too briskly, didn't feel he needed to explain anything to anyone. If they were happy with that, it was their lookout. The LTA – who had been told snappily by Greg before Wimbledon not to let anyone near him – weren't about to get involved in anything so potentially explosive. They simply said they had no influence over Greg, and that, anyway, everything had to go through his management company.

Fortunately for Rusedski, it appeared there were plenty of tennis coaches – either unemployed or worried that they might soon be – out there who wanted to take him on, even though his record of love 'em and leave 'em was in the Zsa Zsa Gabor class. Of those who wrote to the player or his management group asking for the chance to help piece Rusedski's career back together, the credentials of Sven Groeneveld were the most appealing.

For a start, Groeneveld lived in Knightsbridge, a couple of miles away from Rusedski, so getting together for practice would be a piece of cake. Groeneveld had learned his profession at the heels of American guru Nick Bollettieri and had twice coached Mary Pierce, so he came with plenty of experience of dealing with involved parents, and had worked with the former Wimbledon champion Michael Stich, inspiring him to the final of the French Open in 1996, before they parted company.

The thirty-three-year-old Groeneveld had also spent a period of time working for the Swiss Tennis Federation as their development officer, but that task had been as much about administration as court time and his desire was to get back in tandem with a player, preferably one with high aspirations. Rusedski was delighted with the appointment. He had taken on a man with a reputation for being a smashing bloke, but who didn't appear to stay in one tennis relationship too long. Seemed right up Greg's street.

'I had stopped with the Swiss, so I didn't have anything going on during the summer,' said Groeneveld. 'I was visiting Wimbledon, I saw the interviews after Greg's match and I thought this may be my opportunity. I had first spoken with his agent five years earlier when I thought I could offer Greg something, but it didn't work out then. I went to his people at Nike and put in the word that I was available. We had a chat and decided to give it a go.

'I knew what I was getting myself into. Before you accept a job you do your research. I looked at what Greg had done, I knew he had points to defend in the autumn and coming back from the injury it may not have looked too good. But I had had very good success in the past with players in similar circumstances, like Michael Stich and Mary

Pierce. I found this was a time when players were more open to ideas, they want to hear new suggestions and would try things they might have not wanted to do in the past. I took Greg as a really big challenge.'

The talks between Rusedski and Groeneveld took place well outside the glare of the media and the appointment was made quietly, without anything like the fuss created by Pickard's departure. Rusedski was still being treated on a daily basis by his physio Reza Daneshmand, and personal fitness trainer, Steve Green, and all seemed to be knitting together nicely. As I suspected though, he couldn't fully escape the continuing fall-out from his break-up with Pickard eight weeks earlier.

Groeneveld obviously wanted to concentrate his mind on the future. 'We wanted to get healthy, win a tournament, get back in the top ten and qualify for the ATP Finals,' he said, but there was plenty of explaining to be done about the past. Rusedski felt he had come out of the affair the wronged and wounded party.

'Only two people know exactly what happened and only one has talked about it,' he said. 'Only one point of view came out, so people were commenting without knowing all the facts. I didn't have the chance to make my point at all.' Would he tell us all the facts so the record could be straightened back in his favour? No. 'It might come out when I write my own book,' he said. 'I didn't want to create a press feeding frenzy, going back to me, then to Tony, then back to me again. I wanted to keep it quiet.'

Back home in Nottingham, between rounds of golf, Pickard was still following affairs closely. 'Greg knew the ground rules when we started together,' he said. 'He broke the ground rules. And as far as I'm concerned, that was it. I could have stayed there and taken the money, couldn't I? Very easily, but I'm not that type. It wasn't just about the ankle, it wasn't just one thing. I've never discussed it with anyone and I'm not going to. I still have respect for the boy.'

Well, Rusedski did thank Pickard for taking his game up a notch, just as he had thanked Teacher in the same way after they parted company. Within a week of Groeneveld coming on board, Rusedski was remarking that: 'He's a nice, relaxed sort of individual who is closer to my age and can be on the court with me more of the time. He is very intense and into his job, so we are similar in a lot of respects. I want a relationship where if he's not happy with what I'm doing, he can say so and if I'm not happy with what he's doing, I can say so. Hopefully, Sven and I will last a long time, but we'll just have to wait and see. He's definitely done the best job on my backhand of any of my coaches so far.'

The US Open was to test that particular theory. A week before the tournament, Rusedski was sixth in the rankings with an awful lot of points to protect with very little match practice to back him up. Groeneveld laid it on the line. 'We looked at the worst case scenario,' he said, 'and that was if he lost every first round before the Open and in the Open itself, he would be down to between No.25 and No.30 in the world. I told him I knew he could do much better than that. I believed in him and I hoped he would believe in me.'

Rusedski said: 'I didn't know how my ankle was going to stand up but we decided to go for it. I could have stayed in London playing practice sets and working on my physical state but it's not a match situation, where there's so much more stress and strain involved. I think I came through the trial.' In Indianapolis, true, Rusedski toughed out a fierce opening match against the Swede Magnus Larsson, who was nobody's mug and had been in the top ten himself a couple of years earlier, but had never quite managed to carry forward the mantle handed to him by Wilander and Edberg.

It was not the match you wanted on your return on a dicky ankle, everyone agreed with that. Most independent judges felt that victory was an improbability. Larsson could beat anybody on his day and if he was on song, Rusedski – match brittle after so long away from competitive action – might be blown away. What dire consequence might that have on his mood? But Greg demonstrated once more that you wrote him off at your peril, by confounding the doubters and winning his first match back in straight sets. The course had been set again. In the next round he accounted for Francisco Clavet of Spain before losing to another Spaniard, Alex Corretja, who had moved into the top ten and was among one of the most improved and accomplished players of the year.

These results, after so long without raising a racket in competitive anger, were to put Rusedski in an emboldened frame of mind heading back to New York, where he had broken through in major terms in such compelling style twelve months earlier. Pickard still wondered how well he would do. 'The boy's a good tennis player but I don't think technically, he's got it to be No.1 in the world,' said the erstwhile coach. 'Analyse what he's got, a fabulous serve, and his volleying is definitely to a top-class standard. But then, off the floor, I would say he's fairly average. Having the big parts he has, makes up for some of the inadequacies off the ground. Mentally, he's outwardly quite strong, but I wouldn't say he's strong inwardly. That's the bit you don't see. He is very strong outwardly and he's very motivated which makes up for the wobbles. I mean, it's a wonderful façade.'

Façade? Could this be true? It was an intriguing comment but one most people took with a pinch of cynicism. There might be more than a trace of superficiality about the Rusedski grin, but those who had grown to know and appreciate his talents, couldn't possibly agree that he was inwardly lacking. Yes, he gave off signs of nerves at changeovers – those interminable wipes of his face with the towel he munched on as he walked back to the service line, and the even more interminable undoing and doing up of his shoelaces – but not mentally strong? It was as if all of those who wondered exactly what went on inside that complex character had had the veil lifted by the man who had decided they could no longer work together in the first week of the greatest championships in the world.

Rusedski was utterly oblivious to Pickard's comments, as he tried to get enough match practice to give him a chance of winning the most demanding five-set championship of them all. 'Sometimes when you're not expecting to do well, you perform better,' Rusedski suggested. 'If I stay healthy and I'm playing good tennis, I have as good a chance as anyone. I am a positive, optimistic person.' Which was exactly what he said when he left Cromwell Hospital, the afternoon he twisted his ankle at Queen's – and look where that positive, optimistic outlook got him.

After his 6–4, 7–5 semi-final defeat to Rafter on Long Island – where he didn't even have the glimmer of a break point on the Australian's serve – Rusedski turned his attention to a US Open first-round match against Wayne Ferreira, the South African who had beaten Henman in New York the previous year and had been a quarter-finalist at Flushing Meadows as well as reaching the last sixteen on three other occasions.

'I think it is important to build a momentum, not to lose too many sets in the first week, which is what happened last year,' Rusedski said. 'I hadn't lost a set until the semi-finals and that keeps you fresh, especially given the kind of conditions you're going to face in New York. I'm not trying to get too far ahead of myself, though. I have a tough draw, but sometimes that focuses you and you do better because no one expects you to. I expect to go far at the end of this year – if things fall as planned, I should do as well. If not, there's always next year.' And, of course, the next coach.

Henman – still with David Felgate, it went without saying – had spent a couple of weeks sunning himself and swimming in Portugal, the first time he had been completely away from tennis all year. Wimbledon was a huge tournament for any British player but this year, with Rusedski's hop-along exit, the pressure had been focused entirely on to his lean shoulders from the third day. It was a testimony to his abilities that he had handled the situation so well.

Within a week of starting his holiday, Henman was already working on the physical programme left him by his fitness trainer, Tim Newenham. And it didn't, he confessed, take him that long to have the Wimbledon affair out of his system, and begin to get the urge to hit tennis balls again.

His first port of call was to be Los Angeles, and the Mercedes-Benz Open. 'Wimbledon was of no relevance at all now,' he told himself as he flew into the City of the Angels. 'But I needed to make sure my game was right on the button straight away, because although these tournaments were the bread and butter of the circuit, you couldn't be anything less than properly prepared for them.

'LA was a great start for me. There were huge attendances for one thing, and it's a pretty lively place so there wasn't going to be much peace and quiet. I was a little bit unsure going into my first match, I hoped I would start out hitting the ball just as I had at Wimbledon, and that's the way it went. The matches got tougher and tougher, but I became more consistent.' He reached the final, where he faced the local favourite (well Las Vegas was only 272 miles down Interstate 10), Andre Agassi.

Henman had started against South African Grant Stafford, and lost only three games, a result and a sensation which proved to him that he had lost none of the Wimbledon 'feel'. The third round was to prove more explosive, as he faced Jeff Tarango, the local boy from Manhattan Beach who had leapt to international prominence at Wimbledon three years earlier when he accused umpire Bruno Rebeuh of being corrupt, stormed off court and was disqualified. His French wife subsequently stormed up to her fellow countryman, slapped him across the cheek, screaming that he 'deserved a lesson'. Whatever Tarango did subsequently, he would always be reminded of that incident.

There were times in the match when Tim understood why Tarango was considered by many in tennis as a little unusual. 'You're a head case,' shouted one fan in LA, where they know all about shrinks. Henman beat him 7–5, 7–6, and Tarango left afterwards complaining of nausea. Henman was on his way on this, his first visit to the championships. But not everyone was captivated by his progress.

In his column in the *Los Angeles Daily News*, Kevin Modesti chose to put his name to an unflattering piece. 'Tim Henman is an English tennis player,' he wrote. 'And more. He's English cooking. He's

English weather. He's English humour. Dull. Drab. Dry. He's boring even to the English, which makes him, when you think about it, a curiosity in a tennis world of neon personalities.

'I'm thinking of the way Henman is regarded by the press back home,' Modesti continued. 'Here's a column from the *Observer* in England printed shortly after his semi-final loss to Pete Sampras at Wimbledon a month ago. "Prickly, Prissy Perfectionist Who Pulls All the Right Strings," read the headline. The story noted Henman's "somewhat anonymous brand of good looks, impassive demeanour and purposely unprovocative conversation". His coach, his girlfriend and even his parents came in for criticism: "all, apparently schooled in the same defensive discretion that Henman cultivates so assiduously".'

Modesti said he believed the English had it all wrong. 'They should lighten up because Henman is the best thing to happen to English tennis in decades,' he wrote, 'and because their wish for a more flamboyant hero is having exactly zero effect.'

Henman's reaction to the article was typical of that very same defensive discretion. 'I wouldn't say that reading the English press was a popular pastime of mine. If they say I'm not flamboyant enough, that's fine, but I'm sure they would much rather I play the kind of tennis I did at Wimbledon than be flamboyant and play poorly. At the end of the day, I'm not acting out there on the court. What you see is what you get.'

What the people of LA got that week was Henman in bullish mood on the court. He defeated his Wimbledon adversary Byron Black in the quarters, the Frenchman Guillaume Raoux in the semis and then had to face the rejuvenated Agassi on a balmy LA evening. Henman got close, but not close enough. Agassi won 6–4, 6–4 for his tenth consecutive victory in straight sets and his second title in successive weeks. 'It's like letting something ride on a blackjack table,' he said. 'You keep letting it ride, it's getting bigger, quicker. That's the way it feels. It's like every game doubles your confidence, your focus and your intensity. It gets a lot more accomplished.'

Henman accepted that he had been too erratic in his play to expect to beat a player in Agassi's compelling form. Eight aces, seven double faults just about summed him up. Normally so secure on overheads, he missed two at crucial moments. 'I take a lot of confidence from the week and in the final I was playing the hottest player on the tour. But I never strung together a high level of tennis continuously,' he said. 'I played OK, not much better than OK.' Dull. Drab. Dry.

With that, it was a flight across three time zones to Toronto where the officials at the du Maurier Open didn't even allow him the luxury of a day's rest. He was straight on to court against Argentine Guillermo Canas and found himself a set and 5–2 down, precisely the same score as he had been up against Tieleman in the quarters at Queen's when Sue Barker and her BBC team started shuffling about near the side of the court.

Henman was not to be similarly distracted this time. 'It's easy to win when you're playing well, it's much harder when you're playing badly and that's what I had to do to recover that situation,' he said.

Henman gutsed the victory out – and registered a really good feeling inside in the process – before steering himself over a couple more hurdles, beating Albert Costa of Spain and the combative Czech Daniel Vacek in three sets before losing 6–2, 6–4 in the semi-finals to Patrick Rafter, who was on a compelling hard-court roll.

Henman was in a pretty good groove himself but before he'd had time to enjoy the sights and sounds of Cincinatti, he was beaten by the gnarled Austrian Thomas Muster, who was still out there kicking and screaming, hoping to knock a few young heads together before his career finally ran out of angst. Henman looked upon his defeat as a reminder that he should take nothing for granted. It also gave him time to have a bit of a rest.

New Haven, Connecticut conjured a picture of tall-treed serenity, of magnificent mansions, of Ivy League schools, of wealth and prosperity. The tennis centre was situated in the grounds of Yale University which oozed all-American class. Ten streets away, it was very different. In fact, the city centre was like most of the metropoles in America. It was downright dangerous. A drive-by shooting outside the Omni Hotel on the Tuesday night, only an hour after I'd checked in, was enough to put me off strolling the streets in search of the concierge's choice of restaurant.

The tournament itself presented a fantastic field, indeed only Rusedski of the top fifteen failed to show. On the Monday came news via the computer that Henman – though defeated in the first round by Muster in Cincinatti – had nonetheless reached a career-high No.10 in the world and become the 100th man to break into the exalted company in the twenty-five years since the introduction of computer rankings. So confusing was the system that David Felgate had to explain to Tim exactly how he'd done it.

It was not only a huge personal achievement, but was the kind of breakthrough that had seemed utterly unlikely when he was losing five first-round matches in the dog days of winter. And he was only 300 ranking points behind Rusedski, so the British No.1 ranking was back within reach and he wanted that. The queue for his autograph at the Pilot Pen booth was as long as anyone's throughout the week and was only suspended when a huge thunderstorm broke directly over Henman's head.

Maybe he was the chosen one. With rain bouncing off the concrete around him, he arrived in the press lounge completely dry, shirt hanging lazily outside his shorts, flip flops on, legs lean and bronzed, contemplating the recent past and his hopes for the future. 'I was very down after Wimbledon, I don't mind admitting it,' he told me. 'There are times when people comment on what I'm doing and what I'm feeling, but they can't really know, they can only scratch the surface. You don't always want to get into the depths of it all because it might hurt you too much.

'I was disappointed because I was playing the best tennis of my career but I came up against a guy who was better than me on the day. That's the way it goes sometimes but getting to the semi-finals of Wimbledon means I'm pretty close. That was the championship my career needed. I don't think anyone can appreciate its importance unless it's happening to them. I definitely enjoy it, I thrive off it but, equally, it was nice to get away from all of the intensity for a little peace and quiet, to switch off from the game and the pressures.'

I wondered whether his performance could be regarded as a sea-change in his fortunes. 'I definitely felt a lot different from the way I did in the two previous years,' he said. 'I felt really confident against Pete and the way I felt didn't come as a surprise to me. I had practised a lot with him and I believed that was an advantage when he came out playing great in the first set. At 6–3, 1–0 down, if I had just accepted that and said "Yes, he's playing too good," I could have been on the receiving end of a pretty quick match. But I felt I knew what I wanted to do on the court and in the past that's something I was lacking. And the way I responded shows the type of tennis I should be playing.

'A couple points were the crux of the match. I fought back well to break him twice in the second set and then I had a game point to take the third into a tie-break. I'm not saying my first serve was the best I've ever produced, but I thought it was an ace, it smacked the line and Pete came up with a brilliant return. On set point I hit a pretty good pass, but he picked off the volley. What could I say? When you're against a player who has won eleven Grand Slams, it shouldn't come as a surprise.

'I felt great when I came back in LA, I was ready to start hitting balls again. The twin emphases on my return were a) I wanted to continue where I left off at Wimbledon and b) the last time I played on hard courts, at Key Biscayne. I was playing so well, yet I was playing so badly this time last year. I wanted to rectify that.

'I'm as good as I have ever been, mentally, physically and technically. It feels good, but I'm not taking anything for granted. I'm twenty-two in two weeks' time and I need to take advantage of that. I still think I can move much quicker and for longer periods of time and that's something I'm working on every day. Tim [Newenham] has had a huge part to play in my physical development – though it can be a bit painful at times, it's got to be done. It's exciting, too, to know that there are years and years of improvement ahead.'

And no need to add the rider 'hopefully'. Back home, the news of Henman's elevation into the top ten was all over the radio, TV and the newspapers. Robert Philip's column in the *Daily Telegraph* did not reflect the overall impression. 'Now I know we have been waiting many a long year to acclaim a genuine British-born tennis hero who can do battle with the best in the world,' wrote Philip, 'but from the reaction which followed Henman's computerized achievement, you could have been fooled into thinking that he actually won something.

'A few days after all this brouhaha – you might well have missed this little snippet of information, so little prominence was it given by a besotted media – Henman quietly dropped back out of the top ten again to No.13. So, given the inconsistencies of the world rankings worked out by a computer, how should greatness be measured? Pete Sampras is the Wimbledon champion and the best player in the world. Tim Henman is neither and, in all probability, he never will be.'

Cheap shot or not, Henman could neither be blamed for the hysteria which greeted his rise to a landmark world ranking, nor should he have been chastized for the lack of an adequate reaction to his subsequent fall. The vagaries of the computer system were such that Henman was on holiday in Portugal in August when his ranking rose to No.11. How did you explain that to the public?

The effects of his elevation in the rankings back home in England didn't reach Henman in deepest Connecticut and he preferred it that way. 'I don't have any interest in what's been said or not said,' he explained. 'although of course you hope there are more positives than negatives.'

'Back in February and March everybody was saying I should get a new coach, a new forehand, a new backhand and a new serve. Those opinions don't matter to me. I only listen to the ones I value, and they have served me pretty well. I know the support is there for me, especially at Wimbledon when it all gets pretty intense. I wouldn't have changed anything about it, but it's nice sometimes to get away from it. There have been a few letters since Wimbledon, mostly saying well done, good luck for the future. There are a lot of people out there believing I will go further and that's nice.'

There had been rumours that, as recognition of his achievement, Henman would be paid handsomely. The *London Evening Standard* had run a story after Wimbledon suggesting that he would receive a £2 million bonus. Henman scoffed at the idea. 'Brad Gilbert (Andre Agassi's coach) came up to me a couple of weeks ago in LA, saying he'd heard I'd be making $3 million, but I told him it was absolute fiction. Stories like this don't do much for your profession. It's not about whether you read it or not, it's about believing it and this was total garbage. I'm sure if my ranking continues to improve there will be something in the end-of-year bonuses but there's no bonus for this. Absolutely not.'

If not richer in his pocket, he was increasingly prosperous in terms of his reputation. There was a sense in the locker room that he was a burgeoning threat – so he might have to start looking in the mirror as he got changed. This was the world Henman himself described as 'pretty selfish', where nobody gave you a dime. He knew what it was all about, he had become hardened to the prevailing attitude, he just hoped it would never change him. 'In an individual sport, that's the way it has to be, you put yourself first and take care of yourself first,' he said. 'This is a great environment to be in, I love it, there can't be many better ways to earn a living but you have to take care of number one. I can't have many complaints the way things are.'

Life was good, so much so that there was no point moaning because the LTA didn't believe it was worth marking the occasion of his rise to tenth in the world – the first time there had been two British players inside the elite – with so much as a by your leave. In fact, other than a call from his parents, the only tangible recognition from home was a fax from Billy Knight.

Pete Sampras, speaking on the Tuesday night at a gathering of the tournament sponsors, noticed that his friend Henman had slipped into the back of the room, and was happily signing the sheaves of paper being thrust under his nose, making small talk to those who loved his accent. Sampras pointed him out. 'There's Tim Henman, a great guy,' he said. 'It's nice to have a real Brit in the top ten.' Ouch.

'The top ten is something I've talked about for a long time and to achieve it is great,' Henman said. 'But this isn't the time to stand still and just be happy with what I've achieved so far. I didn't expect anything from the LTA, just because I didn't really think about it. Those closest to me are pleased, but we're all ready to move to bigger and better things.'

With that he was gone, flip-flopping out to prepare for his opening match in the New Haven tournament against Vincenzo Santopadre, an Italian left hander whose greatest claim to fame is that his father owned one of Rome's finest restaurants. It was not a particularly good day for tennis, a wind blowing capriciously across the bows of the court, tugging at the ball toss, making this a match to get over with as quickly as possible. That Henman did, without too many travails, dropping only five games.

He came back the following day to face another Italian, Davide Sanguinetti, who had reached the quarter-finals at Wimbledon before losing to Richard Krajicek, but hadn't managed to get beyond the second round in his six tournaments since. The second day's work was a touch harder, Henman losing the first set before coming through with increasing assurance, 4–6, 6–3, 6–3.

He didn't know that he was about to take part in one of the most incredible occasions of the year. Krajicek was the opposition, one of the best movers in men's tennis, a true giant of the game, an immensely likeable Dutchman with a game to match. The match itself was something of a minor classic before its extraordinary denouement in the final set tie-break. It would become, according to *L'Equipe*, The Longest Night. Henman had eight match points, Krajicek won it on his fourth. It would take a chapter to describe each point in detail, but, memorably, Henman, leading 12–11, served a grotesque double fault; at 13–13, Krajicek double faulted himself to give Henman his sixth match point, which he saved with a majestic cross-court backhand winner, and the match ended when Henman drove a forehand into the tramlines. The score was 5–7, 6–2, 7–6 (18–16) to the Dutchman. 'What can you say about a night like this?' Henman asked. 'If you thought about it for too long, you'd go mad. I didn't think I made a lot of mistakes, and every time I play Richard, I feel it's going to be 7–6, 6–7, 7–6. It won't be easy to forget this defeat, but I can't afford to think about it every day.'

Henman had lost another match he should have won – a familiar story – which clearly prevented him from breaking through with greater impact. It was a mystery how a player with, quite possibly, one of the finest games in the sport, couldn't close out matches which were the difference between stardom and superstardom.

Tony Pickard, who had never hidden his high regard for Henman the tennis player was perturbed when he saw him toss aside so many gaping opportunities. And, whether he liked it or not, the story would keep coming back to his relationship with Felgate. 'The thing is,' said Pickard that week, 'you find somebody it works with, and you build up a relationship. OK, at the end of the day, the person is someone you believe in or you have him as a travelling companion. That's it in a nutshell. If it works, it's very special. But you must never be satisfied. If you are, then your player will live in what I call the comfort zone.

'In Henman's case, I don't think his game is going to change. If you analyse his season, he has lost against people he should have beaten. I don't think that shows a weakness, necessarily. But he plays too safe. I must say, I would sit back, look at it and ask "why?" because it happens too regularly.

'You can't go on doing that if you're going to be a top five player and right now I would say that's the one area where he has a problem. You could sit down and analyse that in a month, very easily. Then you've got to deal with it. For sure, it will come at the same time – as near as dammit – every match. It's a bit like Stefan (Edberg). He used to get what I called "the droops". The head would go and I knew we'd had it. OK, it took a while to get rid of it, but we did.

'When it happened on court, he'd say to himself "Wait a minute, the old bugger told me that would happen." He was aware. He was prepared. It's all about preparations. On any given day, at any given time, I think Tim Henman could beat anybody. But to win a Slam you've got to win seven matches in a row and I'm not sure he's ready to do that. What you see of him on Monday, you see of him on Tuesday, you see of him on Wednesday, on Thursday, on Friday. To me, if you're going to win seven in a row, you've got to have a bit stacked away somewhere that nobody sees.

'Edberg was always able to go up a notch. If he played on a Monday, it was usually well within himself. Most of the guys out there today play full throttle from the word go, and only Sampras keeps a little bit tucked away in the tank.'

12 If I Can Make It There ...

The words of welcome over the players' entrance to the new Arthur Ashe Stadium Court at Flushing Meadows don't quite have the intellectual profundity of Kipling's *If*.

At the All England Club, it was about treating the twin impostors of triumph and disaster just the same and becoming a man, my son. In the Big Apple, the capital of schmaltz and high living, they had inscribed the words from Frank Sinatra's 'New York, New York': 'I wanna make it, in the city that never sleeps, to find I'm king of the hill, top of the heap. If I can make it there, I'll make it anywhere. It's up to you.' Yes, it was up to them.

Greg Rusedski had almost made it in 1997, showing courage far beyond the call of duty to reach the final where he was beaten by Pat Rafter, who revealed that he had been as nervous as a kitten before the match began. The clearest image of that final day was Rusedski, biting his lip, trying to suppress a tear, as Rafter grinned before the presentation ceremony. Rusedski returned to New York in no fit state to win the toughest Grand Slam title of them all – or so the objective theory went.

He hadn't played enough matches, he hadn't thought of entering a couple of Challengers for match practice, he had a new coach, he said he was OK, but was he really? Tim Henman had reached a final, a semi and a quarter in his preparations. He was ranked No.13 to Rusedski's No.6. They were drawn in opposite halves. Someone in the British press corps even went so far as to suggest that it portended an all-

British final. OK, maybe the g and ts were flowing a bit too freely as we crossed the Atlantic.

The in-form men's player was Rafter – no one else could hold a candle to his current record. Since his tremulous performance against Henman in the fourth round at Wimbledon, the defending Open champion had compiled a sequence of eighteen victories and two defeats, collecting the hard court titles at Indianapolis, Cincinnati and Long Island. Even Rafter wondered whether he might have peaked too soon and viewed his opening round against the mercurial leftie, Hicham Arazi of Morocco, with justifiable alarm. He was to win the game in five sets, having lost the first two and looking as though he was out on his feet. What a turnaround was to happen for this thoroughly nice guy as the fortnight progressed.

Rusedski had lost to Rafter in the semis on Long Island, a defeat which angered Groeneveld to the extent that he decided he should let the player know where he stood. 'It was so close to the Open and Greg just didn't perform,' said his coach. 'There was a lot of pressure on him, that was certain, but I didn't feel against Rafter that he was ever on the court. That was when I stepped in. I wanted to make sure his attitude was going to be better. I felt good because I knew that his ears were open and he listened. It was our first test together. From that moment, I knew I could talk to Greg the way I would need to from time to time.'

The final Grand Slam of the year opened with a remarkable story line – one far removed from hitting tennis balls across a net. Switzerland's Marc Rosset – a ten-year tour veteran – had been beaten in the opening round by Dominik Hrbaty of Slovakia and, disillusioned with his form, considered taking the first plane home. He and his coach Pierre Simsolo were booked on Swissair Flight 111 from New York to Geneva but, at the last minute, Rosset decided he would stay another couple of days and practise. One hour and forty minutes after take-off, the flight perished off the coast of Halifax, Nova Scotia, with the loss of all 229 people on board.

The lives of two men had been spared on a spur of the moment decision. Rosset, thinking of those who had perished, where he might have been, gave a press conference the morning after the disaster, that was full of humility, good grace and plenty of dry throats. His was one life which would never be the same again.

Rusedski's first opponent was the hugely talented but often brittle South African Wayne Ferreira and from there, it got decidedly tougher; a section which would first present him, if the seedings worked out, with Jonas Bjorkman, then Goran Ivanisevic, his nemesis, with Rafter to come in the quarters. Better not even look beyond that. Henman had drawn Aussie left hander Scott Draper – remember him? The Stella Artois champion, a title which Henman would surely have won at Queen's had he not had one of his incomprehensible lapses of concentration.

Henman had never been beyond the fourth round at the Open, a championship everyone loved to hate, players and media especially. The traffic to and from your hotel in Manhattan was crazy at the quietest of times, and at least twice in the fortnight you could bet your bottom dollar that your driver picked the 59th St Bridge when both levels were clogged and the lights were green all the way up Northern Boulevard.

The US Open's scheduling had long been a comic nonsense, bearing no relation at all to the physical and mental needs of the players, dictated as it was by TV channel CBS Sports and its cable affiliate USA Sports in America. Since it had come on board as a major player in the United Kingdom, Sky Sports were consulted as to when they would prefer the Brits to play, which gave the written press the chance to twist a few arms.

It just so happened that for their matches in the first week, both Henman and Rusedski were treated to 11a.m. starts, US east coast time – 4p.m. in Britain, which meant that the early deadlines at home could more easily be met, especially when the first editions so often had to be put to bed without enough live play for the boys to get their teeth into. The press boys rejoiced.

The two Brits were on the practice court together before their opening matches, which suited their needs. There was nothing to be gained by allowing personal differences to get in the way of thorough preparation for a Grand Slam. Rusedski was starting against a right-hander, Henman faced a leftie. In opposite corners of the court, tossing balls back to their men, were David Felgate and Sven Groeneveld. It was hard to imagine a similar session being arranged if Pickard had still been involved with Greg.

Rusedski was first up, on Tuesday morning against Ferreira. The ensuing three hours and eight minutes underlined the determination of both men not to give in to the other. It wasn't pretty, far from it. There were distracting attempts by both to waste time, and therefore disrupt the other's rhythm.

Rusedski couldn't have been as upbeat as he seemed, surely. 'I'm trying not to feel the pressure,' he said. 'If you work hard, then sooner or later it's going to come right.' But, his place in the top ten and his reign as Britain's No.1 player were under threat and only by lasting deep into the second week could he possibly preserve both positions. Rusedski might have insisted that Groeneveld had worked wonders for his consistently under-achieving backhand, but where was the evidence? He seemed one step slow to everything, the backhand was horrendously erratic, the serve unquestionably rusty, and when Ferreira served for a two-set lead at 5–4 in the second, no one gave a red cent for Greg's prospects.

But the South African, who had been known to snatch defeat from the jaws of victory himself, got nervous and handed his opponent a route back via the tie-break which Rusedski won 7–2. A third set consistently interrupted by Rusedski requiring multiple changes of footwear was snatched by Ferreira, who had his second match point in the fourth set tie-break but sent a forehand service return thumping into the net. Rusedski was still in there and how many players, even in such precarious form, would you back against him in similar circumstances?

The fists were pumping now, as Rusedski closed out the one break of serve required and despite missing a smash on his first match point, came roaring into the net to force the final error from Ferreira and raise his arms in triumph to family and friends in the players' enclosure. Sven Groeneveld had an idea how difficult his task would be.

'There were two good signs for me,' Rusedski said. 'I came back from two match points down and I was out there for more than three hours, so no problems, physically or mentally. It is great to have a win, he is a tough opponent. I am not feeling any pressure at all, I am quite relaxed out there. I knew I had a difficult draw. If I win, I win, if I don't then I'll be gone, shall we say.'

Ferreira, as one might have expected, wasn't so complimentary. He was asked if he was surprised how far Rusedski had come in the previous two years. 'Well, Jeez, if I had that serve, I'd also go far,' he said. 'If you don't do well with a serve like that, there's something wrong. I think of Tim as a better tennis player than Greg, a better all-round game. If you had to take away the serve and leave the rest, Tim is much better in my opinion.'

It was an opinion the British press willingly seized upon, but what seemed just as significant to me was when Ferreira, who played with a huge protective black strapping on his right ankle, spoke of the permanent mental as well as physical scars left by such injuries. 'I don't feel sorry for him (Rusedski) about his ankle. Mine is fine, but I still have a lot of pain. I keep playing through it. It is just the way it is. It doesn't go away so I have to keep playing with it.' How long would Rusedski be scarred by his ill-starred desire to please his fans at Wimbledon?

For the first time in three of the year's Grand Slams, Henman stepped onto court the day after a Rusedski victory, with the additional need to win to match the success of his rival. He was ushered onto the Stadium Court Three which, in the days before the building of the new Stadium Court and the re-direction of the flight path from La Guardia from directly overhead the arena, was the one most players wanted to avoid.

Henman's concentration proved to be middling to good. Draper was not an opponent to be taken lightly – he had in the dim and distant past been talked of as a passable imitation of Rod Laver (what an albatross to place around anyone's neck), so Henman wasn't dealing with a nobody. *The Times* headline the next morning suggested Henman was on cruise control against Draper and the fact that the Briton won in straight sets probably gave cause for such optimism, but the match itself demanded a less charitable analysis.

Tim's mum and dad were there to suffer every point alongside Lucy, of course, and in the row behind Felgate and fitness trainer Tim Newenham were Andrew Richardson, the British No.3, perhaps Tim's closest pal on the circuit whom he was trying to entice to change his mind about retirement from the sport, and Felgate's playing contemporary, Jason Goodall.

Henman took the first set 6–3 but when he served for the second at 5–4 with a chance to ease himself into a winning position, he stuttered once again. All the past lapses in the year were being replayed. When the set was eventually forced into a tie-break, my mind immediately went back to New Haven, Krajicek and those eight match points. Henman's did too. There were to be no such feverish alarms this time, though the assistance of a net cord on the first set-point served to offer him a giant helping hand. Once he had overcome that particular wobble, Henman didn't seem too troubled and advanced in straight sets, the third also on a tie-break.

'I think I have fully rested the memory of Krajicek now,' he said. And when asked when he was able to shrug the memory off, he replied, 'By my eleventh beer that night. No, it wasn't quite like that but I was so disappointed when I came off the court. Yet, I knew I was due a match like that against him. At Wimbledon I beat him in three tie-breaks in a four setter a couple of years back, and when we played in Battersea, he served for the match and I was able to turn that around. I didn't dwell on it that much, there were other defeats this year which affected me a lot more.'

The inevitable question about him usurping Rusedski in the rankings was raised. 'I've got a pretty good opportunity (of passing him),' Henman replied. 'Obviously, he is defending a lot of points, but I'm much more interested in the continuation of the way I'm playing. I'm definitely pretty happy.'

The view from the roof of the Arthur Ashe Stadium took the breath away. One of the most famous skylines in the world stretched away, and as the sun set behind the Empire State, was there a more perfect moment to discuss the prospect of reaching the top of the world?

'I don't want to be known simply as a player who can do well at Wimbledon,' said Henman. 'But it's no good having a couple of good weeks here and there, mixing it with periods of poor tennis. I know I'm improving because I sense the guys in the locker room expect more and more from me. You need to show that on a regular basis to be feared around here. I feel as if I'm knocking on the door and heading in the right direction.'

Rusedski resumed his challenge a day later against Bohdan Ulihrach of the Czech Republic. How could anyone know this match would stretch credulity to its limits?

Mike Dickson of the *Daily Mail* described his first-round victory as 'winning ugly', borrowing a catchphrase from Andre Agassi's coach Brad Gilbert, who had reached the top ten himself but was not one of those players whose talent aroused the aesthetic senses. Rusedski's tennis wasn't pretty, either. Against Ulihrach, he was two sets to one down and despite throwing away a barrel-load of break points in the third set, fought his way back, and saved six break points in the final set before staring down another match point. To this moment of crisis, he responded with a fiercely kicking second serve that reared up at Ulihrach, and forced him to play nothing more than a pat-a-cake forehand which flew over the baseline. Rusedski closed the match out by holding his serve to love.

One remarkable week had brought Rusedski through a couple of unprecedented challenges – he had never won two matches back-to-back saving match points in both, and had never won two five-set matches in succession before, 'These things are bound to give you confidence,' he said. 'I know I can go the distance, I know I can win whether I'm two sets down or two sets to one down. I was frustrated at the end of the third set against Ulihrach and went a little crazy, going for my shots. Then I cooled down, brought myself back and stayed positive from there on – playing a good fourth set. He raised his level again in the fifth and got a buzz, but I managed to hold him, contain him. That was important.'

Containing and holding were all very well, but there was nothing in Rusedski's first two performances which intimated a repeat of his 1997 accomplishments. Worse, he now had to face a serve-volleyer from his own mould, in fellow left-hander, Dutchman Jan Siemerink, an opponent he never relished. At least, there was cause for celebration in that Henman (who had defeated Spain's Felix Mantilla) and Rusedski had become the first two Brits to make the third round at the Open since Buster Mottram and John Lloyd in 1979.

In the press seats for the Siemerink match sat Brian Teacher, wondering how much further forward his former protégé had come in the year since they were on the verge of something really special. The venue was the old Stadium Court at Flushing, now shorn of the top two tiers of seating so providing a more intimate tennis theatre – if such a thing existed in New York.

The match began in mid-afternoon, a setting sun causing problems with the service toss, the ability to pick the overheads, to sight the ball properly at all; it ended with the floodlights on – two matches rolled into one. All of this external paraphernalia – now we realized why he preferred to play indoors – was going to lead to Rusedski's undoing, much to the consternation of his father who sat in the front row of the Players' Box and witnessed a performance which offered all the old misgivings about his son's choices in the summer.

The demands of his opening two matches decreed that he needed to get this one over quickly if he was to last deep into the second week. The New Yorkers liked his attitude, he never gave less than full value for the dollar, but he looked desperately unhappy against Siemerink, a player who was a mirror image, mixing moments of inspiration with crushing lapses of concentration and confidence. The Dutch journalists gathering for the final set after Siemerink had pulled it all square, still expected their man to stumble within sight of the tape.

Instead it was Rusedski, debilitated by his previous efforts, who couldn't sustain his levels of intensity. It was crushing for him not to have the energy in his legs to match the commitment in his soul. The fifth game of the final set was of huge significance.

Rusedski missed two easy forehand volleys, responded with an ace and was then foot-faulted on a second serve – not for the first time. He was break point down, but managed to get a forehand volley into court. At the changeover, he lambasted the umpire over the decisions from his line judges. 'A foot fault on second serve, that's crap. I mean, goodness me (maybe he realized every word was picked up on the courtside mike). You should really be proud, are you proud of yourself? You're doing a fabulous job.'

Just then, in shades of Wimbledon, he began to cramp up. He managed to remain in rallies even though he could hardly move without the trace of a limp. The Dutch waited for Siemerink to seize up, but he managed to stay focused. He broke for 5–4 to serve for the match. For the third game in succession, Rusedski faced match point, but a fiercely-struck backhand service return stunned Siemerink who put a half-volleyed reply into the net. On the second break point and another match point, Rusedski summoned another brutal return of serve which prompted a netted volley. Ditto the third match point. Could Rusedski possibly climb another mountain?

An ace down the middle on his fourth match point finally secured victory for the Dutchman in three hours and two minutes. At exactly the time the multi-Oscar winning blockbuster *Titanic* was being shown on American cable TV, Rusedski finally disappeared beneath the surface. It had been a slow and solemn drowning. He kept the press waiting an hour and a half, much to their dismay, given British deadline times. He didn't apologize for the delay, but looked a little sheepish as he walked in. He said he was all right, not feeling too bad. The foot faults were mentioned. 'You should be able to get over those and move on,' he said. 'I wouldn't have been in such difficulty with a better first service percentage today.

'I felt I had a chance to continue but I haven't had a good Grand Slam season, you can't argue with that. I can only strive to get better. I just couldn't get my form back in time. The injuries really hurt me. If I hadn't missed two months, I wouldn't have fallen out of the top ten, but you can't control these things. I just don't like to be mediocre. I couldn't raise my game to the level I wanted to be. I wasn't seizing up, as you say, but I guess I didn't look very nimble out there.

'I have goals in mind, new goals now. Tim will overtake me in the world rankings and as British No.1 – there's a good chance for him to do really well here. Better than last year, who knows? But I don't let anybody relax, whether they are British No.1 or Pete Sampras. I'm going backwards a little bit at the moment but I'm ready to start making progress again.'

Rusedski's Grand Slam record of third-round defeat in the Australian Open, first round in the French, first round at Wimbledon and third round in the US Open was about the mean average for his pro career – though on the back of his quarters at Wimbledon and final in the US Open in 1997, so much more had been expected. Tim had the field to himself again.

Henman's third-round opponent was one of those he should have dusted down and defeated in under an hour and a half. All right, so there are no easy games in tennis any more, or so we are repeatedly told, and the difference between No.11 in the world and No.149 is not as great in practice as it is in written form, but Germany's Michael Kohlmann had no Grand Slam pedigree – he didn't even figure in the ATP's *1998 Player Guide*.

It was the hottest day of the championships: the mercury moved into the nineties, there was sunshine and blue sky as far as the eye could see, but not on Henman's horizon. He won the first set comfortably enough and then, in the second game of the second set, bounding in behind a serve, his right leg gave way in much the same manner as Rusedski's had at Queen's in June. The TV replay made the fall look bad. Henman climbed back to his feet, towelled himself down and carried on.

His tennis was becoming too loose – he was back in one of his 'why aren't I beating the pants off this guy?' moods. There were five breaks of serve in the second set, which Henman clung on to 7–5, but then he fell apart, unforced errors flying from his racket as often as double faults. Kohlmann could hardly believe it as he raced through the third set 6–1 against a player being touted as a potential champion. Sampras and Rafter would have had this guy wrapped up long ago.

Henman turned his wrath on the umpire, shouting that he should 'show more intensity'. Fortunately, he heeded his own message, wrapping up the match in two hours and thirty-one minutes, and winning the last eight points. It had been a perilous haul, but he was back in the fourth round for the second consecutive year and was to face the formidable figure of Mark Philippoussis.

Who knows whether the outcome against the Australian might have hinged on the second game of the match? Henman had held, and then found himself with three break points in the opening service game of Philippoussis. Henman was attacking the net, forcing Philippoussis to have to come up with winners; it was a bold, intelligent strategy. OK, so Philippoussis struck a crunching inside-out forehand winner on the first break point, but Henman should have buried him, only to err on an outstanding backhand opportunity. The Aussie then produced a service winner and an ace.

The moment Philippoussis had Henman's serve under similar pressure, one wondered if he could be denied. The question was answered in the eleventh game when Henman extricated himself from 15–40, but was punished on the third break point, netting a backhand volley. Henman bravely held off the first three set points, but on the fourth a backhand service return sailed long and Philippoussis was ahead.

It was imperative Henman held his first service game in the second set and, from 0–30 down, he did. And then, quite inexplicably, he began to play like a champion-elect, a stream of winners brought him fourteen points in succession, he aced twice in the third game, twice in the fifth and was 5–0 up before Philippoussis could think straight. At 30–30 in the sixth game, a sprinkling of rain doused Henman's destructive rhythm and the players had to scurry off.

In the Philippoussis corner of the locker room, his recently-appointed coach, Pat Cash, worked on his man's psyche. 'Tim was playing like a dream, no doubt of that,' Cash said. 'I told Mark to try to slow him down, to get into the points more, to make Tim have to work a little harder.' Wise words, for sure, but Philippoussis double faulted on the first point after the players' returned, and played an appalling forehand to lose the set 6–0.

Henman won the first six points of the second set, three of them with service winners, and thus the first eight since the resumption for rain. He was climbing all over an opponent who wasn't renowned for possessing the soundest of temperaments. Philippoussis could only cling on, hoping his luck would turn, knowing that when he'd put pressure on the Henman serve before it had promised to come apart. And so, to the crucial fifth game of the set.

Henman was 0–30 down (how he made life difficult for himself), hauled himself back to a game point which Philippoussis countered, when a Henman forehand that appeared to land plumb on the baseline, was called long. Henman was livid; he knew this was close. The umpire, Jorge Diaz, had a split-second opportunity to overrule but did nothing other than call the score. Deuce.

On the next point, Henman opened up the court and, standing in the tramlines, had the chance to put an overhead anywhere he wanted. Instead, he smashed it to the one place where his opponent could lay a racket on it, Philippoussis managed to get enough wrist strength into his shot and a backhand drive landed back behind the stranded Henman. It was the crux of the match.

Henman railed against the umpire at the next changeover, but his anger could not be translated into destructive form on the court, where it really mattered. Instead, Henman, helpless against a torrent of winners, lost his serve three times in the fourth set and was despatched,

finally, by a crunching forehand service return. Henman's press conference followed a predictable path – full of yeahs, you knows,
hopefullys, and maybes. There were few answers to get our teeth into.
'I'm putting myself in contention,' he said, 'so that's a big positive.
Something that wasn't happening at the beginning of the year. So I
want to go away and finish off this year really strongly.

'I think my game in the past six to eight weeks has gone to a new
level and I think it's very close to going up again. At this level, it only
takes a small margin to win or lose a match. I have to eradicate these
types of errors and I think, if I do that, I'm much tougher than I was
to beat. If I get rid of those types of mistakes, then it will get even
harder.'

The sages weren't so convinced. John McEnroe, for one, didn't
believe Philippoussis had triumphed because he was the better player.
'The conditions were very windy and Philippoussis is a stronger man
than Henman,' he said. 'I don't think Henman is scrawny, like he was
a couple of years ago, his legs have definitely got stronger, but you're
talking here about the difference from being a top fifteen player to one
in the top ten who wants to move to the next level.

'They say Tim's a nice guy, but nice guys don't get in the top ten and
stay there. To do that, you've gotta be a hard-nosed S.O.B. Behind
closed doors, Henman doesn't sit there and say how wonderful everything is. He's got an ego, he believes in himself and that's why he's
become a legitimate contender. He's put aside the attitude that being a
good loser is good enough. He's done quite a good job at Wimbledon
because it's difficult for him in his home country and there's more pressure on him than there is on Rusedski, because he's the true British
player. He'll burn it one of these days.

'But he's going to have to keep working hard, twice as hard. I've
never been one to advocate lifting weights, and I think he would be
better served to play more doubles. I believe your legs get stronger by
spending more time out on the court. Against Philippoussis he lost his
way, he got discouraged and then, in the last set and a half, the big
Aussie played as well as I've ever seen him.

'Having said that, I was disappointed in the fourth that Henman got
so negative. He lost his concentration and didn't want it bad enough.
He might look at his strategy and his timetable for next year a little
more closely. He'd played a lot of tennis this summer, and it's difficult
sometimes, when you're abroad, and you miss your own bed, to put
that out of your head. It caught up with him all at once. That's why he
has a big edge at Wimbledon, but nowhere else at the moment.'

Wise words, which Henman and Felgate would have done well to
heed as they settled on their initial playing schedule for 1999. Henman
left New York as quickly as he could, as he had the defence of his
President's Cup in Tashkent, Uzbekistan to prepare for; while
Rusedski stayed on the hard courts, seeking as much practice partnership as he could find, straining for the rhythm he hadn't had since he'd
last been in the States, in March. A new member was added to his ever-
expanding coterie: Ken Matsuda, who had once been fitness trainer to
Michael Chang, arguably the fittest player of the 1990s.

Matsuda watched Rusedski work out, he analysed, he offered
advice. He said he would come over to London in December to spend
a week at the player's side. 'Ken worked with Chang for nine years and
in that time he didn't pull out of one event, which isn't a bad record,'
Greg said. 'He has been helping my recuperation from the ankle injury,
he's working on strengthening certain areas of my muscle group and
he's a man I have great respect and admiration for. I believe he will
help.'

Henman and Rusedski could only eye the remainder of the US
Open with a pang of 'what might have beens'. Philippoussis went on to
play the unseeded Swede Thomas Johansson, winning 12–10 in a
remarkable fifth set tie-break, to defeat Carlos Moya in the semi-final,
and to reach his first Grand Slam final. Siemerink, to the surprise of no
Dutch writer, immediately lost to Jonas Bjorkman, who succumbed to
Rafter, who went on to defeat No.1 seed Pete Sampras in a semi-final
which may or may not have turned on the left thigh injury Sampras
incurred playing a routine volley in the early stages of the fourth set.

The final, then, pitted Aussie against Aussie, not Brit against Brit.
Rafter, the defending champion would play Philippoussis, two players
who had endured the kind of rivalry in the past which made Henman
and Rusedski look like a pair of neighbours squabbling over the height
of the other's hedgerows. To be honest, it was never much of a contest.
Philippoussis didn't do himself justice, his serve worked only fleet-
ingly, and Rafter was more occasion-tough. He won in four sets, 6–0 in
the fourth, and there was no prouder Aussie when he lifted the cup for
the second successive year.

13 The Davis Cup

From the pursuit of individual honour to the greater glory of your nation – the Davis Cup conjured such different images to the treadmill of the ATP Tour. It was not self first, it was the team, the nation, that mattered. Personal enmities, whether real or imaginary, were put to one side. Tim even let Greg hug him. The splendid BBC documentary on the eve of the World Group qualifying tie between Great Britain and India was titled 'Rally To The Flag'. An apt inscription.

Whatever anyone thought of Rusedski's decision to throw one flag in the bottom drawer and drape himself in another, you couldn't take away his overriding passion for the Davis Cup. He positively thrived on the event. Even those players wounded by his arrival on the scene to the detriment of their own international ambitions, were unable to offer evidence to the contrary. If they could look at the situation objectively, they must have known they could never have done as well.

This was to be a critical year for British hopes. Since 1992 – before either Henman or Rusedski had smacked a ball as a professional – Britain had been out of the World Group, the sixteen nations who comprised the Davis Cup elite.

Instead, trailing around the periphery of the real competition, they had been in the Euro-African Zone, tennis's equivalent of the Vauxhall Conference. 'The public don't know what the hell the Euro-African stuff is all about,' said captain David Lloyd. 'We don't either, it's about time we got the hell out of this place and back where we belong.'

Belonging was one thing, achieving something else. But with two players inside the world's top twenty as leading singles picks, Lloyd was in an enviable position. As the year went on, arguments and political in-fighting about the Davis Cup were besetting the Americans. Pete Sampras insisted he didn't want to play in the semi-final because his personal priorities didn't include wrapping himself in the Star Spangled Banner. In Australia, the old Rafter–Philippoussis argument was stirred up over how they were treated differently by the captain John Newcombe and his coach, Tony Roche.

At the final of the US Open, Roche had sat in Rafter's corner, while Philippoussis felt that he should have remained neutral, which was hardly likely given that he, Philippoussis, had said he didn't want to be considered for the Davis Cup. Rafter was an essential member of the team, who made it a prerogative to play. Rafter would not be drawn into the conflict on the night of his ecstatic success in New York, but by the time he had returned to play Davis Cup against Uzbekistan in a World Group qualifier, he remarked once more that he couldn't understand Philippoussis' attitude.

By contrast, Britain were sailing serenely onward and, one hoped, upward. The 1998 draw had placed them first in competition with the Ukraine in April in a Euro-African Zone Group One tie, the winners of which would qualify for a play-off in September for a place in the 16-nation World Group. Defeat would mean another year in the second division of international nations, which had been Britain's home for more years than was good for tennis's reputation. The LTA chose Newcastle, that most passionate sporting corner of the country, as the venue. Henman and Rusedski were the backbone of the squad; as a pair they represented one of the most formidable partnerships in the world. But it was noticeable, in the official photo-call, that when they were asked to pose for the cameras as they sat together at the pre-tie press conferences, the smiles were forced. Yes, even Greg's.

This was a critical moment for him, especially as he would be out there first on Friday morning, to play Andrei Rybalko, who resided in the nether regions of 525 in the world. Rusedski was heavily odds-on, but the one thing about Davis Cup was to forget the status of your opponent, for the event could play nasty tricks on those who supposed they were superior performers. Rusedski required most of the first set to undo the knots in his stomach.

It was not until he had pocketed the first set with the seventh of his eventual sixteen aces that Rusedski felt comfortable. He swung through – dropping only one point on his serve in the second set – to win 6–4, 6–0, 6–4 in an hour and thirty-six minutes and handed the baton across to Henman. A lot more was known about Tim's opponent, for Andrei Medvedev had been a top tenner himself in 1993, the year in which he reached the semi-finals of the French Open. This was to be a true test of Davis Cup character.

Henman took the first set with relative ease, but in the second there were six breaks of serve in seven games, before four in a row were held to love. Henman had a set point at 6–5, but Medvedev produced a crunching serve which almost took the racket from Henman's hand and went on to win the tie-break. Henman took the third set, Medvedev crushed him 6–1 in the fourth. We were down to the wire, and it was here where the 3,500 Geordie crowd raised their own levels of support. Henman brushed his opponent aside 6–1, to leave Medvedev lamenting: 'It will take a miracle for us to win now and I don't believe in miracles.'

Team captain Lloyd did not loosen the screw, instead he tightened it, by confirming his doubles choice of Henman and Rusedski, who actually seemed to relish playing together and duly defeated Rybalko and Medvedev comprehensively in straight sets. For the first time in five years, Great Britain had a whiff of the promised land. The victory placed them in a draw for the World Group qualifiers, and Lloyd got the opposition he wanted – the Indians, the only country in the hat that guaranteed him a home tie. The question was, which surface would the LTA choose? The Indians loved grass, so Wimbledon or Eastbourne was out. There was no point playing on Har-Tru given Henman and Rusedski's record on clay of any colour or consistency. So the best prospect was a true-bouncing, mid-speed hard court.

Lloyd was hoping that Henman and Rusedski would just be coming home off the back of successful hard court seasons in America, that they would be in the groove, raring to go, fresh and frisky. So hard courts it was – with the City of Nottingham Tennis Centre the chosen venue – which Lloyd hoped would be a perfect replica of Flushing Meadow. No point in wasting home advantage.

Of the nations remaining in the competition only Spain could boast players with singles rankings better than Henman's 11, and Rusedski's 15. The Indians would rely entirely on two twenty-five-year-olds, Leander Paes and Mahesh Bhupathi, a pair who had developed an astonishing doubles empathy – they were ranked three in the world and had just reached the US Open semi-finals – but whose singles rankings did not measure up to the British pair.

There was no doubting the relaxed camaraderie of the British team, ensconced at Breadsall Priory, a hotel and country club half an hour from the Nottingham site – Henman played eighteen holes of golf with captain David Lloyd and former pro Leighton Alfred on the eve of the match. The Indians were put in the less idyllic surroundings of the Hilton at East Midlands Airport, adjacent to the junction of the main runway and the M1 motorway – again, no point in wasting home advantage.

As Henman had moved ahead of Rusedski in the domestic listings, he would play Bhupathi on the opening day; Rusedski would face Paes. Lloyd named Henman and Neil Broad as his doubles team, but with the option of changing his mind up to an hour before the scheduled start. Henman didn't want to play the first match if possible – 'I hate getting up that early' – and his wish was granted when Rusedski drew the short straw. His match against Paes would be absolutely crucial.

It was a cold, miserable Friday morning, the average age of the crowd was fifty-plus, the applause polite and restrained. It seemed totally unnecessary for the announcer to remind the British crowd of the rule about unsportsmanslike behaviour from partisan crowds in Davis Cup ties which could be punished by warnings and point deductions against the offending team's players. One could hardly imagine this lot hooting just as Paes tossed the ball to serve. Rattling their false teeth and crisp packets maybe, but intimidating the opposition, hardly. Calcutta it wasn't.

Rusedski came on bedecked in an outfit which would have sent shudders down the spine of the traditionalists – a black Nike top, and what appeared to be grey long-johns. The long-johns came off to reveal an all black garment which was soon to match his mood. He should have been broken in the first game, and duly lost his second and third service games as Paes chipped and charged anything that wasn't struck within a yard of the baseline.

The beauty of the Davis Cup is that its matches hardly ever conform to rational tennis precedent. The competition was littered with improbable deeds, of glorious unpredictabilities. Paes beating Rusedski on the Tour would be a shock; in the Davis Cup, it would be nothing out of the ordinary.

Just then Rusedski's serve came back, and then he broke Paes, prompting a couple of errors on a forehand which had been as reliable as a Rolls. Three love service games followed and the tie was neatly poised at a set apiece. It was ebb and flow, attack and counter, but Paes seemed to have the greater array, the ability to fashion a winning position by sleight of hand one moment, sheer brute force the next. By contrast, Greg was just hanging in there. When had we said that before? So Paes won the third set, Rusedski the fourth with three breaks of serve which meant Greg was to serve first in the final set. What happened? He froze momentarily, missing two backhands, one sliced approach, one volley and serving a double on break point. Paes managed to stave off four break points in the second game. 2–0.

There were plenty of mishits, misjudgements and missed opportunities as the deciding set, draining all who witnessed it, reached 5–4, with Paes serving for the match. Then nerves began to betray the Indian. He went for a ridiculous overhead when a flailing Rusedski forehand was flying the length of two tennis courts longer than the one he was standing in; saw Rusedski thread home his finest backhand pass of the match, and pushed a forehand volley long to suffer the break back.

Rusedski trailed 0–30, as was his wont, but Paes left a lob he could have smashed and watched in anguish as it landed plumb on the baseline. Rusedski double faulted to go break point down, aced his man, executed a terrible forehand for a second break point and aced again. When he netted a forehand to give Paes a third opportunity, it was greeted with a grunting, forceful forehand winner. Paes prepared to serve for the rubber again.

He reached match point, served down the middle, came bounding in for the *coup de grace* only for Rusedski's backhand return to clip the top of the net and land at his feet. There was no way even a player as athletically gifted as Paes could summon a shot from there. The ball died. A backhand pass from the top drawer brought the games level again at 6–6.

And so it went on. Rusedski survived the next game from 0–40 down, he was 0–30 four successive times but hung in there and moved to his first match point which Paes saved with a forehand pass. But on the second, the Indian cruelly double faulted. Rusedski's reactions were as if he'd reached the summit of Ben Nevis – he hugged every man jack of the team, the doctor and the physio included. I suspect, if David Lloyd hadn't got a hold of him, he would have hugged every single member of the crowd. Maybe even the press.

'Let's be honest, I wasn't playing good tennis,' said Rusedski later in the year as he reflected on the occasion. 'I had gone the distance with Paes, he'd played some pretty good tennis and I hadn't performed up to the standard I like. There was so much pressure, the first match of the tie, he served for the match twice, had a match point and my serve throughout the match was almost non-existent. And yet, I won. I think the people can relate to that kind of struggle, because in life, things don't always flow easily. Some people are fortunate that way, but there are times when you have to make your own luck. Maybe people relate to me because I show my emotions out there. I show who I am; it's what they like.'

Back in the changing rooms that afternoon, Henman had watched snippets from the match, but couldn't bring himself to sit down and endure more than a couple of games at a time. 'I would have made myself too nervous,' he said. 'But it is incredible to think that Greg lost his serve three times in that final set; he doesn't usually lose his serve three times in a whole month.'

1–0 to Great Britain. Henman's task was to make certain he didn't slip against Bhupathi, a man who played singles so infrequently that his ranking was down at 363. But once more, the Davis Cup contrived the image of a man with nothing but pride to play for, reaching deeper into his spirit than he would do if he was playing just another player on just another hard court.

Bhupathi was inspired. He opened in a manner so focused, playing with such flair and confidence, he might have been in a trance. Lloyd squirmed uneasily in the captain's chair. Henman was warned by the Greek umpire for an audible obscenity as he dropped serve in the ninth game of the opening set, and when he lost his serve to love to trail 1–0 in the second, it was the Indian coterie who were on their feet, cheering wildly.

Henman had to rouse himself; the crowd wouldn't be of much help. He needed to find a groove, and quickly, before Bhupathi, who was completely unfazed by the occasion, raced away. An immediate break back was vital and Henman then achieved another in the eighth game to tie the rubber at a set apiece. Then Henman took a point with an audacious winner, as Bhupathi struck the ball violently towards his – how should we put this? – private parts. Henman must have read the Indian's intent, because he half turned, thrust his racket out, felt it strike the sweet spot, and swivelled in time to see the ball land in the middle of his opponent's side of the court. The tide had turned.

Henman won 4–6, 6–3, 6–3, 6–3 to leave his captain saying that this had been a 'great day' for the British game. 'The spectators have had nine intense sets of tennis, so they've had value for money as well. Greg didn't play well at all but he's hung around and he's won. I just wanted Greg to slow down a little bit on his serve, but if the train is going fast, it can be very hard to get off it. Tim's match was disconcerting for a set, against a guy who doesn't play singles who was playing absolutely at the top of his game. I just hoped he couldn't keep it up.'

But 2–0 it was, the overnight lead Lloyd had expected – the lead Britain needed if it was to secure promotion, given the form and reputation of Paes and Bhupathi in doubles. Lloyd had to within an hour before the start of the doubles to change his side, but Rusedski was still feeling the effects of Friday's endurance, so it was to be as per the initial announcement – Henman and Neil Broad against a team they had beaten in their only previous meeting, on the way to Olympic silver.

Paes and Bhupathi looked like a team. Much had been made of the kit worn by the Brits: Rusedski's black and grey, Henman's light blue with V-neck slipover and now the broad Broad, with bandanna askew and shirt askance. Paes and Bhupathi weren't exactly in national colours, but they wore the same lime green-navy blue ensemble.

It was to be hoped that the ITF might look at the question of team playing kit in the Davis Cup. If they were to preserve its mystique in world tennis at a time when debate was intensifying about changes to its whys and wherefores, then why not insist on making the event even more special? It had grown from an event for two nations, the United States and Great Britain, in 1900 to 129 in a century of competition, and yet the feeling was it needed a culture change. If the teams could wear matching suits and ties at the press conferences and official functions, why couldn't that be extended to on court as well, which is where the public got to see them and sense the spirit of one-nationship?

A letter sent to me by one of those watching that Saturday afternoon confirmed that the consensus in the crowd was how untidy the British team looked. That Henman and Broad lost in straight sets wasn't much of a turn-up for the books, even if it did raise the tie to a new, fascinating level. They were handsomely outplayed by the handsome Indians.

As with any game of doubles, it had its moments of eccentricity, of errors, of great comradeship, of sheer delight. Paes and Bhupathi were a touchy-feely team, flicking the tips of their fingers on each shot, whether a winning one or not. Henman began supremely, serving like a dream, dominating almost all the rallies and keeping his partner in contention. Broad seemed fazed by the whole occasion.

It was remarkable, then, that Henman should forfeit all three of his service points in the first set tie-break, which the Indians pocketed 7–2. The first break of serve, Broad's, arrived in the eighth game of the second set and there was no way the Indians were going to lose with such an advantage. Once again, they prevailed in a tie-break, winning 7–6, 6–3, 7–6. Paes knew it was still an uphill battle. 'We have a lot of work to do tomorrow, at least I know I have, against Tim,' he said.

Paes had not been happy with some of Henman's behaviour in the doubles – he had twice struck a ball at Bhupathi and not offered the kind of acknowledgement or apology one tends to associate with the sport. The Indian journalists warned us that Paes, who felt his friend had been offended, was really fired up and the first set underlined their message.

There were four breaks of serve, the fourth when Henman served for the lead, but he managed to squeeze home in the tie-break. The second set was altogether more easy, even Greg came out to witness it. But Paes was a fighter and Henman knew anyone who had beaten Sampras in singles this year had to be a pretty decent player. The Indian hung in there for all he was worth.

Paes broke to lead 2–0 in the third set, inspired by one Indian voice who shouted 'The crowd's right behind you, Leander.' Henman angrily smashed a ball into the net, but it snapped him out of his funk. Paes was visibly slowing, but it made him no easier to sweep aside, for he was able to stay in rallies courtesy of his respectable groundstrokes. The match, growing more tense by the minute, descended into tie-break territory again. Paes twice edged ahead, Henman responded, reaching match point at 6–5. There then followed the rally of the match at the moment of the match, Henman finally exhausting a man who was spent, as near as made little difference.

'Definitely the best Davis Cup match I've played,' said Henman later. 'These are high-pressure situations, don't let anyone tell you differently. I can remember my first Davis Cup tie, that was a shattering experience, losing to Romania in Manchester, and this is shattering in a different way. I can't wait for the World Group. No disrespect to those nations we've been playing, but it's going to be a lot more fun to play the likes of the States, Sweden, whoever we draw. The World Group has been on our agenda for a long time, but it doesn't stop there.

'I would have been ready to play a fourth or a fifth set today, if I'd lost the third (we were glad he was so sure). I hope this acts as a great incentive to other players, because we do need more than just the two of us out there. I think that Miles (Maclagan) has a great opportunity to come through and take one of the places but now some more younger ones need to start pushing along.'

There was something about Henman during the Paes match which riveted me, almost as much as the tennis. I was told that he likes to know where people are, where his coach is sitting, where he can make eye contact – he zeroes in on things at court side which may go some

way to explaining that when people or objects are out of place –
remember Sue Barker and her camera team at Queen's – Henman loses
that focus. I sensed that, against Paes, I was that focus. After almost
every point he struck, he looked up to where I was sitting, frozen rigid
with the cold, in the press seats. There was no hint of recognition on
his face, no raising or lowering of the eyebrows, just a short, near
sinister glance which spoke of his absolute intensity. I decided – for
Britain's sake – that I shouldn't move a muscle, for fear that I would be
blamed should Henman lose. We won.

Rusedski didn't come into the press conference to share in the glory,
delighted that he didn't need to play the fifth rubber, as it had been
rendered inconsequential by the outcome of Henman's match. He was
asked, though, by the BBC's Iain Carter, if he would say a few words
on the success of the squad, and the fact that the place back in the
World Group was assured. The answer was that he would talk, so long
as Carter didn't ask him about 'the injury'.

What was happening? Was there going to be yet another question
mark over his progress for the rest of what had already been a year of
almost unremitting exasperation? We waited to find out.

The rest of the world was consumed – or should have been – by the
Davis Cup in the same week Britain was nuzzling up with the big boys
again. The semi-finals assumed diametrically different poses with
Sweden defeating the Spaniards whose higher personal rankings
mattered little on a quickfire indoor court; while Italy, blessed with
nothing these days in the class of Pietrangeli or Panatta, went to
Milwaukee and gave the United States a roasting.

Imagine the British team without Henman or Rusedski. The
American captain, Tom Gullikson, hampered by the dismissive
gestures of Sampras, Agassi and Chang, was left to pick from second
stringers, though Todd Martin's world ranking of 29 at the time
deserved immense respect. There was talk of Jim Courier, a stalwart of
the competition, returning from injury to play singles, but Gullikson
preferred the new young prince of the US teeny-tennyboppers, but
nowhere near Davis Cup-honed, Jan-Michael Gambill. Martin lost to
Andrea Gaudenzi, Gambill to Davide Sanguinetti, and the doubles
went in five sets. The Americans were humiliated, on home soil.

John McEnroe, who had made his singles debut for the USA in their
4–1 victory over Britain in 1978, said to me during the US Open that
he would love to be considered as a possible future captain 'but it
would need a brave USTA president to do it'. Now, in the light of this
shambolic defeat, he railed against the attitude of a nation he led to five

Davis Cup triumphs. 'Tom (Gullikson) has had the job for five years and his team has just got butchered,' McEnroe said, 'It should be moved around. Give it to Stan Smith, he walks tall and commands respect. As for myself, I'd like it, but frankly I don't think it's on the cards. I don't want to be in the position of having to deal with players who don't care. So what if I got Sampras to play next year? He's already proved he's too selfish to care.'

With that, the scene changed to the Kensington Hilton hotel on an October afternoon, with Stefan Edberg drawing the World Group for the 1998/9 event – the centenary of the Davis Cup. In 1899, when Dwight Davis, a graduate of Harvard University, donated a silver trophy for an annual tennis match between the US and Great Britain, he could not have dreamt the competition would mushroom to involve a record number of nations.

Edberg's own Sweden were seeded; he drew them the Slovak Republic; then came Germany, also seeded, against Russia. David Lloyd had described the decision of the Davis Cup committee not to seed Great Britain as ludicrous, pointing to the respective rankings of Henman and Rusedski. Then, while Lloyd was on the golf course in La Manga, Edberg pulled out the piece of paper with Britain's name to be placed alongside – who else? – the United States with British home advantage. Dwight Davis's dream reincarnated. After an hour of tortuous procedure as the draw droned on, tennis had burst back into life. The prospect of Sampras v. Rusedski and Agassi v. Henman with the reverse a couple of days later, lived on in the heart, if not the head.

Neither of the American players was willing to say if they would commit to the Davis Cup in 1999. McEnroe bemoaned their attitude. 'We should turn this tie into a festival for the event, a festival for tennis, this should be a visionary time. But, by their attitude, they're going to kill the sport in America,' he said. Tennis in Britain, one felt, could hardly be more alive.

And it was in Nottingham, too, that the seeds were sown for the healing of the wounds between Tim and Greg. On the Saturday evening, Lucy Connor, Fran Ridler and Sven Groeneveld got together with Jan and David Felgate and Lucy Heald for an evening out. Lucy Connor, as befitted a drama student, rose to her feet in the restaurant and burst into song, so well in fact that the entire patronage rose as one to applaud her. The party continued back at the team's hotel.

Jan, Fran and the two Lucys decided they would sing a song together at the Lawn Tennis Writers' dinner at the All England Club in December. It didn't come off in the end – maybe the occasion wasn't

Right: What do I do now? Greg Rusedski pondering his next move in his 1999 Australian Open second-round defeat to qualifier Paul Goldstein. ACTION IMAGES

Left: The clasp of friendship – Sampras and Henman meet at the end of the 1998 semi-final. ACTION IMAGES

Below: Will he get as close again? – Tim salutes the Centre Court crowd after his semi-final defeat to Pete Sampras. ACTION IMAGES

Left: The Rusedski serve, the most powerful single weapon in men's tennis. PROFESSIONAL SPORT

Right: The Henman first serve, which provided so much debate and concern over the year. PROFESSIONAL SPORT

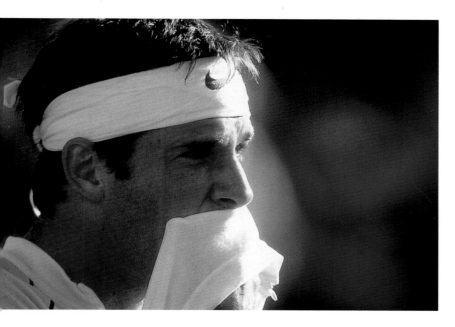

Top: A typical image of Greg Rusedski wiping the perspiration from his top lip with his tennis shirt. PROFESSIONAL SPORT

Below: The ATP trainer Bill Norris tends to Rusedski's aching shoulders during his first round defeat at the 1998 French Open. PROFESSIONAL SPORT

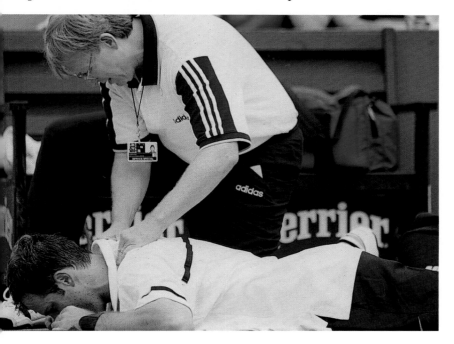

Above: The best of rivals captured at the 1998 US Open
PROFESSIONAL SPORT

Left: The only time Tim and Greg met in 1998 – in the finals of the ATP Tour World championships in Hanover. Greg won in straight sets. ALLSPORT

Top: The former British No.1 Jeremy Bates, who never reached the heights of Henman and Rusedski. PROFESSIONAL SPORT

Below Left: Sven Groeneveld, the amiable Dutchman who believes that, at his best, Rusedski is unbeatable. ACTION IMAGES

Below right: Chris Wilkinson, the third ranked British male – over 170 places behind Tim and Greg at the end of 1998. PROFESSIONAL SPORT

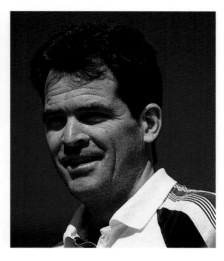

Top: The British boys together – against the Ukraine in the Davis Cup tie at Newcastle in April. PROFESSIONAL SPORT

Below: Fancy seeing you here – Lucy Heald, Tim's girlfriend, interviewing Tim in her role as a producer for Trans World International. ALLSPORT

Right: In happier times…Tony Pickard and Greg Rusedski at the start of their partnership, which was to end so controversially at Wimbledon.

Below: Tim Henman wins his deciding singles against Leander Paes at Nottingham.

Below: David Lloyd, the man who first spotted Tim's talent, and went on to prosper from it as Davis Cup captain.

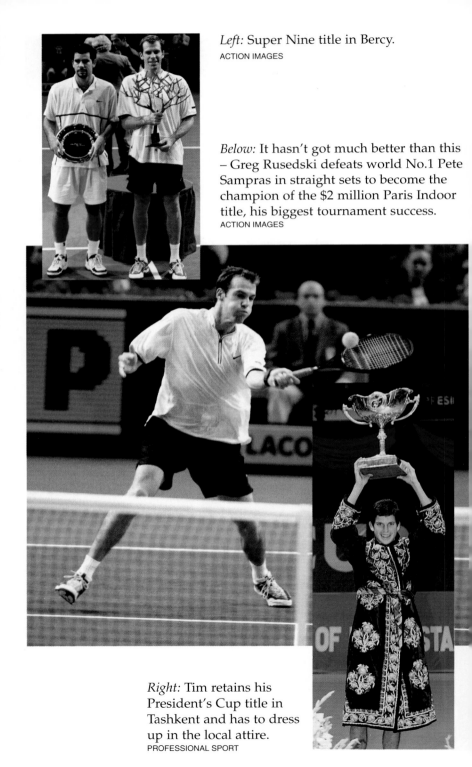

Left: Super Nine title in Bercy.
ACTION IMAGES

Below: It hasn't got much better than this – Greg Rusedski defeats world No.1 Pete Sampras in straight sets to become the champion of the $2 million Paris Indoor title, his biggest tournament success.
ACTION IMAGES

Right: Tim retains his President's Cup title in Tashkent and has to dress up in the local attire.
PROFESSIONAL SPORT

right, but there was an overwhelming sense of togetherness for a
fleeting moment in late September. Though neither Tim nor Greg was
involved, this was the first time, or so Jan Felgate for one, believed, that
a genuine relationship between the two players became a possibility.

The two remained vastly different in so many respects – personality
aside. The feeling in tennis was that Tim, with his political contacts, his
attitude in the locker room, his large following and his image as a
genuine nice guy, was a member of the sport's inner sanctum, while
Greg, who was still battling with sponsors, didn't have people he could
turn to on the circuit, and struggled to cement long-term relationships
with anyone but his coterie of physios, coach, girlfriend and family
back in Canada, remained very much an outsider.

Jan Felgate wondered whether this new informality might lead to
the extension of an invitation to Greg and Lucy for drinks at
Christmas. In the end, it didn't.

14 The Long and Winding Road to Hanover

The Grand Slam Cup had come to being in 1990, the year that marked a dramatic shift in the political fortunes of the players. The Association of Tennis Professionals won a ferocious battle with the Men's International Professional Tennis Council for control of the tour and engineered a position whereby it ran the men's tour for the players, on behalf of the players and with the players. The ATP decided it should indulge in its own end-of-year championship, to boot.

The ITF could – indeed should – have stood back and let the players have the floor. The ATP finals would never have the clout of Wimbledon and the rest of the Grand Slam quartet, however high the ATP tried to build them up. There would be prestige attached, certainly, and the thought of having the best eight players in the world under one roof was extremely appealing.

What did the ITF do? They decided to organize the Greed is Good Cup. The best brains in the tennis business procreated yet another championship in an already overcrowded season, calling it the Grand Slam Cup, as if the Slams themselves weren't prestigious enough. The idea of this new humdinger was to bring together the four Grand Slam winners and those with the next best records in the majors, to contest a championship which offered a small fortune to those who already had enough money to survive the loss of a few points in the Dow Jones.

Boris Becker described the prize money on offer when the Grand

Slam Cup came of age in 1990 as obscene, an attitude which won him great praise. But the lure was too much, even for Becker, who contested the Cup five times in his home city of Munich. In 1997, he received a wild card entry into the event, a decision which flew in the face of the event's principled objective.

And what was the tournament doing in the last week of September, in a calendar already brimful of events which the public couldn't understand, following immediately after the Davis Cup in which so many nations with participants in the Grand Slam Cup had been competing? It wasn't as if the event was held at the end of the year, as a true finale after the Davis Cup final. The ITF were hurting no one but themselves.

And, what's more, they were in a desperate fix in 1998. Pete Sampras, the Wimbledon champion, cited the injury he had collected in the US Open semi-final against Pat Rafter as a reason not to play (though he would appear the following week in the Swiss Open in Basle); Rafter himself said that he was drained after the Open and representing Australia in the Davis Cup; Carlos Moya, the French champion, preferred the pickings on offer to support a fledgling ATP tournament on his home island of Mallorca.

Which left Petr Korda, who, with the best will in the world, wasn't exactly the kind of player who would drag the denizens of Munich out to the Olympiahalle for a night's tennis. What should the organizers do? Cancel? God forbid. They decided instead to offer a wild card to Andre Agassi, whose last Grand Slam final appearance was in the 1995 US Open.

For the sake of the publicity which Agassi's presence would obviously generate – and his image soon presented on every lamppost and at every bus stop in Munich – the ITF had to sell their event on the face of a man who shouldn't have been there in the first place.

Agassi eventually earned the official runners-up prize money of $1 million for reaching the final of the Cup where he lost to Marcelo Rios, who had reached a Grand Slam final in 1998, though he'd disappeared from the others almost as soon as they'd printed the draws. Tim Henman was having misgivings about participating the moment the exhilaration of his victory over Leander Paes had worn off, and he realized he'd have to be on the first plane the next morning.

He knew all about the politics of the situation. He was a member of the organizational structure of the ATP Tour, as one of the ten representatives on the Players' Council – to all intents and purposes the players who carried out the wishes of their fellow competitors.

Henman was on the Council as the member for the players ranked 11–25 – and he could always confer with his coach, for David Felgate was a member of the ATP Tour Board of Directors.

Indeed, such was the liking for Henman throughout the sport, that many players had willed him to stand as replacement for Alex Corretja as President of the Players' Council, a titular position which would have made Henman the most powerful spokesman for the players' interests in the world. He declined the opportunity on the premise that the hours required to do the job properly would have damaging repercussions on what he was all about – becoming the best player he could be.

What purpose was served by a potential President of the Players' Council of the ATP playing in the ITF's Grand Slam Cup, only Henman could know. 'I view it as a bonus week,' he said. 'I will have a relaxed attitude going into my match [he was to play the Swede, Jonas Bjorkman]. Win or lose it's a nice cheque. So why not take it?' It was hard to argue with Henman from a financial point of view, but it was clear from his attitude that here was an athlete entering a prestigious event with little or no motivation to win it. Surely, there should be no other reason to play a professional sport unless the attitude was focused entirely on winning. Henman did himself – and probably the ATP Tour – a disservice by agreeing to play in the first place.

His 7–5, 6–4 loss to Bjorkman from 5–1 up in the first set, was utterly predictable and he confessed afterwards that he was wrong to have appeared at all. 'It's a mercenary event with no ranking points,' he said.

Henman had played nine weeks of tennis with only the briefest of pauses for breath, and Munich was a tournament, albeit a very affluent one, too far. He came home to rest a while (with £60,000 prize money) and take the weight off his feet. Felgate could get a ticket to see his beloved Arsenal at home to Panathinaikos at Wembley in the Champions' League. Everyone was happy.

Rusedski was also delighted with the Arsenal victory, but more elated with his own late choice of the Adidas Open de Toulouse, to get himself back on points-stacking track. If the British No.2 was to find a way to qualify for one of the eight places at the ATP Tour World Championships in Hanover in November, he probably had to win a couple and reach the finals of at least another of the six tournaments he had entered. It was the tallest of orders, even for a player of his legendary never-say-die attitude.

He was granted a wild card into Toulouse and was immediately installed as top seed in a field littered with extremely competent performers. There would be no walking away happy with a loss and a nice cheque here, every point had to be worked for. The champion in Toulouse would earn for five victories almost precisely half of Henman's reward in Munich for one defeat. And they wondered why the general public had difficulty coming to terms with the machinations of world tennis.

At the outset of the Toulouse Open, Rusedski was fourteenth in the rankings, three places and 275 computer points behind Henman. To qualify for Hanover, both had to be among the top eight points earners in the calendar year from 1 January. Henman was eighth and last in the field in this, the first week of October, behind Rafter, Rios, Sampras and Moya, who had already confirmed their places, Agassi, Corretja and Kucera. Krajicek and Korda, both soldiering on despite the effects of injury, Kafelnikov and a revitalized Ivanisevic, were snapping at Tim's heels.

Hanover might have been in Rusedski's sights, but it was a distant vision. He was more interested in a consistent run of form, to defend as many of the points as possible he had accumulated in the same period in 1997, when he won the title in Basle, reached the final of Vienna, the semis at Paris Bercy and the quarters in Stockholm. Extremely tough times lay ahead. 'To get back in the top ten by the end of the year would be satisfying enough,' Rusedski said. 'Getting to Hanover would be a huge bonus, but I'm not really looking at that.' Conversely, getting to the World Championships by right had become Henman's *raison d'etre*. The tables might have been turned from the previous year, but Rusedski wanted to look further than any domestic squabbling.

He needed to be back on court winning, not just to satisfy himself and those nearest and dearest to him, but in terms of generating support from anyone who might be prepared to invest in his playing prospects and personality. His racket contract with Wilson was over and his clothing agreement with Nike expired at the end of October. The only contract left running was that with Austin Reed, the premier British clothes company.

'It's difficult,' Rusedski admitted. 'The timing of the injury around Wimbledon was all wrong. If I get back playing well, I'm sure there will be companies wanting to get involved with me. We will have to wait and see. I'm just getting on with it. That's all I can do.'

He seemed, as he had always been, a slave to adversity. The game gave him nothing for free, everything had to be earned. The only thing that came easy to Greg was that darned smile. 'When I was growing up, my parents made a lot of sacrifices for me and I knew every time I stepped onto the court, I wanted to give my best. It wasn't like I *had* to win; but they expected a good effort out there and I felt a little of having to give back all the support they had given me. You think of it and it gives you the extra drive, the extra desire.

'There is a tough balance between being given nothing and being given everything. You need certain things to succeed in life, but sometimes it's better if you don't have them. My life has always been a challenge. Obviously, I would have liked it to have been easier, but the only way that's going to happen is if you stay healthy and make sure you keep improving.'

Rusedski wasn't on court until the final match on Tuesday evening, hoping there might be a quorum in the stands to provide him with the backdrop of an atmosphere. The evening crowd in Toulouse – about 150 people – had been perked up by its first sight of a seventeen-year-old Swiss by the name of Roger Federer who played a quite magnificent match to dump Guillaume Raoux, one of the home favourites, out of the event for the loss of four games. We had witnessed in the Wimbledon junior champion a player of great temperament and stunning self-assurance, a top-tenner in the making, for certain.

Rusedski wanted to get back into that company for all he was worth. The last time he had played indoors – on a court that suited him down to the ground in Battersea Park – he had lost having had match points against Marc-Kevin Gollner. So who should be his first opponent when the tour went back inside? Gollner, of course.

The match, to tell the truth, had all the charm of a pistol whipping. One smacked down a serve, the other clobbered a return, and so it went on for two excruciating tie-break sets. Rusedski won them both. Indeed he wasn't to drop a set all week until he reached the final. Andrei Medvedev, Arnaud Clement, and Nicolas Kiefer were put out of their misery to an impressive degree, before Rusedski came up against the man who had beaten him in the US Open, Holland's Jan Siemerink.

Ironically, Siemerink had been asked to stand by as an alternate for the Grand Slam Cup. If he had been called in to the event and lost in the opening round, he could have done himself a fiscal favour, but he remained in Toulouse, and didn't do so badly for himself, taking the final 6–4, 6–4. Rusedski was down on himself for losing, but it had been a long time since he had been this close. Things were beginning to start to fall back into place.

Henman spent a few days back home after his Grand Slam Cup experience before heading for the picturesque Swiss town of Basle. The events were going to come thick and fast for him now, so a time for mature reflection and a few deep intakes of good old English air were essential. Every day, he was confronted with a different set of arithmetical prognostications showing how well he had to do to reach the World Championships.

Sticky starts were nothing new to Henman throughout the year, so when he dropped the first set of his opening match to Australian Jason Stoltenberg, he wasn't exactly surprised, nor downhearted. He prevailed in three, courtesy of three service breaks in the final set, then put to flight the flighty Moroccan left-hander, Hicham Arazi, who had given him such a roasting in Hamburg back in the spring.

The results elsewhere were working in his favour. The defeat of the still-struggling Petr Korda by Germany's Nicolas Kiefer meant the Czech would lose ground in the race for Hanover. Richard Krajicek wasn't due to re-appear on the Tour until the following week in Vienna – six weeks since he had withdrawn from the US Open with a recurrence of a knee injury which would ultimately require surgery, though he had kept putting the date back.

Henman purred on through the week to reach a semi-final against Thomas Johansson, who had had three match points to reach the last four in New York before falling to Mark Philippoussis. It was the same section of the draw from which Henman had been favoured to emerge until he was blown away in the fourth set by the big Australian, but that setback was well behind him now.

The semi and final in Basle proved to be seminal experiences for the British No.1. The court for the Swiss Indoors was notoriously slow, which was expected to play into the hands of the likes of Johansson, one of the new breed of Swedes who was much more Wilander than Edberg. Look for loopholes in your opponent's play from the back of the court. Wear them down. Serve and volley with the utmost caution.

Henman hadn't lost his serve in two matches, and there was a greater feeling of solidity about him now, especially from the back of the court. He wasn't rushing, he wasn't trying to be too aggressive and then losing patience if aggression failed him. This was an altogether more composed, formidable, focused Englishman. A single break was enough to secure him a foothold, but Henman was then punished for trying to be too elaborate.

The execution of the drop shot from the back of the court has to be inch-perfect to defeat any top-ranked player. Henman had played an audacious, backward-spinning effort in the first set, but then got too cocky. Each of the four times he attempted a repeat in the second, Johansson reached it and played a winner. A first service overrule at 2–3, 30–40 (these umpires picked their moments) loosened one of those coils in the brain and before it had been re-set properly it was set-all.

Johansson had reeled off five consecutive games and held two break points on Henman's opening service game of the final set for what would surely have been a crushing sixth. A service winner – Henman's first serve was striking its mark again – and a superb backhand volley steadied jangling nerves. Then, smartly, Henman broke for 3–2. Johansson's body language began to indicate that he felt he couldn't win, but when Henman served for the match at 5–4, the Swede stiffened his resolve, unleashed a couple of ferocious passes on the backhand and squared the match. He twice nosed ahead in the tiebreak, too, but three consecutive errors, one off the forehand and two, incredibly, on his double hander across the incoming volleyer, handed Henman the match 6–3, 2–6, 7–6.

The final would pit him against Agassi for the first time since the final in LA back in late July. The two men had chatted in Toronto the next week, Agassi asking Henman if he would take a little piece of advice on his game. Henman, not one to take these suggestions at absolute face value nonetheless listened to what Agassi had to say.

The gist of Agassi's message was that Henman should be more selective in when he should stay back and when he should come to the net. Aggression purely for the sake of it might work on grass, but if Henman was going to be a fully moulded player, he had to appreciate when to stay back, and to pick his moment better to come to the net. It was a message that stuck and, ironically, the moment it all came together for Tim was the very next time Agassi was on the opposite side.

The first two sets were as near to perfection as Henman had ever touched. 'It was as though I could do anything, at times it was a bit unnerving,' he said. 'But, frankly, it wasn't a surprise. I had done it before in practice and I'd got near to it in matches against lesser players. Being able to sustain it for long periods against someone of Agassi's talent – I think it goes to show what can lie ahead for me.'

At floor level, it was quite a sight to behold; in the commentary box, Frew McMillan, for Eurosport, was suggesting he had never seen the Thames running as pure as Henman. 'It was a master class, especially from the Henman backhand,' McMillan, one of the game's most erudite analysts, confirmed later. 'Some of his performance was quite divine.'

Of course, there had to be a letdown. Henman couldn't keep it up for three consecutive sets in a best-of-five final; for a start, Agassi had his pride to consider. A straight-setter would look bad in the record books, it would mean the kind of psychological shift in the balance of power Agassi didn't want. No one gave ground easily in this sport.

So Agassi battled back, enough to win the third set and then break Henman for a 2–1 lead in the fourth. Then came the crux. Even Henman sat at changeover and wondered whether his best shot hadn't been good enough, but he re-focused, stayed in the rallies again, picked his moment as Agassi had said he should, and forced his way into a 4–2 lead. Agassi, smarting, responded to take the Henman serve. 4–3. He served his ninth ace to hold at 4–4; Henman scored his nineteenth, to lead 5–4. Agassi needed to hold again to keep the game alive but Henman was irresistible now. He had the scent of a remarkable victory and steadied himself to move to a couple of match points. A brilliantly fierce rally ensued, Henman chasing down Agassi's bullets from the baseline, then tossing up a lob which called for a smash from the baseline. Agassi sized up his options but blasted the ball wide. Henman raised his fists – Felgate let out a roar.

'Great play, Tim,' Agassi mouthed as the two shook hands at the net, before the American, distraught at losing after giving his all, bounced his racket so hard on to the ground at his chair, that it took a wicked bounce and flew into the crowd. Thankfully, no one was injured. 'I had never categorized Tim as a top-ten player before today,' Agassi said later, 'now I'll have to.'

A short hop across the Alps to Vienna brought another week of vivid contrast. Why couldn't both Tim and Greg succeed, or both fail in the same week? It always seemed to be one or the other stepping into the limelight while the other hit a roadblock. Henman's winter slump was countered with a title and two finals for Rusedski; the summer was Tim's delight, as Rusedski toiled with the disruption to his fitness and the break-up with Pickard. Henman had now won back-to-back titles for the first time in his career as Rusedski struggled to make up for lost time and ground. Would they ever get the opportunity to play each other on the professional tour?

Once again, in the CA Trophy in the Austrian capital, where all but one player in the top ten was present, the only way they could cross swords would have been if both had reached the final, which, given the tournament's pulling power, would have required a couple of Herculean efforts. Rusedski was taken all the way to a third set tie-break in the opening round by Yevgeny Kafelnikov, a victory which was as sweet for him – incredibly his first over top-ten opposition in the entire year – as it was for Henman, considering how adjacent were he and the Russian in terms of ranking points. Henman was aware, too, that a solid week would almost certainly see him rise to a career-high No.9 in the world.

Rusedski defeated Thomas Muster in straight sets and Henman accounted for a couple of durable Swedes, Magnus Gustafsson and Thomas Enqvist (the second in three extremely tight sets), so that they could both relish a Friday quarter-final. Henman would play the world No.1 Sampras, a repeat of the Wimbledon semi-final, while Rusedski would play Patrick Rafter, a repeat of the 1997 US Open Final. Revenge would be particularly delicious.

Rusedski was the man to sample it, taking Rafter apart 6–3, 7–6, a victory as thorough as anyone had enjoyed over the Open champion for months. This was Rusedski touching the heights of his game again, a crisp, effective put away, with volleying of a calibre he hadn't relished since he had reached the finals in Indian Wells in March. And his backhand, too, so long a predictable weakness, pinned Rafter down time after time.

Victories came little sweeter, especially as Rusedski had to put up with a noisy interference from the crowd who remembered his collapse in the final to Goran Ivanisevic the previous year and clearly objected to him having beaten local hero Muster in the third round. As he served for the match at 5–4, a distinct off-putting cry rose from the cheap seats. Rusedski lost serve and complained to the umpire. 'I thought the whole thing was pretty disgusting,' he said. The din died as he secured a place in the semi-finals with 'a very important match and a very big win for me'.

He was to be the only Brit in the semis. Henman wasn't so much beaten by Sampras as crushed, as one would an irritant mosquito. He played an excellent first point, finishing off a twenty-stroke rally with one of those flashing high backhand volleys which had become something of a trademark, and then crumpled against a vicious onslaught of Sampras at his imperious best.

Henman lost 6–0, 6–3 but there could be no quibbling and, to be fair to him, he didn't quibble. 'Pete was so aggressive on every point. These sort of performances we see from him every so often speak for themselves. As Pete said to me as we shook hands, I've had a good run. I have a week off now, which I need and I'll be ready for the remainder of the season.'

For the starry-eyed pupil, it was a reminder of who remained the master. This was no tap on the shoulder, but a swift kick up the backside. One immediately thought back to Rusedski's comments on the developing 'friendship' between Sampras and Henman, about Sampras being happy to practise with Henman, let him get close, because he knew he would never lose to him. It offered intriguing food for thought. Henman came home to headlines in successive days which looked as if a sub-editor who worked for *The Times*, had a shift on the *Observer* on a Saturday afternoon. 'Just how good is Tim Henman?' one day, was followed by 'So how good is Henman?' the next.

It was a testament to the player's progress up the rankings for a sixth successive year – he had started in January, remember, at No.17 and these two articles were written as he was about to reach a career-high No.9 in mid-October – that such a question should be posed. Henman might have won two ATP tournaments in succession, and led his country to a place in the Davis Cup World Group, but there was nothing like a seismic defeat, even by the world No.1 in explosive form, to set the tongues wagging.

Julian Muscat in *The Times* said that to judge Henman on this reverse was about as valid as condemning Canute for failing to repel the tide of rising waves but that didn't prevent him saying this: 'He (Henman) precipitated his failure to make a match of it by his inability to correct some glaring errors within his game. A great deal of his progress over the past four months is due to his improved first service. He had established a rhythm that largely eliminated his penchant for throwing the occasion's gift of a game.'

But against Sampras he was swept aside and never allowed to settle. Rhythm? Forget it. It might have helped if the Henman first serve had reached even 50 per cent but, as the nerves increased, many second serves sat up and begged to be hit. Sampras required no such generosity. If Henman had thought he was building up to his real breakthrough in top five terms, the sheer brutality of the Sampras performance shattered such illusions in the short term.

Jon Henderson, in the *Observer*, drew on the observations of others in the game. Tony Pickard, Mark Cox, Nick Bollettieri and Sampras's coach Paul Annacone gave their thoughts on the progress of Tim Henman.

All four men hugely admired the British No.1, but stopped short of an unequivocal endorsement. Cox, as one involved in the Rover Junior Tennis Initiative in Britain, and thus with a vested interest in the future development of tennis players in the country, wondered whether outside influences might conspire to undermine Henman's progress.

'The higher up he goes, the more he will have to handle the super-star way of life – demands on his time, distractions away from his tennis,' he said. 'More and more people crave valuable time and there is a danger this will impinge on the development of his tennis ability. He has to be able to retain his single-minded focus on playing the game.'

Pickard preferred to pinpoint what he still regarded as weaknesses in the Henman game. 'If Tim wants to stay where he is now, I don't think he'll have a problem,' he said. 'But for me, if he's going to advance, he has to address two things: his concentration and the way he uses his ability. He should be starting to stamp one particular part of his game on his opponents but he isn't doing that. He's playing everybody everywhere, if you see what I mean. All the great players have made one part of their game a little bit different. Borg played exceptionally from the back of the court, so did Connors, he was another genius. McEnroe served and volleyed, he changed the system, Lendl and Wilander were perhaps the best baseliners of the decade, Edberg and Becker imposed their particular games on their oppo-nents. If Tim is looking to go forward, he must promote one aspect of his game which would make it more effective and would also help him achieve the consistency he lacks at present.'

It was noted by Annacone that, at the age of twenty-four, Sampras had won six Grand Slam titles, while Henman was still seeking his breakthrough at such an exalted level. 'I think it's a blessing to play a number of different ways as Tim can at the very highest level,' he added. 'But I've always felt that players like him, with so much versa-tility, are going to develop a little bit slower because they have to figure out when to play which style of tennis.'

Bollettieri, whose renowned training camp in Florida had tended to turn out baseliners by the score, but which eschewed the versatility Annacone regarded as essential, picked on a couple of technical faults. 'When Tim's serve and volley are on target, they are among the very best in the world, and he can do anything with his backhand, he hits his forehand very flat and very aggressively, a bit more spin and vari-ation might help. And when running wide to his right, his backswing needs to be more compact. Bollettieri had noted what he thought were 'visual negative signs' in Henman. 'He should try to be more like the basketball legend Michael Jordan. When he has just missed seven shots in a row, from his facial expression and body language, you'd think he'd just made seven.'

So, you paid your 90p and you took your choice. Good, bad or indifferent, everyone wanted to have their say. Henman's game was ripe for dissection. The man himself had read neither piece when I broached the matter with him, and my brief precis of the contents didn't entice him to go home and read them, either. I could think of a number of sportsmen who would have spent the weekend poring over every word, fretting about what message he should be interpreting from such critical acclaims of his work. Henman refused to be ruffled. 'I read less and less, if at all,' he said. 'I'm ranked No.9 in the world at the moment – I hope it gets better soon – so I don't have a particular worry about what certain people might think about me.

'I don't want this to sound big-headed because I'm not that way at all, but there are certain people who matter to me: David Felgate, my coach, Tim Newenham, my fitness trainer, Lucy, my girlfriend who probably knows me better than anyone, my parents, Jan Felgate, and a few others. There are a couple of journalists whose opinions I respect, but outside of that, I don't take any notice.

'I remember when I was younger, I said I wasn't really interested in other people's opinions and I said it more than I really believed it. Now, as I've grown older, more and more people talk about me and write about me, and I realize that what they say and think is largely irrelevant. So, it's not worthwhile thinking about it or getting upset if people don't like what I'm doing.'

These were tough words from a twenty-four-year-old, but no one could argue that Henman didn't have his head screwed on straight. If he was going to make a success of his life – and who would say he wasn't doing just that? – he would have to be as single-minded as the sport demanded.

Rusedski, meanwhile, was awaiting his semi-final, against Karol Kucera, a man he had beaten on the previous two occasions they had met, with left arm emboldened. Not only that, if Sampras were to defeat his compatriot Todd Martin in the other semi-final, a Rusedski–Sampras final would have whetted British tennis appetites, even if it created not an iota of interest across the pond.

But this was to be another afternoon when Rusedski would come unstuck. Kucera had been a ballboy for 1986 Wimbledon semi-finalist Miloslav Mecir in Bratislava, and had obviously learned much from the fluent body language and wondrous camouflage of shot Mecir had perfected when he reached the world top ten in the late 1980s. Kucera was taking his relaxed mood to extraordinary levels, commuting home each night across the border to Slovakia until he reached the quarter-finals.

Though Rusedski powered to a 4–1 lead in the first set he was pulled back; when he had a set point in the tie-break, it was overturned; when he sped away in the second set, he was lured in, as if on a leash. He couldn't break Kucera's tantalizing spell, even though the tenor of his performances during the week suggested his stay outside the top ten – and he had dropped to No.18 – would not be long.

Intriguingly, it was his first serve which let him down, especially on that set point. Giving Kucera a second chance was like offering him a piece of the finest Viennese cake – he wolfed it down. The improvement shown during the past two weeks on the Rusedski backhand was cause enough for him not to be too disheartened by his 7–6, 6–4 defeat. Henman wasn't best pleased with the outcome either, as it meant that Kucera took his seventh spot on the Road to Hanover.

I suggested in my report for the *Sunday Telegraph* that, as a consequence of his defeat to Kucera, Rusedski had done Henman a disservice – a statement for which I was taken to task in a reader's letter, which asked me to ponder:

'1. Why on earth should Rusedski give any thought to how the outcome of his matches is going to affect Tim Henman? Surely, as a top professional player, his only responsibility is to himself, but if you are going to criticize Rusedski on Henman's behalf for losing to Karol Kucera, you really ought to thank Greg for beating Yevgeny Kafelnikov in the first round in Vienna, a result which enabled Henman to move above Kafelnikov in this week's rankings.

'2. Would Henman feel that *he* owed Rusedski any favours if the positions were reversed? Tim's attitude to Greg has hardly been one of sweetness and light since they began duelling for the top spot in Britain, and his sneering dismissal of Rusedski's achievement in reaching the 1997 US Open ('I wouldn't have minded his draw'), together with his whinging when Rusedski picked up various Sports Personality of the Year awards, hardly leads one to believe that Tim would be first in the queue to help Greg out in any way.

'3. Has Rusedski not done Henman a big enough favour already this year by spending two months on the sidelines following an injury, thereby greatly facilitating Henman's return to the British No.1 spot? (Incidentally, I have yet to hear Tim admit that Greg's absence from many of this summer's tournaments played any part in the reversal of their rankings.)

'4. If Henman and Rusedski should end up playing each other between now and the end of the ATP Tour season, would you expect Rusedski to roll over and let Henman win, so as not to impede Tim's chances of playing in Hanover?

'5. If Henman fails to qualify for Hanover, both you and he might be well advised to reflect on his eight first round exits from ATP tournaments this year, rather than blaming Greg for failing to do Tim's work for him.'

All the points raised were coherently and strongly argued, even if they smacked of anti-Henmanism of the highest order. Here was a Rusedski camp follower, for sure. The basic tenet of the argument was sound – that there was only one person you could truly rely on to get anywhere in this sport, and that person was you. Others might assist along the way, wittingly or unwittingly, but to survive in professional tennis meant to be consumed by it, to do it your way, and not be sidetracked.

Henman could fortunately rely on some unwitting help from Sampras to make things feel a little better in Vienna. The American's straight-sets victory over Kucera in the final further underpinned his own desire for a record-breaking sixth successive year as the world's No.1. 'It's an important goal I'm trying to achieve,' he said, 'which means that whatever I need to do, I'll do (this was Sampras's second stop of a five-country tour of Europe). I have a chance to make it, and that's really all I can ask for. It's up to me. I can't expect the other players to lose. It's definitely important and, what's more, it's something that might never be achieved again.'

As Sampras left for his next port of call, the French town of Lyon – where he was to pull out during a quarter-final when he felt a couple of nasty twinges in a back arched time and again in the pursuit of glory – Henman and Rusedski had returned for some R&R at home. As McEnroe said: 'The travelling is relentless these days and there's still nothing like your own bed.'

The time available for refuge was scant, because the European indoor circuit was reaching its frenzied peak. A week in Stuttgart for the Eurocard Open was followed immediately by the Open de Paris, both Mercedes Super Nine championships with pots of gold on offer

– over £2 million in prize money, prestige by the bucketload and, more important than anything at this time of the year, precious points.

The only certain conclusion which could be drawn before the October storms blew us to Stuttgart was that Henman would qualify for the World Championships if he reached the final. Rusedski, it appeared, would have to win both events to stand an earthly. Six players had now confirmed their places, Spain's Alex Corretja joining the throng with his victory in Lyon. Seven more were vying for the last two seats at the table – Kucera, Krajicek, Korda, Kafelnikov, Ivanisevic, Henman and Rusedski.

Henman's second-round victory over Mark Woodforde was little more than a formality, and now he faced Jan-Michael Gambill, the beach-blond young American who had denied him in the quarter-finals in Tokyo in April when he had been the highest seed left in the tournament. It was one of those scorned opportunities which blighted Henman's year. This week would bring a potentially expensive repeat.

A year previously, Gambill wasn't even inside the top 200. He was playing a series of Challengers which took him to tennis outposts such as Puebla in Mexico, Burbank in California and finally to Las Vegas where Andre Agassi, who was trying to decide whether he wanted another crack at the big boys of tennis, joined him in the field. Twelve months from then, incredibly, Agassi was back to five in the world. Gambill's own reputation was growing too, though he might have hoped for a more gentle introduction to Davis Cup tennis when, instead, he had the misfortune to be selected for the semi-final defeat to Italy, which brought the wrath of the nation – well, those who noticed the score – down upon his head. But Gambill had not lost the desire to represent his country, and noted that he might be playing against Britain in 1999. 'It's going to be a rowdy atmosphere, I hope I'm there,' he said.

There was nothing about Gambill's game to concern Henman although he had a distinct, unshapely double-fisted groundstroke attack, with such an exaggerated grip that he was able to exert disguise almost beyond the moment of impact. But the exertions had taken a toll on his back. He said he was looking forward to December when he could go to Hawaii and indulge in some body surfing. If Gambill's game wasn't fearsome, his entourage looked far more dangerous. The boy's father Chuck was his coach, his mother Diane sat behind the umpire's chair, clicking pictures, while a family friend named Ursula screamed and clapped her support in a distinctly English accent. 'This time, Jan-Michael, this one,' she shouted as he walked back to his chair, walked away from his chair, prepared to serve, you name it, she was shouting. Henman consistently shot her dark, disapproving looks.

The whole occasion was tailor-made for Henman to fall flat on his face. He gave off negative vibes, there was nothing rhythmic about his movement or stroke-play. An illustration of his capricious mood came in the sixth game of the match on the Henman serve. He was 0–40 down, produced three consecutive aces but then frittered the next two points away. He broke back immediately, took the set into a tie-break but then lost the first four points, double faulted twice and thus had to start from scratch again.

He blasted Gambill aside in the second set, breaking him twice, but was continuously on the back foot in the final set, making copious errors on the forehand wing. Once more, a tie-break loomed and, quite astonishingly, Henman was 4–0 down again before he had time to get himself together. Then he double faulted to trail 5–1. The game was lost. He smashed his racket into the ground, which emphasized both his frustration and that of those watching who had seen him fall by the wayside once again.

'I'm still happy with the way I'm playing, and the situation I'm in,' he said, when reminded that Krajicek, Kafelnikov and Ivanisevic were closing dangerously to within striking distance of his spot on the qualification trail. But given the frailty of his performance against Gambill, the British press weren't as optimistic. The general opinion was that Henman might be thinking and speaking positively, but he was deluding himself.

'The winner this week will end up getting 500 points, the winner in Paris will get 500 points and in either Stockholm and Moscow it will be 300,' he said. 'There are still plenty of points for me to pick up. But all these guys have won indoor tournaments in the past, they are capable of doing it again. But I'm very happy with the way I'm playing. I'm 300 points and something in front of Korda (who was having a desperate run of results) and a little bit more in front of Krajicek (who was getting back to his more venomous form and had delayed knee surgery in an attempt to reach Hanover).' When Gambill quit on his chair after five games of his quarter-final against Sampras, complaining of more pain from his bad back, it made the hurt of Henman's defeat even more acute.

The road to Hanover was like a steeplechase, and they still had a couple of water jumps left to negotiate. Still in the chase was one runner who had been lapped but who wouldn't stop trying to make up for lost ground. Greg Rusedski.

There were precisely forty-two spectators on Court One in Stuttgart when Rusedski started his second-round match against Australian Jason Stoltenberg, who was being coached on an occasional basis at Wimbledon by Warren Jacques. The crowd peaked at fifty-seven, troughing at thirty-three. It was not as if the match wasn't enough to sustain the people's attention span.

It said everything about Rusedski, with flashes of torment, distress and unsuppressed anger. It was to span three tie-breaks, although it should never have been allowed to travel that far, Rusedski watching five match points disappear at 5–4 in the second when the Australian went for broke and his opponent's left arm began to twitch. Rusedski let his temper get the better of him in the tie-break, believing he had heard the German umpire Rudi Berger call 'let' on the first service point, though the cry was clearly 'fault'. Rusedski was suffering from a cold, and his hearing had been impaired. He stewed on that perceived injustice for too long.

There were no breaks of serve in the final set, Rusedski taking the tie-break thanks to Stoltenberg's tenth double fault and a couple of topspun backhand passes which proved how much that shot was beginning to improve. There would now be a greater test as the world No.3, Pat Rafter, waited for him in the last eight. 'I just managed to stay in there,' said Rusedski, 'but I just didn't want to lose this match. No disrespect to Jason, but if I'd played like that against a top player, I would be out. I guess sometimes you can want it too much – winning that is. I need to tighten up in a few areas, I need to close out matches like this one sooner, but it's better to be over keen than under keen.'

Back at the hotel, Sven Groeneveld was waiting to deliver a few home truths. It was a sign that the new coach was certain of his ground. Rusedski, who didn't relish lectures, listened intently. He was told that he should be more mellow, not get himself so upset, hang loose a little. He was exerting far too much pressure on himself. Relax. It was exceptionally sound advice. 'What I admire about Greg,' said his coach, 'is that he doesn't try to hide behind things. He admits to the facts. He sits down, we talk about things calmly. He is a very honest and straightforward person.'

All of these characteristics helped him against Rafter, who might have been the king on hard courts in the summer, but didn't pose quite the same menace when he had to play in a confined space under a roof.

Rafter without that zinc cream smeared across his cheeks didn't cut the same, fearsome opposition. But he was still the No.3 player in the world and could finish the year as No.1.

This was a match which epitomized the need for a break from the treadmill. The two players spooned simple volleys over the baseline and squandered passing shots which should have been comfortable makes for players of their calibre. Rusedski proved once more to be an aggravating opponent. He was never ready when the umpire called 'time' to resume play, choosing that moment to have another swig from the pink stuff in his water bottle, undo and then re-tie his shoelaces, or take a bite from his banana.

In the first set tie-break, leading 3–0, Rusedski decided that his racket string needed attention, but the ballgirl couldn't find his 'String-a-ling', the device players use – or should that be only Rusedski, Henman and Sampras ever seem to use – to fiddle with the face of their racket. Rusedski had to walk to his bag, unwrap a package and carry out his repairs with a new 'String-a-ling'. Rafter was quietly fuming at the other end of the court. 'Take your time, mate,' he called down the court. Rusedski, a look of pained hurt across his face, said something back, got himself together, and won the first set tie-break – his fourth of the week.

Rafter saved break points in the fourth game of the second set; Rusedski was 0–40 down in two successive service games, but refused to buckle. A second tie-break was in the offing, and this time Rafter snatched it 7–5. But Rusedski managed to hold his body, soul and 'String-a-ling' together in the third, to secure a place in the quarter-finals, 7–6, 6–7, 6–4. Rafter had won the US Open five weeks earlier when he was full of the joys of summer. Now, he looked bleary-eyed and spent.

'It's mental tiredness, pure and simple,' he said. 'It's been a long year. I just want to get through Paris next week, go home to Bermuda to re-charge the batteries and see how I'm feeling. I don't even know yet if I'm going to come back for Hanover, but don't take that too seriously, mate. You can't get out in the sunshine here, and that affects me. I don't like it indoors so much.' Nor did his opponent's antics cheer him up. 'Greg is playing a lot smarter than he was a year ago but it's pretty easy to get confrontational with him,' Rafter said, flashing a smile for the first time. 'I think you know what I mean, mate.' He didn't have to explain further.

Rusedski saw the result as a successful lesson in man-management. His own. 'I played my game more professionally today,' he said, 'I took my time and didn't let things get to me. I played proper tennis and if I'm going to win, I'm going to win at my game, no one else's.

But, such are the vagaries of the sport, that, the next day, Rusedski was a pale, unconvincing, lethargic shadow – meat and drink for a player like Jonas Bjorkman. The Swede didn't even have to be anywhere near his own best to win the quarter-final; indeed, if there was ever printed a textbook on tennis errors, this match alone would have filled a dozen chapters. Rusedski rushed and stumbled over so much that the crowd began to cat-call. But maybe even they suspected something was wrong. 'I didn't have any movement today,' said Rusedski after his 6–3, 6–2 defeat in just over the hour. 'I could easily have been out after my first match here, so I take heart from reaching the quarter-finals, but I just didn't have it. There was no gas left in the tank. At least I didn't do what a couple of others have done here this week, and thrown in the towel. I gave him enough of a battle, and with a couple of days off I'll be ready for Paris next week.'

Rusedski's own World Championship ambitions were also running on empty. He had collected enough points to stay in with an outside chance, but the pointer was moving towards the red zone. Just for the record, he was asked what he made of Henman's prospects. 'I would say he's 99.9 per cent certain, unless disaster strikes.' A couple of us in the interview room exchanged glances. Was it our imagination, or didn't he say 'unless disaster strikes' with one of those silly grins on his face?

Disaster was rising, and maybe about to strike, in the powerful shape of 6ft 5in Dutchman, Richard Krajicek, who had always proved such an indomitable opponent of Henman's. Krajicek was putting off an operation on his damaged left knee until such time as his body couldn't take any more. It was a dangerous gamble, but he was intent on giving Hanover one final roll of the dice.

He now faced Pete Sampras in the final, holding a 4–2 head-to-head record over the tournament favourite. Sampras had few nemeses in the world, but Krajicek was certainly one of them. Even the medium-paced court in the Hans Martin Schleyer Halle – which drew compliments from all the players – could not absolutely negate the strengths in these two men's right arms. There was only a single point against serve in the first five games and that was a Sampras double fault.

The smart money was on three tie-breaks to decide it – we had to make do with a couple. The only time serve was broken in the entire match came in the tenth game of the second set when Sampras once more proved the more brittle – though he didn't help himself with three more doubles. Krajicek wasn't playing badly for an outpatient.

Sampras folded in the third set tie-break. He clawed back two match points, but lost on the third, 6–7, 6–4, 7–6. He was visibly distressed. 'I've never been one to bullshit people, and not tell it like it is,' he had told me earlier in the week, when we sat in his hotel suite in Stuttgart, discussing the pressures of trying to remain No.1 in the world for six straight years.

'I'm pretty pissed with this result. Richard seems to have the better nerve against me when it comes down to the pivotal points; when he's on, he can be pretty devastating. I felt like I was playing really well this week, I felt fresh today, mentally and physically and the key for me now is getting ready for next week (the Open de Paris) and that's a true test of whether I can re-group and stay mentally strong.'

Sampras's foremost challenger for the No.1 berth, Marcelo Rios from Chile, had lost in seven first round matches in the year – 'one pointers' as they are known in the trade. What crazy, mixed-up system was it that indulged a player losing so many opening rounds, yet still gave him the opportunity to be proclaimed the world No.1? Sampras felt strongly that in order to be No.1 – the 'one-pointer' statistic aside – you had to have won a Grand Slam championship, and the nearest Rios had come in 1998 was the Australian Open final when he was shamed by his lacklustre performance against Petr Korda.

This week, Rios was to withdraw before his quarter-final against Yevgeny Kafelnikov, having jarred a hip flexor while kicking a tennis ball during his practice session. No one was sorry to see him go – except Henman. The extra points for the Russian, and Krajicek's victory over Sampras, were like a hole in the head for Tim's World Championship ambitions. To make matters even harder, on the final Sunday in Stuttgart, Krajicek's straight-sets victory over Kafelnikov leapfrogged him over the English challenger into eighth place with the prospect of another significant points haul in Paris to come. Qualification was coming right down to the wire.

The draw sheet for the Open de Paris was scanned more closely than any other in the year. Where were the pitfalls? Where might one have a less daunting ride? Henman received a bye into the second round, where his opponent would be Arnaud de Pasquale, a blond French teenager, brimming with potential. Players said they didn't look past the next match, but Henman probably knew victory would confirm a third round meeting with Kafelnikov, with a probable quarter against Rios for the winner. De Pasquale, though extremely talented, didn't have quite enough quality to stay with Henman; Kafelnikov defeated the Swede Magnus Norman in three tight sets.

Kafelnikov, who still chastized himself two years later for blowing that famous match at Wimbledon, had said to me in a conversation at New Haven in August that he didn't think Henman was as strong or talented as his ranking suggested. 'He's not made it yet,' the Russian said. 'He may not be as good as he believes he is.' Henman went on to win their September final in Tashkent in straight sets.

On the eve of the match in Paris came heartening news for the British player when Krajicek pulled out of his match against the Swiss, Marc Rosset, when leading 5–2 in the final set, citing more twinges in his troublesome knee. Krajicek had decided he would have his operation immediately, ruling himself out of Hanover, preferring to concentrate on getting himself right for 1999.

Henman thus knew that victory over Kafelnikov would guarantee him a place in the finals, because the Russian could not then gather sufficient points to overhaul him. Kafelnikov turned up the heat in the interview after his victory over Norman. 'I have been playing so badly this year, I don't deserve a place in the finals,' he said. 'The pressure is all on Tim now, it will be interesting to see how he copes with it. There is nothing for me to get worried about.'

It was with such abandon that Kafelnikov began his match against Henman, to lead by a set, 4–2 and with a break point. At this crucial point the net cord intervened and the Russian was denied what would have been a crushing breakthrough. Even then, the likelihood was for a drubbing for the Brit, but nothing is ever as it seems in tennis and suddenly the Russian's game, which had seemed so perfect, especially off the ground, began to disintegrate. Kafelnikov was tightening – Henman couldn't believe his fortune. The net cords twice more worked in his favour, he sped into a 5–1 lead in the final set, and was on the verge of victory. It was then that Rusedski's 'unless disaster strikes' phrase from Stuttgart, was to sound particularly prophetic.

On the verge of victory Henman stumbled. He served for the match and lost his serve to love, frittering away shots as if he thought it didn't matter. Kafelnikov held and Henman had lost ten points in succession. He served for the match again at 5–4, produced two aces, and stood at match point with Hanover beckoning. He struck a first serve as destructively as he would have wanted, but Kafelnikov responded with a return so ferocious, it was past Henman's racket before he'd had time to prepare for his volley.

With that riposte went Henman's chances, even though he steadied himself and managed to take the final set into a tie-break. Kafelnikov won it decisively, 7–2 with a flourish of compelling forehands. Henman was heading home, contriving yet another defeat from the jaws of success and leaving those of us who had witnessed it pondering once more how far his undoubted talent would eventually take him.

'I had the match in hand at 6–3, 4–3 but it turned so quickly, I hardly had time to notice,' said Kafelnikov. 'Then, I'm down 5–1 and I'm going to walk off a loser, but Tim plays a loose game at 5–2 and that was the turning point, because I felt I would get the chance on some second serves at 5–4.' Kafelnikov was encouraged to suggest he felt it bad of Henman that he didn't apologize after he had been the fortunate party over a series of net cords. 'We're so friendly off the court,' he said, 'I don't understand that. If you go on the court and compete against each other, we should respect also each other and if you hit the net consistently, then you should say something – "Look Yevgeny, I'm really sorry." He never said so. I got frustrated. But it's pretty understandable the way he's behaving right now. He thinks he should be in Hanover. He's deserved it the way he's performed this year. He should be the one who competes in this event.

'I haven't had any victories over a top-ten opponent this year, and this was going to be my last chance, I thought. I played with an extra motivation. If I win tomorrow (against Marcelo Rios) I'm going to finish in the top ten for the fourth consecutive year and that's a big achievement for me.'

The Hanover machinations – who would, who wouldn't, who would be fit, who wouldn't be – continued to be fiercely debated over a bottle or three of Brouilly in the restaurants around the Bercy Stadium. The ATP Tour press relations crew in Paris tried to make our life a little easier with daily bulletins but, bless 'em and their computers, did little more than help confuse the situation. As of 5 November – and Tim Henman must have been feeling the heat as would a Guy atop the burning bonfire – the situation on 'The Road to Hanover' was as follows:

Player	Points	Fact
1. Marcelo Rios*	3670	Plays Santiago next week.
2. Pete Sampras*	3476	Looking to finish No.1 for sixth year in succession.
3. Patrick Rafter*	3315	Can still finish No.1
4. Andre Agassi*	2879	Can still finish No.1

Player	Points	Fact
5. Carlos Moya*	2819	Does not play next week.
6. Alex Corretja*	2798	Plays Moscow next week.
7. Karol Kucera	2579	Plays Stockholm next week.
8. Richard Krajicek†	2548	Undergoes knee surgery next week.
9. Tim Henman	2427	Can't qualify until Stockholm and Moscow draws are released.
10. Yevgeny Kafelnikov	2134	Plays Moscow next week.
11. Petr Korda	2114	Plays Moscow next week.
12. Goran Ivanisevic	1980	Out of race.
13. Greg Rusedski	1941	Must reach final here to keep hopes alive.

(*Already qualified for the World Championships. †Out of race through injury.)

Within a couple of hours of releasing this information it was about as redundant as last evening's fish and chip paper. Korda, whose terrible run of form meant he now couldn't reach Hanover, had withdrawn from Moscow, citing the 'flu. Rafter, as he had suggested the previous week in Stuttgart, had had enough of tennis for the year, he needed surgery on his knee and was thus, pulling out of Hanover – his No.1 dream in tatters.

'I've been aware of a problem with my left knee for a while, it comes and it goes,' he said. 'The doctor has suggested rehab for a few weeks. I'm disappointed to be missing Hanover, it would have been my biggest opportunity to reach No.1, which is something I've been striving for the whole year. We all want to make it there. But I hope 1999 will be a long and prosperous year, and I'm going to do every-thing I can to be ready for the new season. I'm going to London to start rehab, then to Bermuda and finally, back to Australia.'

What were terrible blows for Rafter and Krajicek – further evidence of what the ceaseless toil of the professional tennis player could take on his physical resources – was like a breath of fresh life to Henman. Now, it seemed, he couldn't possibly not qualify. Should Rusedski, who had reached the semi-finals in the Open de Paris with a thumping straight-sets victory over Sweden's Magnus Gustafsson, lose to Kafelnikov in the last four – then Henman could not be caught.

The outcome of the most remarkable year of his life could rest for Henman on his great rival losing – not to him, but someone else. But Rusedski was in no mood to lose, indeed, never in his career had he been in such a positive frame of mind. He had come to Paris talking up his prospects of returning to the world's top ten, but few people seemed willing to listen to him. The emphasis had been either on Henman breasting the Hanover tape, or how much more the wilting body of Pete Sampras could take as he homed in on his sporting Utopia.

Sampras had come close to pulling out before his Open de Paris quarter-final against Mark Philippoussis, and was spared only when the medical staff – whose work earned them an ATP award for medical excellence – confirmed he didn't have a disc problem, which would have meant dangerous repercussions had he kept playing. He taped up the lower section of his lumbar region and continued relentlessly on what was described in France as *Il voyage en solitaire*, beating both Philippoussis and then Todd Martin in the semi, in straight sets. Kafelnikov, whose own form was resurgent, had done him a favour by knocking out Rios, who was heading back to Chile for the Santiago Open, on clay. Whether or not he would worry about returning to Europe for the World Championships remained the subject of intense debate.

Rusedski against Kafelnikov in the other semi, was a tight affair, full of dramatic interludes and classic rallies. What was staggering was the succession of baseline contests won by the British player. 'No more jokes, please, about the Rusedski backhand,' wrote Richard Evans, in the *Sunday Times*. Indeed, the shot once deemed the worst in his repertoire had a new-found quality about it. Kafelnikov, a wily fox, kept thinking he might wear it down, but couldn't. He was passed more emphatically, and more destructively, than he had been for a long time.

The Russian didn't help himself when he conceded a penalty point for breaking his racket, giving Rusedski the crucial break of serve in the opening game of the final set. In the eighth game, the crowd became vehemently animated when a Kafelnikov forehand down the line, which might just have clipped the outside, was called out. What might have been 15–30 on the Rusedski serve was called 30–15. Umpire Rudi Berger pleaded for quiet, but the more he did, the more insistent became the whistling and jeering. 'Sometimes I don't like the French,' whispered Philippe Bouin, of *L'Equipe*, as both players stood complaining at the umpire's chair. But what could Berger do?

Rusedski took the bull by the horns and simply served through the din. He won the next two points, one of them with an ace, and served out the semi, winning 6–3, 4–6, 6–4 for his date with the defending champion, Sampras, whom he had not beaten in their previous six meetings. Cue the match which might change the course of Rusedski's life.

The wonder was that the British player showed not a trace of nerves from the outset. He knew what the match meant to Sampras, everyone in the arena did; but not so many were aware of the self-belief and astonishing will that had been channelled through Rusedski's career from the moment his dad Tom used to stand tin cans on poles and ask Greg to knock them over.

This was Rusedski's chance, one he had come close to taking in the past. He was to play the match of his life. It was plain from the outset that Rusedski was just as driven as his opponent. He knew he couldn't give Sampras too many second serves to zero in on, but when the American did nail a couple of returns, Rusedski's volleying, high and low, was exquisite.

Rusedski secured the first set when Sampras' own, usually tumultuous second serve betrayed him. He saved four break points in the opening game of the second, then watched the favourite extend to a 4–2 lead. Unaccountably, when serving for the set, Sampras played a shocking game, double faulting twice more. The set entered a tie-break in which Rusedski hammered in five first serves. Sampras's nerve went first, and there was nothing left in the tank for the third set. The storm could not be denied. Rusedski emphasized his victory with a superb ace down the T. The score 6–4, 7–6, 6–3; the effect, a high from which Rusedski never wanted to come down.

I was immediately reminded of the way that Sampras had treated Henman so contemptuously in Vienna a month previously; of how he might have wanted to do the same to Rusedski, but found an opponent who matched him, and often mastered him, who wouldn't accept second best, who stayed strong when most people would have buckled at the knees.

Rusedski was on the front page of *The Times* and *Daily Telegraph*. Tennis was a hot issue. There had been no more notable victory for a British tennis player in the thirty years of Open tennis. Never had a Brit won a Super Nine event, the next best thing to a Slam and the ATP Finals themselves on the tournament calendar. Rusedski was tempted into talking about becoming No.1 in the world one day. Tony Pickard – asked for his comments – suggested he shouldn't have done that, because, in his time, the likes of Lendl and McEnroe had never talked about what they were going to do. They just went out and did it. But Greg's adrenalin rush was overwhelming.

'I know he really wanted the match as well, which makes it even more special because he wants the No.1. This was by far the best I've played. I knew I had to raise my game, even from yesterday against Kafelnikov. The excitement of the moment, and having beaten Pete, it's an unbelievable feeling.

'I'm a much better player, my game has come on leaps and bounds. Sven has been very patient and really got me to work on the areas I needed work on. My returns are much more solid, and I think I can play on slower surfaces better next year. I've been very consistent since my comeback, I've not lost in a first round and only once in the second. Every week, it's been quarters, or semis or the final. I've been losing to top-ten players and there's nothing to be ashamed of in that. This week, I've brought myself up to another level.'

Sampras was asked what was giving him more trouble – his back, his racket or Rusedski? 'My hat is off to Greg,' he replied. 'He outplayed me for the most part, I had my chance but I kinda let it slip away a little. He returned my serve and passed me extremely well. His movement is better. He's pretty complete when he's on and he pretty much kicked everyone's butt all week, but not every week is indoors on a quick surface. You have to be consistent on all surfaces. One match doesn't mean you're going to be No.1 in the world. There's a lot of competition out there.' And didn't Sampras know it.

'I certainly hope I can get to Hanover fresh and feeling good about the way I'm playing. I got outplayed today by someone who was hot, and you have to accept that. You only have so many chances against Greg. He was a bit too good, you have to swallow it and move on. But the match was pivotal. A win would have put me ahead (of Rios) by quite a bit, and now I have to get myself back to re-group again for Wednesday in Sweden (for the Stockholm tournament). It's not easy to get up emotionally every week.'

There was nothing wrong with Rusedski's emotions. His second tournament victory of the year earned him a handy £245,000 and it was pointed out that the trophy handed to him resembled the antlers on a Canadian moose. There was still no getting away from the ancestors.

In the short-term, the result of his victory was confirmation of Karol Kucera's place in Hanover and virtually assured Henman of his berth. If Kafelnikov, taking his weary body home to Moscow to play in the Kremlin Cup, successfully defended his title and amassed a significant haul of bonus points, Henman would have to reach the semi-finals in Stockholm. Rusedski would join Henman in Hanover if he could match Kafelnikov's gains in the week, but would qualify automatically if he reached the Stockholm final, though that might require him to beat Sampras in the semis. The only definite conclusion to draw was that one of the British players would qualify and the other would be commandeered to stand by as an alternate. It was that close, that tense, that dramatic.

On the Monday morning, on the BBC's *Breakfast News*, Pickard was beckoned from his home to appear in the Nottingham studio to discuss Rusedski's victory. The story of their Wimbledon split was dragged back into the public domain, as Pickard knew it would be, and though he visibly bristled when it was put to him that Rusedski might have improved since they parted company, he neatly sidestepped the chance to agree with the questioner. Pickard's greatest concern was the quality, or rather the lack of it, of those players behind Greg and Tim. 'The Federation (LTA) have got to wake up to the situation they have here and give the talented young kids a chance,' he said, 'or else there will be nothing to show for the progress the top two have made.'

Rusedski made the point in his Paris interview of stressing the contribution made by Groeneveld, which would have got Pickard's goat, even if it hadn't been meant to. Player and new coach did not go out on the town on the Sunday evening, preferring a quiet night at The Barfly on Avenue Georges V. 'We had one beer each and a nice little talk,' said Groeneveld. Greg, abstemious for professional purposes, was flying as high as a kite inside.

'A lot of people have underestimated me all the way along, they said I couldn't get back,' he said, 'Sven has been great. I had a bad ankle injury, and he didn't mind waiting for me. We talked every day on the phone, and he's helped me a lot with my return of serve, my backhand groundstroke especially. I've beaten four players in the top ten, Kafelnikov twice, Rafter twice and now Sampras. He thinks my game can be better, the maturing process still has time.'

Groeneveld concurred. 'I honestly believe that if Greg plays his best tennis, he is unbeatable,' he said. 'Pete is a very proud player, we knew he would be very hard to beat. We discussed a couple of things beforehand, that Greg should pressure Pete on his backhand especially. He (Sampras) won't go in with a sliced backhand, he'll roll it and roll it and we thought that was a little bit of a weakness. I wanted Greg to keep his service returns simple as well, not go for too many winners, just keep the pressure on.

'As the match wore on and the tactics worked, Greg began to go for more shots and a couple of his topspin backhands passes down the line were exceptional. If he feels he is improving, he knows he can rise to any level.'

No extra stimulation was required once you stepped off the plane at Stockholm airport for the final leg on the regular season. The scene as the plane banked to land was of the Christmas card variety, with fir trees covered with a light dusting of snow. Winter was fast approaching. The chill took your breath away.

The field for the Scandia Open had been reinforced by Sampras' decision to ask for a wild card, his sixth of the year, though the ATP rule-book stipulated that five was the maximum. Sampras got around the rules by claiming a special dispensation. The ATP gave in and gave it to him probably because, like the rest of us, they couldn't stand the thought of Marcelo Rios becoming the world No.1.

It was alleged in the Swedish papers that Sampras had been paid a generous sum to participate, but it was not money well invested. The world No.1, clearly fatigued, looking as grey in the face as the colour of his Nike towelling suit, promptly lost in the opening round on Wednesday night, to the Australian Jason Stoltenberg, who had given Rusedski two tough matches in Stuttgart and Paris. Suddenly, in the space of four days, Sampras had lost successive matches and his No.1 ranking was in serious jeopardy. He smashed his racket for the first time any of us could ever remember when the first set disappeared. He would have turned the air blue had it been in his nature.

'Jason played tough, he knows what he's doing,' said Sampras, who was in his press conference within five minutes of the end of the match. 'It took me a while to get my bearings out there, which didn't help. I'm a little bit exhausted now, I want a little break and to get away from the game. It's the end of a long road trip. I don't think it was the wrong call coming here, I wanted to give myself the best chance possible of finishing the year No.1.'

Henman and Rusedski were not bothered by such high falutin' considerations. They had their own backs to watch. In effect, unless the two British players reached the final weekend in Stockholm, they could be undermined by the antics of Kafelnikov at home in Moscow. Henman got through his first round against Sweden's Mikael Tillstrom with next to no problems, then faced Wayne Ferreira of South Africa, who had defeated him in two of their previous three meetings. Kafelnikov would be playing Sebastian Grosjean of France at the same time.

I was charged with the task of relaying messages on how the match was progressing to Felgate as he sat trying to concentrate on every nuance of Tim's form. Grosjean won the first set – great for Henman. Grosjean lost the next two and the match Henman couldn't afford to let Ferreira win, or his chance might be gone. It was a match designed to twist your emotions: every which way.

Tim was tight. Ferreira was hardly playing free himself. The first set would include six breaks of serve, several loose forehands from Henman and move to yet another tie-break. Henman, who had played his previous three 'breakers' so carelessly, was drilled in this one, and broke in the first game of the second set to establish an advantage he managed to hold, finally breaking Ferreira again to triumph on his second match point.

Felgate was back out with his pencil, paper, draw sheet and mental calculator. It was now clear that if Tim defeated Sweden's Magnus Gustafsson in the quarter-final on Friday night, he was a certainty for Hanover, whatever Rusedski (who had beaten Tommy Haas of Germany and Vince Spadea of the US to reach the last eight himself) did here, or Kafelnikov engineered in Moscow. Everything was back in Tim's hands.

Rusedski would play first on Friday, against his old Canadian foe Daniel Nestor, the man who had risen to become his country's No.1 player once Rusedski had taken his leave. Rusedski always had trouble playing a fellow leftie, he knew that Nestor – whose all-court game was sharply honed by his doubles' expertise – had one of the most formidable serves in the game, and the fact that he was Canadian served only to complicate matters further.

That there was an edge to the match was clear. Nestor was as undemonstrative as Greg was the epitome of anxiety. Nestor plodded back to the baseline and across it between points, Rusedski beckoned the poor ballboys countless times for his towel though it never seemed to make positive contact with his forehand when he went to dry his brow. Rusedski had to save four break points in the fifth game of the opening set, which, hardly surprisingly, required a tie-break to resolve. Greg won it 7–2, finally breaking free from the chains of caution.

Then he tightened up. Nestor's serve began to bounce, spin and skip, especially when it flew wide to the Rusedski forehand in the advantage court. Nestor broke to lead 2–0, had a break point for a 4–0 lead denied him by a complete mishit from Rusedski which landed in, then broke to love anyway for a 5–1 advantage. The crowd was beginning to give Rusedski the bird.

After three games of the final set, with neither man giving the slightest ground, Rusedski called for the ATP trainer. Was this to be yet another injury blow? With his ninth ace, Rusedski held to love for 3–2, sat down at his chair, breathed deeply and settled on how he might break Nestor for the first time.

Nestor led 40–0 but then double faulted. Rusedski sneaked another point, then another to take it to deuce. He had a break point, but Nestor nailed a backhand volley. Nestor aced, then double faulted. Rusedski had a second break point, Nestor produced a service winner. Rusedski had a third, responded to with an ace, a fourth, another ace, a fifth and finally, Nestor cracked. Having squandered eight points for 3–3, Nestor trailed 4–2. The match was in Rusedski's pocket.

There was no exchange of words at the net, simply a limp shake of the hand. The eyes didn't meet, this result was a desperate disappointment for Nestor. He could have been the one to deny Rusedski his Hanover berth, and what a pleasurable experience that would have been, but Canada's honour could not be defended in the manner he would have wanted. Greg seemed to want to mend bridges. 'Daniel is a player who should be higher rated than he is,' he said. 'He has a fantastic serve, the one that kicks out to my forehand is one of the most difficult to return in the game. I just thought, in the end, I had the greater intensity today.'

Rusedski also said in his press conference that he had damaged his right glutus maximus, which, in layman's terms, was a pulled muscle in his buttock. He had been prescribed aspirin and Vitamin C to help alleviate the pain. The physio believed he would be OK 'in two or three days'. He couldn't say how he might be for the following afternoon's semi-final, against the rapidly-improving Swede, Thomas Johansson.

But, as far as Friday was concerned, Rusedski had done his job; and so had Kafelnikov in Moscow, trouncing the Frenchman Guillaume Raoux 6–1, 6–1. Now it was Tim's turn. He had never lost to Gustafsson in four previous meetings, one of which had been on the self-same court a year earlier, in the round of sixteen. But the emotions were vastly different now. Anders Jarryd, a stalwart of the Swedish Davis Cup team throughout the 1980s, moved into the seat just behind me: 'Magnus loves this court and the ambience here. Tim is in for a hell of a hard time,' he said. He was not to know, also, that if Henman won, he qualified for the finals as of right – but if he lost, Rusedski would be through, as of his right. The rivalry had come to this.

Henman blazed a trail, confidently holding his serve and immediately breaking the Swede, who, aged thirty-three, was often the oldest player in tournaments he entered. Henman became edgy when a cameraman moved at eye level (memories of Queen's back in the summer) as he was serving in the fifth game and squandered a 40–0 lead to deuce before taking the game. He won the first set in thirty-eight minutes. Halfway there.

At 15–15 in the second game of the second set Henman missed a routine put-away backhand volley, which gave Gustafsson the incentive to nail his next backhand service return and set up a winning pass. As Henman's forehand gave way under attack, the Swede broke to lead 2–0. Henman broke back, but he had been rattled, a feeling underscored when he missed a simple smash from right on top of the net at 30–30 in the sixth game. Gustafsson pounced again and it was 4–2. A third set would decide it.

The crowd was being roused by a couple of elderly Swedish gentlemen who had brought huge blue flags with their distinctive yellow cross into the stadium. There was wild cheering at every point their man won; a strange hissing noise when he missed. And kids seemed to be swarming everywhere, especially into the front row of the area at the back of the court, from where Felgate was trying to establish an unfettered line of semaphore with his player.

Henman broke to lead 4–2, relaxed, and was 0–40 down before he could think straight. A forehand winner rescued one break point, but Gustafsson was still rock solid from the back of the court, and he promptly broke back. Then, serving at 4–4, Henman was a break point down, the relinquishment of which would have meant his opponent was serving for the match. His first serve was netted, the second seemed to take an age to land, then reared up, forcing the Swede to have to play an ungainly double-fisted backhand return which he plonked into the net.

The crowd, once so animated, had become eerily silent. Clearly, a tie-break would decide the outcome. 'Go for it, Tim,' shouted an English voice. The crowd picked up its clapping.

Tie-breaks had been the bane of Henman's life. Given the nip-and-tuck of this dramatic night, most of us there sensed this one would be desperately tight. What happened? Henman held the first point and Bill Ryan, one of IMG's most prominent tennis managers, asked if I knew it had been statistically proven that 70 per cent of tie-breaks were won by the player winning the first point. When it got to 6–0, it would have been a statistical nightmare – and a nightmare in any other sense of the word – had Henman thrown it away. No problem. Within five extraordinary minutes, Henman had won 7–0, and when Gustafsson's final shot drifted into the tramlines – just as well he didn't have to contrive a winner himself – Henman went into a half-leaping, knees-bent, right-arm pumping celebration which confirmed that he'd learned something from getting close to Sampras.

This was what the second half of the year had been all about. Ever since Henman had lost in such despair in the semi-finals of Wimbledon, the target had been the ATP World Championship. Not many gave him a chance when he went so often to the brink only to keep staggering back; he had been helped when others fell by the wayside, true, but this was a moment of sheer self-satisfaction. There were a handful of Englishmen in Sweden with him on this special night who delighted in his achievement, who shared in his pride, who had played their part along the way. But only Tim Henman could appreciate totally the sense of personal fulfilment.

As only he could know how deep was the despair when he lost to Sampras on a beautiful English summer's evening on Centre Court, so those in attendance merely guessed at the feelings welling up inside the Kulinga Tennishallen 133 days later as the snow fell upon Stockholm.

'I enjoyed seeing that last forehand go wide,' Henman said, 'because the best way to describe these last few weeks is mental torment. I lost 7–6 in the third set in my last two tournaments so you can imagine how I felt when I knew I had to win this one. There are all sorts going through your mind. It's been a new type of pressure, it's been really tough, which makes getting to Hanover extra satisfying.'

A few minutes later, the official press conference formalities completed, I was ushered into the locker room deep beneath the court, where Henman was having a rub down to try to draw the tiredness from his legs. There were no special friends around, coach Felgate had said his piece and left while physical trainer Tim Newenham was happy to leave his client to the Swedish masseur. It wasn't the scene of jubilation one suspected might have greeted you – and certainly nothing like those associated with an FA Cup giant-killing. No champagne, no exultation. Just a satisfied human being. And a spent one.

'I knew, once I'd seen the results from Paris, after I'd been match point away from qualifying against Kafelnikov myself, that it would prey on my mind. It would on anybody's,' he said. 'I had to try to put it out of my mind, come here and do a job. And, I was still confident with the way I was playing, even though I'd had some rough results.

'You've got to have self-belief and I've never been short of that. There might be moments when the doubts and negative thoughts creep in, but you have to stop yourself and say "That's history." There was nothing I could do about what had happened before, the only thing I could control was this week and that's what I've done. I've earned my place the hard way.

'The pressure was building and building but I kept telling myself I was better off in my position because Greg and Yevgeny were chasing and that was always going to be more difficult. I have thrived on these situations, you have to rise to them and try to enjoy them. That's what I do. I think back to the beginning of the year when I was having a bad time, but never once did I get down on myself. I knew I was going to come out of the slump. There were other, more recent, rough weeks, when not only did my results not go well, but other results didn't go for me either. Even then, I had to keep the same belief I had back in the spring.'

It was back then that the spotlight was turned, almost blindingly, onto his coach. 'That's the beauty of the press, I suppose,' Tim responded. 'Sometimes they are out on a mission and for those five weeks or so, he was their target. I was thinking about those sort of things last night.'

Henman was watching Sky News in his room in the splendid Grand Hotel when the tear-stained face of Liverpool manager Roy Evans flashed up. Here was a thoroughly decent man, who had done his utmost to bring success to a club where he'd spent thirty-five years, knowing it was time to move on, but finding the words almost impossible to come by. 'It was terrible to see it,' Tim said, 'and at that moment, I remembered why I so enjoyed being an individual, not a public company. I'm not employed by anyone, I'm self-employed. I'm an individual sportsman, I do what I want.

'Roy Evans undoubtedly had a big influence but he wasn't out there on the pitch, he couldn't kick the ball for the players, he had to watch and hope. I've got people helping me but at the end of the day, I win or I lose, it's as simple as that. I appreciate there are plenty of other people giving their opinions – they were all saying back in March that my coach had to go – and I think it emphasizes the point about how many people I listen to where my career is concerned. When you break it down, there are very few. If something works, why change? That's something I learned through those pretty dismal months.'

They seemed so long ago, but at the moment of emotional release, the impressions which came back most vividly were those which you would have thought he had long banished. He said: 'If you'd have said to me in mid-March that I would qualify this year, I would have looked at you out of the corner of my eye, a little bit strangely. It just goes to show that if you keep working, you can turn things around. I look at it from the point of view of being determined and very ambitious – I've spent half a year striving for one target. This win has pretty much assured me of being a top-ten player at the end of the year, and that's more progress.

'If I hadn't made it to the Masters (Henman's shorthand for the ATP Tour World Championships), it would have been on a par with the letdown at Wimbledon. It's been so long drawn out. I played Sampras for three-and-a-half hours in that semi-final, and I dwelt on it for a couple of days. This has been three weeks, with matches every day and it's been painful at times, working towards it.

'Greg had won earlier in the day, Kafelnikov had won, so it was my turn to play catch up. Coming into the match against Gustafsson, I remembered that I'd beaten him the four times we'd played and I suddenly found myself thinking, "Is this going to be the first defeat?" Why should I start thinking about that? What was he thinking? He'd never beaten me, he couldn't be feeling too confident himself. It was an unbelieveable atmosphere, a court which had only been three-quarters full for every other match and now they were three deep at the back of the seats. I did well to hold it all together, the same as it was back in March when I'd lost to Wayne Black in Indian Wells. I have to say then that I had serious doubts, pessimism was crowding in. I put on a brave face, but that wasn't how I was feeling inside. I didn't know where the next win was coming from.'

Since that day at Indian Wells he had played sixty-two singles matches on the ATP Tour (including the Grand Slams), winning forty-two of them, reaching the semi-finals of Wimbledon and winning titles in Tashkent and Basel. There were a few hiccups along the way, but the response he was able to summon added to his conviction that more than the occasional visit to Hanover was on the cards.

There was still a trace of a pulse in Rusedski's ambitions, and, to add to the intrigue of a fascinating week, Rusedski would have to play a Swede, Thomas Johansson, in the semi-final the next afternoon, knowing that the atmosphere would be just as intimidating, the pressures just as colossal, but that if he were to win, he would qualify as well. The baton had been passed back from right-hander to left.

Tim allowed himself a glass of red wine in the splendid bar at the Grand where Stockholm's trendiest people came to drink and talk the night away, and that was the extent of the celebration. He was tucked up by 10p.m., getting his body clock tuned for his semi-final against the American Todd Martin – and the intriguing prospect on a snowy Sunday in Sweden of the first all-British men's final in the history of Open tennis.

Those hopes – and a lot more besides – were to be summarily dashed in a few hours on Saturday afternoon. Henman lost to Martin – not surprising, given the circumstances, but a blot that raised questions the player himself found difficult to answer. Martin was broken in the first game and survived a break point which would have put him 3–0 down. Henman looked composed as he duly took the opening set in forty minutes. Then, quite incredibly, he came off the rails completely. Martin broke to lead 2–0 in the second set, then broke again for 4–0. Henman was at the back of the court, skipping around, telling himself to stay focused, stay in the match. He broke back for 4–1, only for Martin to nip any hopes of a recovery in the bud by breaking again for 5–1. As the match drifted out of Henman's control, he would be broken five times in six service games, something unheard of from a top-ten player.

One of Henman's racket strings broke on the final point of the match and a forehand service return lobbed gently back into the net. Martin, one of the nicest guys on the Tour, slapped Henman on the back after they had exchanged pleasantries. Henman was so confused that he forgot to shake the umpire's outstretched hand. He was in the press room within a couple of minutes, sweat trickling down a face whose ashen complexion betrayed the exhaustion of a week which meant so much.

'I came here to qualify for Hanover and that's what I've done,' he said, 'but because I qualified didn't mean this tournament was over. I wanted to finish the job off but I just didn't have the adrenalin of yesterday. It's disappointing to me that I didn't have the levels of commitment I should. There has been such a focus in the last three or four weeks, Hanover has been so close, that some might argue that this result was inevitable. I would find it very difficult to accept if that was the case.'

There was a week to get such damning thoughts out of his mind. He would dash to the airport to fly home that evening, which meant that girlfriend Lucy, who had come out to Stockholm on Saturday morning, would be back in Barnes before she'd had time to see anything but the airport, the back of a taxi and an indoor tennis court.

Enter Greg, knowing what he had to do. When Johansson won the toss and elected to face the fastest serve in the world and Rusedski held with a couple of aces inside a minute, a frantic pace had been set. But, as with Henman, the opening signs were illusory. Rusedski double faulted twice in the third game before throwing in an ace and a service winner on a second serve, but Johansson's nerve was sure. He broke to lead 2–1 and the games flew by until Rusedski pieced together a compelling reply, helped by a net cord at 30–30, to break back at 5–5. What did he do then? Give Johansson an opening he greedily accepted to retrieve the advantage and serve out for the set.

There were four break points in the second set, all of them to Rusedski, but he couldn't come up with the inspiration to take them. So, like Henman the night before, he would have to endure a tie-break with hardly a soul in the place wanting him to win. Rusedski wasn't up to the task, although he did have a set point at 6–5, rescued by a quite wonderful forehand pass by Johansson at full stretch, the acclaim for which almost took the roof off. The Swede proceeded to ace his way to a second match point, controlled the decisive rally and finished a 7–5, 7–6 winner.

Rusedski, like Henman, did not bother with a shower before meeting the press. A man who had been full of fun and keen to make small talk all week had lost his sense of humour. He claimed he didn't move as freely as he would have liked but, most importantly, he was shattered to have come so close, from so far back, only to stumble when in sight of the tape.

His situation wasn't helped by the way Kafelnikov was shattering all his opponents in Moscow. Marc Rosset, the giant Swiss, pulled out in the second set of the semi-final, which left Ivanisevic as the opponent who now held the British player's Hanover fates in his hand. Rusedski said he knew what the outcome would be.

'Kafelnikov will win, no doubt,' he said. 'The scores in the past few days there have been ridiculous given the pace of the court. If Goran starts serving aces tomorrow, they'll confiscate his passport. They won't let him out of the country. It has come down to fractions in the end, and I didn't quite have it in me to make up all the ground I lost. Looking back, those two months out of the game stopped me finishing the year in the top five.'

The result Rusedski feared duly happened, Kafelnikov winning the title in Moscow to claim the eighth spot, though Ivanisevic had his chances, and good ones at that. Each one he missed must have felt like a kick in Greg's guts. Rusedski wondered whether he really wanted to travel to Hanover as an alternate. He wasn't going to make the same kind of dramatic impact there that Henman did the previous November, when he arrived on private jet from the British nationals. But there was $40,000 on offer just to spend a week practising, and a hefty fine if you didn't show. Rusedski showed.

15 The ATP World Championships

David Felgate could have been forgiven for wanting to chuck handfuls of snow in the air to celebrate the moment of Tim's achievement. He had said to me earlier in the year that he would only feel truly vindicated when his charge had won something. Reaching the ATP Finals was surely a time to release those emotions.

Instead, Felgate was quiet, contemplative. 'Tim finished ninth in the points standings and if he had beaten Martin, it would have been eighth and he'd have qualified for Hanover by rights,' said the coach. 'I know he's made it into the finals, but I'd have felt much better if he'd have beaten Martin. I'm sure by the time tomorrow comes around I'll have put it out of my system. Tim's done fantastically well. The Swedish players seemed to be genuinely delighted for him that he'd qualified. They were all coming up in the locker room, wishing him well.'

He continued: 'I know a lot of people want to know everything there is to know about Tim, but the truth is, there isn't really anything to tell. He is what he appears. That's a bit dull for you I know, but we are dealing with a truly top-class professional sportsman who doesn't let anything interfere with what he believes is right for him and for his career. I admire him for that. He's been through a lot this year.'

And now, here it was. Hanover. All the hassle, all the heartache, all the pain along the way was worth the ATP Finals. Not the classiest joint on the tennis tour, but to the professionals, it was an Elysian Field. Or should that be an Elysian GreenSet hard court.

Each of the elite eight players had their own chauffeur-cum-body-guard and hostess. Nothing was too much for the championship organizers. Marcelo Rios duly arrived from Santiago, Pete Sampras from his ten-day break in the sun and Andre Agassi had blown into town. Tim Henman was chuffed to be in the field, Greg Rusedski, the reserve, was champing at the bit to play. The only problem was, this was a world championship which would not crown a world champion. The winner of the $3.3 million event would not necessarily finish as the No.1 player in the world.

Sampras led Rios going into the championship by the thread-thin margin of thirty-three points – precisely the same number by which Rusedski had finished the regular tour adrift of Yevgeny Kafelnikov. The figures were symptomatic of how close the game had become at the top, a concertina effect which meant that any of those in the field could have more than reasonable designs on finishing the following year in the top three.

The World Championships were played in a round robin format, with the eight players split into two groups, the Red and the White. Each player would face the other in his group once over four days, with the top two qualifying for the semi-finals. The winners of those would then meet in the best-of-five-set-final.

Agassi, who had won the title in 1990, but couldn't knock Stefan Edberg from his perch as No.1 in the process, was in the finals for the sixth time, but ricked his back practising with the Spaniard Alex Corretja. He therefore missed the official launch, where the remaining seven players, plus Rusedski as alternate, posed in their smart suits for the team picture. Rusedski was introduced at the function as 'coming here direct from Canada'. He looked distraught at the mistake. We couldn't see if Henman was smiling behind the curtains as he waited for his introduction.

The top two, Sampras and Rios were kept apart in the draw, as were Nos.3 and 4 Carlos Moya and Agassi; Nos.5 and 6 Alex Corretja and Karol Kucera; and Nos.7 and 8, Henman and Kafelnikov. No one wanted to draw Sampras but three would be disappointed. Henman was among the fortunate four. Sampras was bracketed with French Open champion Moya, Karol Kucera, and the man he blitzed in the 1997 final, Kafelnikov. Henman was grouped with Rios, Corretja and Agassi.

Henman was ready. 'I feel very proud to have made it to Hanover, but now I want to do some damage and win it,' he said. 'I had a good indoor run (eighteen wins and eight defeats) at the end of the season, so there's no reason why I can't finish off the year in style. I won't need any motivating – these are the World Championships.'

The stage for the event was Hall 13 of the Hanover Messe – a huge glass-fronted contraption in the middle of nowhere some five miles out of town. There were more idyllic vistas on the travelling circus but few of the players had time to consider the lack of aesthetic beauty in the surroundings. Here were the top eight players under one roof. For all the glamour of the Grand Slams – Sampras, for instance, had triumphed at Wimbledon without defeating a top-ten player – there was no escaping the talent he would need to see off if he was to secure his place in the sport's Valhalla.

First up was Kafelnikov against Sampras. Kafelnikov's opening double fault was symptomatic of the nervousness which overcame him throughout a set in which the American flowed, free of the inhibitions he'd shown in Stockholm. A few days at home in Florida had obviously been good for the soul. Kafelnikov was completely out of kilter, serving nine doubles, being foot-faulted twice, and incurring a code violation for an outburst of foul language. Only once did he manage to break the Sampras serve – to love, no less – only to throw away the advantage by losing his own in the very next game. Sampras secured his 6–2, 6–4 victory when the Russian dumped another forehand into the net.

'The win today was mental for me as much as anything – I knew I couldn't afford to feel flat. This is a very, very big week. All the top guys are here, the level of tennis is going to be great. I didn't want to dig myself into the kind of hole I did last year [when he lost to Moya in his first round robin and had to win his next two to qualify]. I don't want to say that my performance today was a statement, but I was definitely very focused.'

As if to underline the class of the field, Moya and Kucera then proceeded to engage in a fascinating match, spreading magic across a captivating two hours and twenty-eight minutes. The Spaniard emerged with a commendable victory and eagerness to face Sampras the next day. 'He cannot be the best from the back, so I'm going to try to keep him there,' said the Spaniard. 'I have time to think about my shots on this court, I don't tell you how many chances I will have, but he needs to be careful.'

Henman knew he could take no outrageous risks against Rios, his opponent on the first evening session of the Championship. The Chilean had defeated him twice, in the semi-final of Key Biscayne after which he knocked Sampras off his No.1 perch, and again in the Italian Open for the loss of a mere four games. But Henman knew that, indoors Rios didn't possess quite the same menace, and that, quite possibly, his heart wasn't in the event. While Sampras wanted the prize desperately, he ate, slept and breathed it; Rios acted as though he couldn't care less if he was No.1 or not. It seemed a shrug of the shoulders for him.

The same bunch of Chileans who had been flown to Miami in a hastily-chartered jumbo jet from Santiago for the final weekend in Key Biscayne seemed to have found their way to Hanover. The entrance for the two players, through brandished Chilean flags and dry ice, was more usually found at a boxing match. Immediately, the gloves were off. Henman opened with a flourish, holding his first service game to love, but Rios' serve was equally secure and it became a match of missed opportunity from the baseline.

The British press searched for signs of immobility in Rios, looking for things they hoped they'd see, that he was pulling up short, maybe. And was that a grimace, a twinge? The Chilean's timing was definitely awry but the consensus was that for Henman to win the match, he had to win the first set. The moment he gave Rios an opening, the aches and pains would have mysteriously cleared.

The turning point came in the twelfth game. Henman was gifted a point when Rios allowed a looping backhand to go over his head, when he might have put it away. The ball landed smack on the baseline. Tim raced to 0–40. On his first set point, Henman, forced to pursue a Rios lob, swatted the ball back over his shoulder. Able to retrieve Rios' limp attempt at a smash, he forced his opponent into a backhand error. The crucial first set was his.

Henman was in trouble once on his serve, in the third game of the second set, but saved it with a delicate cross-court forehand winner, which he greeted with one of those low, discreet punches of satisfaction. It was then that someone switched all of Rios' lights off. He lost his serve twice to trail 5–1, leaving Henman with a fabulous opportunity and the German crowd with an increasing sense of anger towards the limpness of Rios' challenge. Henman served the match out for a 7–5, 6–1 victory as sweet as any other in his life. The world No.2's sweeping, pony-tailed mane was indeed a scalp to be prized.

'I came out here, I was aggressive and I took my chances,' Henman said. 'I knew I had a lot to gain and nothing much to lose this week.

I wouldn't say that my tennis was amazing, but it was to a very high standard, and very consistent. Rios is a good front runner, so I knew I had to serve well, which I did. A result like this does wonders for your confidence, whether he was carrying an injury or not.'

The other two players in the group met later in the day. Agassi had been having physical problems of his own, and we went through the same process, of trying to work out if he was impaired as he ran down shots against Corretja. There was one long 'aaargh' from Agassi when he bent into one first serve, and we wondered if that was a sign that all was not well, but he broke the Spaniard in the eleventh game, survived a break point, and then produced two emphatic, unhindered serves to claim the first set.

But Agassi could not race away from his opponent. He was broken for 5–3 in the second, and Corretja's eleventh ace squared the match. When Agassi lost his serve to trail 2–1 in the final set, he whispered something to the umpire at the changeover, walked over to Corretja's chair and said he couldn't continue. Later that evening, he was to be on a private jet back to Las Vegas.

Which meant that Rusedski was in after all. Not only that, he would face Henman. He could forget about being the resident practice partner – though no one had much use of a left hander with only Rios of the initial eight playing that way. Now Greg was due to play Rios on Thursday, but, a few minutes before he was to walk on court – with all his work in practice designed to counter fellow left-hander Rios – he suddenly found he was playing the right-handed Albert Costa.

The Spaniard had flown in from Barcelona that morning to be the second alternate, just in case anyone else pulled up and, well wouldn't you believe it, Rios announced he couldn't compete any more. The result was not only that Rusedski would have a new opponent to face, but also that Pete Sampras would retain his end-of-year No.1 status for the sixth year in succession. He learnt the news in his hotel room, as he sat tucking into a plate of pasta with no one to share the moment – 'I was with all my friends, I was on my own,' he said, in a moment of classic insight into how lonely his existence had become.

Sampras defeated Moya in straight sets to compliment his first victory in the group over Kafelnikov. He would top the group, so would play the runner-up in the group now occupied by Henman and Rusedski in the semis. Could both Brits qualify? It was possible, but implausible. Rusedski knew he would have to win both matches

– against Costa and Henman – to stand any chance because the rules were designed specifically to make it more difficult for an alternate to reach the semis. In effect, Rusedski started with one hand tied behind his back. He would suffer through playing only two matches to the other's three.

Next up was Henman against Corretja – who had each won their first match. A loss here would not be a mortal blow, but Henman knew he would have to face Rusedski in the third and didn't want to have to beat him to qualify.

Corretja had beaten Henman in their only meeting, at the Paris Indoors the previous November. The improvement in both players had been vast. Henman and Felgate decided that their strategy against a player who operated almost exclusively from the baseline was to rush the net behind chipped approaches, and force the Spaniard to make a succession of winning passing shots. It would take excellence and courage, the need to stay focused even when the ball zapped back past him, as it was certain to do on occasions.

The first two sets went all the way to tie-breaks, Henman sneaking the first with a single 'mini-break' when one of those chip-charge approaches forced Corretja to thump his backhand wide; the Spaniard responding to take the second when Henman's forehand began to unravel. It was more than ever a test of inner belief, and Henman's was bountiful. He broke the first two Corretja service games in the final set, at one stage screaming 'Come on, come on,' to himself above the support the Spaniard was attempting to extract from the crowd. The Englishman held himself unwaveringly steady to win 7–6, 6–7, 6–2 in exactly two-and-a-half hours. At first, he wasn't certain he was through to the semi-finals, but once the complicated arithmetic had been worked out, he was thrilled at achieving the initial target he had set himself for the championship.

The after-match talk came round to the demands of the game on the players. 'The schedule doesn't make it easy,' said Henman. 'The vital thing is to stay as healthy as possible. You've got to be strong in a lot of areas. You have to have a strong game, you have to be strong between the ears, you have to be strong physically. I did my fair share of mileage today out there with him. I'm satisfied to be through to the semis but there's a lot more tennis still to play.

'I'm playing Greg tomorrow and everyone knows we have a pretty healthy rivalry.' (Henman brought up the word 'rivalry', the press didn't.) I don't like losing matches but I think we will be extra keen to beat each other. We're both very, very competitive. It's the World

Championship. There's two British guys going out to battle for it.

'In the past couple of years, we've both come a long way. I think at times we both feel like we want some others to come along and start taking the headlines away from us. Not that we don't enjoy it, but there's plenty of room for that. We've been practising recently at Queen's, and as far as I can remember, in six sets, there hasn't been a single break. I think we're very level, which is a diplomatic answer, but an honest one.'

In the evening, Rusedski duly completed a 7–6, 6–1 victory over Costa, where what was going on in his mind was never evident to those of us at courtside. 'I was choking like crazy, there was no ifs or buts about it,' he said to me at the end of the year. 'I am playing a guy who has a 0–16 record indoors, I'm in the World Championships, and there's so much at stake, in terms of points, money, ranking, everything. I couldn't have asked for a better situation.

'I had ten set points in the first set and I was choking. There's nothing wrong with that, because I kept trying. If people go out on the court and say "It's too much, that's it" and give in, that I can't respect. There's nothing wrong with an honest choke.' Fortunately, Rusedski was able to clear his head and swept through the second set.

He knew that victory over Henman on Friday would confirm his return to the top ten, so the edge the British press wanted was there. Henman may have qualified for the last four but Rusedski had to win to have any chance (and then hope that Costa would upset Corretja). The prospects were remote, Greg knew that, but that wouldn't stop him going for it. He even joked that Tonya Harding – the 1980s American ice skater found guilty of involvement in a baseball bat attack on her rival, Nancy Kerrigan – would be arriving on the next plane to Hanover to take care of matters.

'Heh, it's the Commonwealth title,' said Rino Tomassi of *La Gazzetta dello Sport*, Italy's leading sports paper, 'that's what they're playing for, isn't it?' Rino had written before the event that the Brits were only attending in the hope that Henman would play Rusedski. As far as we were concerned, that was the final. That was the event. Nothing else mattered.

Six months after they had been due to meet in the semi-finals at Queen's – until Rusedski did his ankle and Henman crumbled to Laurence Tieleman – the two Brits would finally get to grips in 1998. It had been a long time coming. How would they react? Rusedski led the pair on to court and, in fairness, he had Henman where he wanted him from that moment on. Henman was never in it, there was no tightness in his game, he missed the most routine of put-aways, he looked unbelievably anxious. David Felgate, who would usually be perpetually in motion in the box, mouthing exhortations, waving a motivational fist, sat with his arms folded across his chest.

In twenty-five minutes, the first set was Rusedski's, 6–2. He had lost three points in his four service games, while breaking Henman twice. Would there be any semblance of a comeback? Not a bit of it. Henman was disgusted with himself, as evidenced by a couple of the trademark spits he often indulges in when he misses shots he should make. He kept looking across to Felgate, but the return stares were blank. There was no message to impart that would get Henman out of this fix.

He lost his serve twice more to trail 5–1, but suddenly realized he could be on the end of a deeply humiliating scoreline, and raced to 0–40 on Rusedski's serve. Rusedski forced a backhand volley winner, an ace, and a fluked forehand off the frame to retrieve to deuce. Henman spurted again, and, on his fifth break point, tempted Rusedski into a volleying error. 6–2, 6–4 looked an awful lot better on the scoresheet than 6–2, 6–1.

Where does that rank in your list of all-time great, or not so great performances? Henman baulked at the first question, but retained his cool. 'I think it's irrelevant where it ranks, it was a disappointing performance. A lot of attention is being paid to the rivalry. I won't dwell on that one too long, I've got a semi-final tomorrow. I think we both wanted to win. On the day my performance wasn't good enough. Having said that, he did play pretty well. I don't like to lose.

'I haven't served a lot of double faults this week (there were six in the Rusedski match). Maybe I was going for it a little too much. I'll probably go out on the practice court later and hit some balls, to get some rhythm back into my serve. I'm still going into my match against Moya tomorrow with a lot of confidence. I know a lot of people wanted to see us have a tight and hard-fought match. Greg had more to play for, his performance showed that. But it was another chance to improve my ranking, and I missed out.'

He was asked (by a Spanish journalist) how good his relations with Rusedski were. 'Yeah, good,' he replied. 'There was definitely a spell earlier in the year when we weren't getting on particularly well. I think, at times, that was blown out of proportion by the press. But now, we do. We definitely get on better. We have a pretty good time in the Davis Cup. I think it's a lot better.'

Henman could still end the year ranked fourth in the world if he won the title; Rusedski had to settle for ninth – not bad considering he had only been fit for two-thirds of it. 'It's unbelievably satisfying,' he said. 'To get there is one thing, but to stay there for two years, I think really establishes me as a top-ten player now. With all the aggro I had this year, with the departure of my coach and the injury and everything, I can't be more pleased or satisfied here to have come into the World Championships with the best players in the world, to win two matches, and to be undefeated. You can't ask for more.'

Could there have been a more incongruous completion of the year for Rusedski in tennis-playing terms than beating Henman to secure a top-ten berth? I wondered whether there was any additional motivation because, for the first time since they broke into the upper strata of the game, Rusedski would finish *behind* Henman in the year-end rankings? 'I'm not worried about that anymore,' he said. 'When you play each other, obviously you want to win. But I'm looking more at getting somewhere I've never been before. I've been to four in the world, I'd like to get into the area where it's three, two or one. That's my objective for next year.'

Henman had to come back the next day to face Carlos Moya for a place in the final. His parents had flown in from London at the crack of dawn on the Saturday morning and watched, as I did, his midday practice session with Sampras on the stadium court. The signs weren't good. Henman could hardly keep a ball in court; Sampras shot a couple of worried glances at his friend, and tried to make light of his errors. They would come back to haunt Henman in the match proper.

But you had to pinch yourself. A week earlier, I had been watching at Telford as Mark Hilton and Danny Sapsford contested the semi-finals of the British Nationals, and here we were, at the World Championships, with a Brit in the semis. The chief guest at the Nationals, was the President of the LTA, Sir Geoffrey Cass; here it was the new Chancellor of the Federal Republic of Germany, Gerhard Schroeder.

The semi-final was an affair consumed by nerves; it appeared that the tennis shoes of both players had been coated in treacle. Neither moved smoothly, both shot anxious glances towards their corners. In the third game, Henman managed to get in two first serves out of twelve and when he had two break points in the sixth game – both of them on Moya second serves – he couldn't capitalize. The next game – the seventh – Henman was bouncing the racket strings against the palm of his hand in that troubled manner of his as he made a couple of volleying errors. Then, the British player made a dreadful forehand error from mid-court, spraying the ball wide, to give Moya the advantage. The first set was the Spaniard's in fifty tentative minutes.

Henman's response was courageous, holding from 0–30 in the opening game, then breaking for the first time to lead 2–0, and holding to love for 3–0. Nothing would be straightforward though, even if Henman had two points for a 5–1 lead. When he could take advantage, his mind wandered, and he served two double faults to trail 0–40 in the seventh game. Henman then produced three fabulous serves, two inducing errors on the return, the third an ace. He steadied himself to serve out for the set.

The start to the final set was also an English flourish. Henman attacked the net, produced a couple of winning smashes, and immediately broke, confirming the advantage by holding for 2–0. He only had to hold his serve four more times for a place in the final. Moya was giving off more negative vibes, though Henman wasn't through yet, not by a long chalk. The break back came in the sixth game, though once more the seventh was potentially crucial. Henman raced to 15–40, two more break points from which the Spaniard couldn't possibly have recovered, had either been taken. Henman tried a backhand lob which landed long, then netted a volley attempting to cut off a powerful passing shot. Moya held.

So did Henman, from break point down, in the next game. Moya served, another break point. Had Henman taken it, he would have been serving for the match. It was then that Moya's serving arm might have tightened, but he conjured a half-pace offering to Henman's backhand, which required the British player to reach up, and the half-court return was cut off with a forehand which left Henman spreadeagled behind the baseline.

Moya held for 5–4, Henman for 5–5, and Moya for 6–5. As he walked back to serve once more, Henman flicked a ball at one of the cameramen jostling for a position to capture the final drama at courtside. Once more – as at Queen's – he had been distracted, perhaps fatally. Moya was rock steady now from the baseline and produced two punching backhands past the incoming volleyer. Match point. Moya's thumping forehand service return down the line brought a brutal end to Henman's year.

A total of fifty unforced errors from Henman rather summed up the nervousness which betrayed him. I wondered whether his performance was a hangover from his previous night's defeat to Rusedski. Henman said not. 'It has been a really intense, sort of jam-packed last six months,' he said. 'I've enjoyed it, but I'm looking forward to a short break, then getting back on the practice court in December. I've established myself in the top ten but my feeling at the moment is that it's not good enough. I've got to go to the next level.'

With that, tired and drawn, he tossed the hand-held microphone onto the leather sofa on which he was sitting, rose slowly to his feet and walked out of his final press conference of 1998.

As did his pal Sampras a couple of hours later. The world No.1 had match points against Corretja, but the Spaniard proved himself to be an astonishingly courageous athlete, indulging in a couple of twenty-plus stroke rallies from the baseline to sap Sampras' strength, and finishing him off in the final set tie-break, to confirm an all-Spanish final.

It is worth noting that the final developed into a classic of its kind. Moya won the first two sets at a canter, and then Corretja conjured visions of Ivan Lendl, his first idol, recovering from a similar plight against John McEnroe in the 1984 French Open final, to win in five. 'If your idol can do it, why not you? Come on, don't give in,' said Corretja to himself, refusing to countenance doubts. The outcome was one of the gutsiest performances I had ever seen on a tennis court, like the seventeen-year-old Michael Chang at the 1989 French, as Corretja summoned reserves of energy from who knew where.

He slowly clawed his way back, taking the final of the final event into a final set. It see-sawed one way, then the other, before Corretja prevailed in exactly four hours, falling to his knees as the last Moya shot sailed over the baseline. The twenty-four-year-old – the same age as Henman – raced behind the advertisements at the back of the court and threw himself full-length, Klinsmann-style, into a posse of family and friends.

Corretja had triumphed 3–6, 3–6, 7–5, 6–3, 7–5, and had reached a career-high No.3 in the world. 'I am really mentally strong,' he said. 'All through my life I have considered myself a winner. Today, I think it was my ambition which made me win. It was the first time in my life I had come back from losing the first two sets. Of course, I will carry on working hard. I know reaching No.1 will be really tough, really difficult, but if I'm No.3, it means I can be No.1. I didn't want to finish with a small trophy, I wanted to finish with this one,' he added, brandishing the greatest prize of his life.

Corretja's coach handed him his mobile phone. It was the president of Spain on the line. And, I have to admit, my mind wandered forward to the day it might be Tony Blair calling Tim or Greg on the first Sunday in July.

16 Year's End

The Monday evening after Hanover, at the David Lloyd Racket club at Raynes Park, Greg Rusedski stepped out to play an exhibition against Boris Becker for the families and dependants of the IRA's bomb outrage in Omagh, which had claimed twenty-nine lives in the summer. The German Ambassador to Great Britain was present to watch the tennis, as was Northern Ireland's First Minister and Nobel Peace Prize joint winner, David Trimble. The solemnity of the cause was in marked contrast to the light-hearted atmosphere of the occasion.

This was Rusedski at his best, giving the public what it wanted, amusing his audience by entering into a discourse with Becker during rallies, signing autographs for them until writer's cramp overtook him, disarming ladies both young and old who swooned over his omnipresent grin. A cheque for £30,000 was handed to the trustees of the Omagh Fund.

I wondered why Greg had been asked to take part by the event's organizers and not Tim Henman – and my mind went back to why he had become the 1997 Sports Personality of the Year. Greg was at ease with the people and they were cosy with him – Tim would have found it unnerving to try to be something he's not. A showman. It was hard to imagine Henman switching racket hands and making himself look ridiculous by playing left-handed. Rusedski didn't care a hoot. Neither did Becker.

Henman, looking every inch the dapper young, smart-casual millionaire that same evening, sat on a sofa between golfer Severiano

Ballesteros and snooker's Stephen Hendry for a recording of the BBC's
On Side.

Inevitably, the subject of a Brit becoming the world No.1 was raised.
'I think I can speak for the both of us,' Henman ventured, 'when I say
we have a great opportunity next year, which makes it a very exciting
time. My year really started at Wimbledon, so I've reached No.7 in the
world on six months' work. If I put the full eleven months in 1999,
there's every chance for me. Greg was out injured for three months and
he finished at No.9.'

Both players were committed to starting the year back in Doha and
therefore had to turn down the Football Association's request to make
the draw for the fourth round of the FA Cup. On 14 December 1998
Rusedski sat down with his coach, Sven Groeneveld, physio Reza
Daneshmand, physical fitness coach Steve Green, and Michael Chang's
former fitness coach, Ken Matsuda, to plan the journey ahead.

Groeneveld detailed the team's aims: 'Taking everything into
consideration, I think Greg is getting near to as good as he may ever
be. The whole team have met and talked about what we think we
should do for the next year. We have pointed out some weaknesses
and we're working on those. Greg isn't the kind of person you can
force something on, he has to develop it himself, like his backhand
topspin. But you don't have to repeat anything a thousand times over
to him, either, he works things through in his own mind. I don't
believe we're in a hurry, we have our time and we spend it gradually
improving him.

'Ken Matsuda has been brought in specifically to work on Greg's
footwork and balance, so that he flows on the court. Greg does use a
lot of energy during points. He is naturally fit but he also uses a lot of
energy that's not necessary. Ken's knowledge of the game in his area
means he is teaching Greg to conserve that energy for use when he
really needs it, which is going to be vitally important in two-week
Grand Slams when it's hot, it's demanding and you have to win best-
of-five matches. Greg wants his game to be more efficient and that's the
task we have for the year ahead.'

The year just completed was one of discovery and re-discovery.
Rusedski had started at six in the world, and finished ranked ninth. But
he knew he was a far better player; and we who followed him knew it,
too. 'I had probably the best start to a season ever, reaching the final in
Split, winning in Antwerp, breaking the world record for the fastest
serve in Indian Wells and having the chance to be No.1 in the world at
Key Biscayne,' he said. 'The clay courts were absolutely miserable, I

had only one win, then I got to the grass and felt everything was coming together, until the little slip.'

The trip to Turkey with Daneshmand remained the year's biggest bone of contention. 'I just went away for two days with my physio,' Rusedski explained. 'I didn't want to be specific about where I was, I just wanted to be out of the spotlight, away from the pressures. I went away to relax, where no one could get hold of me.

'It was more a mental, than medical purpose, because for anything to heal, you have to be mentally right. No matter what a doctor can do, if the patient is in a good mood, with a positive feeling, he will heal faster than someone in a negative frame of mind. When I travelled, I had everything taped up so the swelling wouldn't increase. I had the top physio who I believed in, with me. I received round-the-clock treatment. Here was a person who sacrificed two days' work, someone it's impossible to get an appointment with for two months without a referral, and even if you have a referral, you might not get the appointment. I was great in my mind, and I knew I was in the very best hands.'

I relayed John McEnroe's remarks that the idea of flying anywhere with a dodgy ankle a week before a major championship was a stupid gamble. Rusedski had read them. 'I didn't know McEnroe had a doctorate in medicine,' he replied. 'Is there anything he doesn't know the answer to? I see he's telling us now that he can beat everyone on the tour, so we're waiting excitedly for his comeback. I'm sure there are tournament directors queuing up out there with wild cards for him into the doubles so he can prove his point.'

Rusedski went on to discuss his injury and the team around him in more detail. 'Everyone is allowed their opinion, but I believe in the people around me. Reza has been there since 1996 and I have complete and utter faith in him. He has been a constant for me, like Steve Green. I know there are those who have said I change coaches too frequently, but I have to have a set of people around me who are positive. There is so much still to be learned about medicines and how they can help. There's not one set way and I want to be surrounded by people with open minds.

'I think what happened with Tony (Pickard) at Wimbledon was well orchestrated. He wanted me to be treated at Wimbledon by the ATP physios, but I had my own physio. He *knew* Reza's work. Back in December, we were practising indoors at Wimbledon and it was so cold, for a time, I couldn't move, I couldn't walk straight. I hobbled my way to see Reza, he fixed me up and told me I couldn't serve for a week.

'So Tony knew what he did, but he didn't believe in it. With the greatest respect to the ATP guys, Reza knows my body better than anybody because I work with him on a constant basis. I said to Tony "No, Reza's doing it," because I felt strongly about it. That's where most of the problems arose. You just had to see his client list to know he must be doing something right. Reza is a good friend and he's always been there when I've needed him, sometimes at a cost to his other clients.

'The thing that disappointed me most with Tony was the way he treated my physio. He didn't deserve the criticism he got. I could handle my own situation no problem, but Reza got hurt and that wasn't right. I remember after the first day against Draper at Wimbledon, he was giving me a light bandage in the locker room, some ultrasound and a massage to get the circulation going and Tony was in there trying to tell him his job. That's what I found hard to understand and cope with.

'Tony is a great coach, tactically fabulous, he was good for me, but that was telling someone who had been in the profession for twenty years that they didn't know what they were doing. That made no sense to me. I look back at what happened with Tony as doing me a favour.'

Rusedski's resurgence in the autumn was an astounding tribute to his own idealistic powers of self confidence and his 'My Way is the Right Way' philosophy. Nobody could ever accuse him of not believing in himself. The appointment of Groeneveld acted as the spur he required at just the right time. 'The minute I was back on the court, I was hitting two million groundstrokes a day to get my backhand topspin better,' said Rusedski. 'I had to improve my return of serve as well. It didn't all come together right away but I look at my record after coming back in Indianapolis, and I had twenty-eight wins and eight losses, which was the best finish of any player.

'I have come through all my trials a better player. I have proved a lot of things. I had a great year in 1997, reaching No.4 in the world and a Grand Slam final, but 1998 was even better. I feel I have exploded back onto the scene – I was playing great tennis at the end of the year. I didn't get as high as I was, I didn't reach a Grand Slam final but this was, ultimately, a more satisfying year for me. I know there was controversy, but it's not a big deal if you know what is right, you feel what is right and you do what is right. I know certain people haven't liked the decisions I've made, but if you handle them properly, you hold yourself with dignity, then you will be OK.'

Once again, as the embers of the year flickered, so Henman and

Rusedski went about winding down in their two distinctly separate ways. Henman, his girlfriend Lucy, David and Jan Felgate travelled to Skibo Castle in Scotland for a few days of rest and recuperation. Rusedski was doing the TV rounds; it was difficult to turn a page in the listings and not find his name attached to some show or other. He was a guest on Ian Wright's *All Wright on the Night, They Think It's all Over* – where he came through a pretty rough ride over his accent – and the Comedy Awards (which wasn't being considered as a replacement for the British National Championships). To some, it would have been overkill, to Greg it was simply being natural, being himself.

'Tim and I are totally different characters,' he said. 'That's what makes us and our world so exciting. I suppose I'm a little bit more outspoken, a little more chatty shall we say. He's chatty, too, but in a more reserved way. I don't think he'd go on *Fantasy Football* for instance, but I love it. Our sport needs personality, I like to take risks in life, it's more my philosophy than Tim's, I think.'

Image is vital to both of them, yet they go about portraying theirs in contrary ways. Greg and his Lucy have posed for *OK!* magazine in their Chelsea flat; Tim would never think of agreeing to anything so intrusive. His agent Jan Felgate said: 'Image isn't something we spend all our time studying, but it's fair to say that a lot of Tim's sponsors want someone with an image which sits well with their product.

'It works because Tim is perceived, rightly so, as a classy, determined person. He doesn't like people getting too close, there are a lot of things he would never be comfortable doing. He's been invited on to every game show and every talk show you could name and most of the time he says no. He would never want to leave himself open to any embarrassment. That isn't likely to happen on *A Question of Sport*. I don't think you'll ever see him on *Noel's House Party*. He was asked this year if he'd introduce the girl group All Saints at a concert in Hyde Park. I knew the answer before he said no. He's not interested in being known for anything other than his tennis.'

The two men had their fan clubs, both well supported, both besotted with their own man, and not exactly enamoured of the other. Rusedski was accepted by the public at large more than he was by those inside tennis; Henman was seen as more distant in public terms, but he was very much a member of the sport's 'family'. Rusedski didn't have favourites in the press; Henman had one or two he courted and who, in turn, openly courted him. Sven Groeneveld rarely ventured outside the coach's domain of locker room and practice court; David Felgate was a regular visitor to the press rooms of the world, eager to swap gossip, but more concerned to surf the Internet to find out what was happening at Arsenal. Both players said they didn't mind what was written about them, it was what they and their coaches said that mattered.

The press trod a difficult line. After years when they had only British mediocrity upon which to base their judgements, the landscape had changed. John Roberts of the *Independent* remembered what it was like and what it had become. 'There was no expectation before, we relied on Jeremy Bates in the late 1980s and early 1990s to reach the odd quarter-final here or there and it wasn't easy for him to be the one left trying to keep the tinder glowing,' Roberts said. 'We heard rumours about this guy in Canada, but we were a bit sceptical. All we knew was that he might be a top fifty player and he had a big serve.

'The only big name we had was Wimbledon. But Greg had done well up to a point in Canada and he wanted to do better – the environment he arrived in was so different. He had a latent determination and started straightaway to make the kind of impact which fascinated us. His arrival definitely took the pressure off Henman, who was about to supersede Bates and become Britain's lone ranger. I didn't think his game was ready for that, nor was he mature enough to handle everything that went with being British No.1.

'Rusedski played Petchey at Queen's that first year and lost in straight sets. I was one of those who joked that he obviously had all the credentials to be British. Then came his entry on Centre Court at Wimbledon wearing the Union Jack bandanna, which didn't endear him to the other players, both British and from elsewhere. Pete Sampras took great delight in beating him in the quarters. But, in domestic terms, Greg had become Tim's stalking horse, Tim had something to aim for without too much pressure on him.'

Roberts recalled a conversation with the former *Guardian* correspondent David Irvine at the Nabisco Masters (the forerunner to the ATP finals) in New York ten years earlier, when Jakob Hlasek, representing Switzerland, but of Czech descent, was one of the eight final qualifiers. 'Hlasek was a solid player, good physique, sound temperament, he was never going to be No.1 but he was a good top-tenner. I said to David that we didn't expect to find a world beater in Britain but it would be nice to have someone like Hlasek. David said, "We'll have to go to Czechoslovakia for one." That wasn't exactly my point but little did we know, we'd go to Canada instead.'

Irvine was one of those who had been most vehemently opposed to

Rusedski's importation, to the extent that he preferred to send his colleague Stephen Bierley, to cover Rusedski's controversial 1995 debut as a Brit on Centre Court. A year later, Irvine having retired, Bierley watched from the same seat as Henman defeated Yevgeny Kafelnikov, recently enthroned as the French Open champion, in the match that turned his career around. 'I suppose most people imagined Tim was going to lose, but I can remember the astonishing sense of achievement there was when he won,' Bierley said. 'Earlier in the spring, I'd dismissed his defeat in the Italian Open in a sentence at the end of a 750-word report. I could never do that again.

'What we have to remember is that both Tim and Greg are exceptional players and, while it's not a question of getting blasé, we have started to expect them to stay where they are. Even when we criticize, as from time to time we do, it has to be seen in the context of their positions in the world order. I imagine people didn't criticize Jeremy Bates to the same extent, questioned the relationship between him and his coach, or picked on his backhand topspin, as we've done with Tim and Greg.

'I think that Greg gets lifted by criticism. If there's something going wrong, he uses it to spur him on. He doesn't sulk, he doesn't say "Oh my God what am I going to do now." It's more "To hell with them, I'll show them." He has this constant, unnerving capacity to surprise. After everything he'd been through in the year, who would have thought he would have beaten Sampras in Paris?

'Tim also did remarkably well to recover this year. I think back to this year's Australian Open and his first round against Golmard, a performance which, by his own admission was bloody awful. He said he couldn't hit his hat. It was then that the bandwagon started to roll, people looked for the reasons why, and picked on Felgate. The argument that he should go wasn't based on much, more that the expectations surrounding Henman had grown to such a massive extent. Tim had said he wanted to be a top-ten player, and top-ten players didn't lose like he was losing.

'But, he's turned it around, with Felgate. His ranking has improved from No.99 to No.29 to No.17 to No.7, who can argue with that sort of rise? Now we have to see if he can maintain that upward progress. I think that 1999 will be a very critical year for Tim because every match he plays will have so much riding on it because he's a top ten player and the rest will be gunning for him.'

A top-ten player. Two top-ten players. It felt a trifle disconcerting to say it, let alone write it down. The last time any of us thought the idea out loud was back in the late 1980s when a blond, uppitty lad from

Taunton called Andrew Castle arrived on the scene after four years of being worked ruthlessly in the American collegiate system. He was homesick, and he wanted a chance to show what he'd learned. (He was another player brought up outside the LTA system.)

Castle was full of himself and with justification. He told it as it was and tennis recoiled a little, but he was the breath of optimism we needed. In the second round of the 1986 Wimbledon championships, he reached two sets all against the vastly experienced Swede, Mats Wilander, only to lose 6–0 in the fifth. The praise Castle was accorded the next morning knocked his socks off. It earned him sponsorship contracts, TV appearances, the press swooned, the crowd loved him. 'But I lost 6–0 in the fifth,' he kept reminding us. We didn't want to hear. There was no greater illustration of how much the country yearned for a summer saviour.

Castle first set eyes on Henman in 1990 when he was brought down to Australia by Davis Cup captain Warren Jacques. 'Jeremy (Bates) and I were in the main draw in Melbourne and Jacquesy thought it would be useful for the younger players to have a hit with us,' said Castle. 'I remember setting eyes on this scrawny little thing who'd run for miles, scampering around picking up stray balls and then recounting us with statistical gems about tennis. He was so precocious, so talented and such a student of the game. You couldn't help but be entranced.

'I don't think I'd ever met anyone quite so English. He is conservative with a small 'c', he comes from a privileged background, he never had to worry that there wouldn't be enough petrol in the tank to get him to practice. But, despite all the privileges, he's got down in the dirt. I recall a quote, I think it was from Einstein, that if a = success then a = x + y + z: x is work; y is play; z is keeping your mouth shut. Tim works, plays and keeps his mouth shut.

'Greg is more of a prickly character, he gets under people's skin. I don't think he sets out to be offensive, but if you are in the same arena as him, it's possible to feel as though you are being offended. Having said that, I've grown to be a real fan of the way he does things. His tennis may not be natural, but there's a brutal strength in that serving arm and you marry that with his incredible desire and that's some player. Sampras wasn't there to make up the numbers in the Paris final and Greg was all over him – a phenomenal performance.'

The reaction from the British players still out there slogging away remained along distinct party lines – Henman was the favoured man, Rusedski would have to struggle like mad to win them over. The National champion Danny Sapsford put it with clear emphasis: 'I don't look upon Greg as being British at all. I'm sure he wants to be accepted, but no one really gives him the chance. I guess it was the LTA's ploy to bring in someone in the top hundred because they were getting a lot of stick about not having any decent players. I don't know if they thought the situation would change if they brought in a foreigner who suddenly decides to be British, but if that was the case, it was crazy. A delusion.'

Sapsford went on: 'Tim and Greg are in a different class to the rest of us, I look up to them, but I'm not in their league. We need three or four more guys to be pulled up by them, guys in their age group, like Richardson, Maclagan and maybe Lee. But it hasn't happened. They inhabit a different planet. I said to my wife at Wimbledon this year that I didn't think I would live to see an English player win it. I went to the semi-final, the atmosphere was unbelievable and Tim was fantastic.'

What if Rusedski got there first? 'I would welcome it, but not with the same level of enthusiasm I'd have for Tim. I suppose you could say I would be neutral. Could you expect anything else?'

Epilogue

The Annual General Meeting of the Lawn Tennis Association was held on Wednesday 9 December 1998 at 2p.m. at the Queen's Club. A watery sun greeted the administrators of the British game who arrived to congratulate themselves on a 'remarkable year'. Britain had never before had two male players in the top ten and there was another record windfall from the omnipotent Wimbledon. Self-congratulations and large sherries all round.

It wasn't until the twelfth paragraph of his speech that the president of the LTA, Sir Geoffrey Cass, mentioned Henman; Rusedski had to wait until the nineteenth. He went on to say that he was 'delighted to be president at a point in time when the standard of our top men is the highest it has been for sixty-two years'. There were two ways of looking at that remark. Henman and Rusedski had indeed placed British tennis in a situation unique in its history. But a short scan further down the computer rankings told a far more unflattering story.

Never before had there been two men in the top ten, but never had the third-placed British male been so far adrift either. Chris Wilkinson, approaching twenty-nine years of age, languished at 184 in the world, having set himself a target of getting inside the top 100 before he called it a day. There was a single British male between 200 and 300, Miles Maclagan, exactly 100 places behind Wilkinson, and then came the rest. Barry Cowan was at 309, Nick Gould was down at 323. Jamie Delgado, the player David Lloyd had reckoned would be the star of his Slater Group, was the tenth-best Brit at 426. Danny Sapsford, the national champion, was ranked 558th. Hardly the highest standard for sixty-two years.

The women's situation was even more dire. Sam Smith might have beaten the former Wimbledon champion Conchita Martinez during the

1998 Championships to reach the last sixteen, but she hadn't won a match on the WTA Tour between that day and the end of the year. Her ranking would almost certainly crash through the floor from its 31 December position of 58 unless she pulled her game and her emotions around.

Henman and Rusedski were so far out in front, it was a substantial embarrassment. One might have thought that with this situation, the closing down of the National School at Bisham Abbey, the apparently endless quest to find a Performance Director for the LTA, and what had happened to the feted 'Partnership with Business' for the sport, there would have been someone who wanted to say something from the floor. Henman himself might have been keen to know why there wasn't one indoor centre to cater for the many schools and universities in the city of Oxford, his home town. Instead, the only 'hear hears' during Sir Geoffrey's speech were registered when he praised Wimbledon for the immaculate organization of their splendid championships, even though Sir Geoffrey himself admitted that he was worried about the long-term development of British players. 'It shouldn't be forgotten that it's the LTA's job to spread the tennis word in the country, elite success is only one objective,' he said. 'I realize that the success of Tim and Greg has put us under greater pressure, but it's a good pressure to be under.

'I don't mind being given a hard time, it goes with the territory. Whatever I do, people are always going to be more interested with the extraordinary or the sensational, rather than look at the run-of-the-mill things we have to attend to, because they aren't sexy. There is a massive amount going on beneath the surface. Just because we earn a substantial amount from Wimbledon each year, doesn't mean we will produce winning tennis players.

'Success will ultimately spring from how many people, and of what calibre, are involved in the game. It doesn't matter what coaches do, you can't turn someone who doesn't have any idea of natural racket control into one who has. You don't create a Nastase or a McEnroe. You could be coached by Gonzales, Laver or Newcombe for fifty years, but you've either got it, or you haven't. If you do have the physique, the racket-handling flair, then you also need those personal characteristics of burning ambition and absolute determination. That's quite a difficult mix to find in one person.

'I don't know all the answers. But I think the situation has something to do with the nation as a whole getting softer. Very few people have to lift themselves up by the bootstraps to feel as if they're doing something, the situation is not as challenging as it once was. Tim and Greg are out there each week, succeeding against all the odds, in a world where they know people want to kill them every time they step onto the court. That's a hard, hard world.'

Could the right mentality be found in Britain in people other than the two headline-hogging inspirations? The evidence wasn't bright. Henman and Rusedski had been stacking the results up for over three years, but the impact of their progress on the country which wallowed so fully in their success was negligible. Paul Hutchins, now trying to raise tennis's profile through the Rover Junior Initiative, saw little in the pipeline which made him confident of future top-ten material.

'Hand on heart, there isn't a feeling that other players are looking at Tim and Greg, saying "I want some of that." We used to talk about the attitude when we didn't have any players in the top ten, now we're talking about it when we've got these two leading the way,' he said. 'Where it has been inspirational is among the eleven-to-fifteen-year-olds, they feel there's someone up there to aim at. That's the boom area, if there is one.

'Of course, there's been an unparalleled interest in the media, and that has to help the perception of parents and kids about the sport. On the other hand, it isn't reflected in sales of rackets or tennis balls, of increased club membership or the number of people playing the game apart from the eleven-to-fifteen age group. I would love to be sitting here saying that Tim and Greg have made a major impact on the British game, but I'm not. It's a continuing frustration and worry for someone like me, who's so heavily involved in the business of tennis.

'It is in the clubs where there has to be a change. They are the biggest negative aspect – most of them are sleeping giants, many are dozing, some are brain dead. I'm involved in the National Senior Club League and the Rover Junior Club League and even there, the flame is not alight, as yet. What the LTA has to do is light the flame of club tennis, to ignite the coaches at those clubs, in those who are involved in junior development, in order to capitalize on Tim and Greg.'

Doubts abounded. David Lloyd was back on his hobby-horse of independent schemes, like the one which had unearthed Tim Henman. His idea was that the LTA should act not as a coaching entity of itself, but as a sporting trust, funding initiatives. 'Every three years, those who set up their schemes would go to the bank and say, "These are my results, can I have any more money?" If the results were rubbish, the bank would tell them where to get off. If they were successful, they produced, the bank would reward them. That is a fact of life.

'We have all these squads around under the LTA auspices and who judges them? How can people within the LTA criticize the squads, when they picked them themselves? It's a nonsense. We need a healthy, creative, competitive, coaching system. Give people £300,000 over three years to set up their schemes, let them produce a balance sheet, show us their results, and see how good they are.

'Instead of which we have this gigantic central core which leads to bad management, costs too much money, and does away with responsibility. I like to run businesses as a circle, with the strength on the rim, not the centre.

'The Slater Scheme was on the outside. We had good players, great coaches and it stopped only because we couldn't get the players because the LTA made it impossible for them to come to us. That's another reason why the independent squad method is so good – it's not a monopoly.'

The LTA was told to forget Henman and Rusedski, in a manner of speaking. 'They should be taken out of the equation,' said Lloyd, 'because what the LTA has to do now has nothing to do with them. They present a false picture of the state of the game. In reality, the situation is as bad as it's ever been. There are some decent young players, like Matthew Smith, Lee Childs and David Sherwood, but that's not enough. We need more. The LTA's argument is that their results are very good, but that can be misleading. Jamie Delgado won the Orange Bowl at fourteen. Ten years on, he's making up the numbers. We can't be complacent just because we have two world-class players.'

The country suffered for not having a good enough tournament structure, and certainly not enough on clay courts, the only surface on which to be taught, to understand and to have drilled into you, the basics of the game. Henman and Rusedski couldn't play on clay either, but the powers-that-be overlooked that. Every indoor centre built had fast carpet or cement as its surface, young players were pigeon-holed too soon. Henman and Rusedski served and volleyed by nature, so that had to be the way.

Ian Barclay from the soon-to-be-closed LTA National School, had been pleading for indoor clay courts for years, to little avail. 'If the instincts of our players is staying at the back of the court, we should give them that chance,' he said. 'We don't have the material to follow the top two, quite honestly I would prefer it if their idols were Alex Corretja or Marat Safin, rather than Tim and Greg. I don't have one player in my group who you could shove onto a Wimbledon grass

court and who could win a couple of matches. I haven't seen any 6'2"
unbelievably gifted serve-volliers.

'Tim and Greg have spoiled it, in a way. If Tim had decided to play
golf, he'd have been as good as Nick Faldo, he would have captained
the British field hockey team. He has that freakish ability, he's a naturally gifted boy, you only have to see him with a ball. He has an
unbelievable touch, flair, hands, but it still takes more than that to win
Wimbledon. He doesn't have Greg's big serve for a start. I'm hoping
for the sake of British tennis that he does, but I still think it's in the
balance.'

At the Lawn Tennis Writers' Association annual dinner on 11
December 1998, Tim Henman won the Special Services Award which
had been Rusedski's the previous year. The two of them sat together at
the top table. It was only right and proper. Henman also won the
Player of the Year award from the LTA; David 'The Trouble With Tim'
Felgate was Coach of the Year.

A couple of nights later, Tim and Greg were seated together again,
in wicker chairs at the BBC Sports Personality Award for 1998. The
two of them were nominated in the most sophisticated poll ever undertaken on the night, with over 500,000 people voting by telephone in the
final ten minutes of the show. I wasn't surprised that Henman was in
the top six – the Wimbledon semi-final, his qualification for the World
championships, No.7 in the world etc, etc, but Greg, the defending
personality, was there again, after what had been a traumatic year –
obviously he was still a tennis player for whom the British public
retained a deep affection. His Wimbledon had been little short of a
nightmare, he had split acrimoniously from his coach, he had gone out
of the top ten, but had bounced back, demonstrating all that old grit
and determination. Rusedski reappearing in the top six nominees was
as thought-provoking as the award going to a kid who scored a couple
of great goals in a terrible World Cup campaign for England.

Henman and Rusedski were conspicuously rewarded for their
talents. Indeed, it was something of an irony that in the year when
Henman's rise was the most spectacular, when he was the one who
broke the twenty-five-year wait for a British Wimbledon semi-finalist
and when he qualified for the ATP World Finals as of right, he should
have earned $1,448,770 (around £905,480), to Rusedski's $1,460,437
(around £912,770). What's seven grand between friends?

It was said at the end of the year that Henman who had played 88
singles matches in 1998, more than any other professional 'was a gold
field waiting to be mined'. The gold rush would be triggered with a

1999 Wimbledon victory, to which his sponsors would all contribute immense bonuses. The reckoning was that should all fall into place, Henman could earn close to £4 million in the upcoming year, which would make him the fourth richest sportsman in the country, and number one in his sport.

All of Henman's sponsorship deals – it is estimated that he makes over £2 million from those alone per annum – were firmly in place. He wore Adidas gear, used Slazenger rackets, sported a Midland Bank patch on his shirt sleeve, drove a Mercedes and represented Robinson's Aces. The entire spectrum was covered. Rusedski entered 1999 without a new clothing contract, his old Nike deal having expired the previous October (though he and Groeneveld were still wearing their matching dark brown, Darth Vader-like hooded sweat tops). He was preparing to use his old Wilson rackets in Australia, though he was negotiating a new deal as the New Year approached. The very British clothing company Austin Reed maintained their sponsorship and, in the week before Christmas, it was announced that he had completed a world-wide marketing agreement with the veritably British Jaguar Cars. The company presented him with a top-of-the-range XK8 convertible, finished in sapphire blue metallic with an ivory interior. It was suggested that Rusedski would earn precisely the same in 1999 as he had in the year just ended, which would take him out of the top-ten British earners, where he had been level tenth with Henman on 31 December 1998.

There was one branding relevant to both men. They were absolute quality in a relentlessly cut-throat world. Whether you preferred one to the other – and I started out on this odyssey with a mind free of obligation or preference – it was impossible to underestimate their twin achievements. The sight of Rusedski writhing in agony at Queen's clutching his left ankle and seeing him, turning at the net, hardly able to hang on to his racket his arms were shaking so much, in a victory salute to Sven Groeneveld when he defeated Pete Sampras in the final of the Open de Paris, spoke of an inestimable fighter.

Henman's recovery from the agonies in Australia and the condemnation of his coach, his place in the last four at Wimbledon, qualification for his first ATP Finals and yet another career high end-of-year ranking, told of the immense character which lay beneath those angelic boy-next-door features.

In the week leading up to Christmas, both players practised, morning and afternoon, court work and gym work, at Queen's Club, in preparation for their first journey of the New Year. Henman, under the supervision of his fitness coach, Tim Newenham, had put on an extra four kilos of upper body weight and was now at 76 kilos, exactly where Newenham wanted him. Maybe now, the service which he needed to rely on for the push towards a Grand Slam championship would stand him in powerful stead.

All the talk as tennis entered 1999 was of the foul stench of drug abuse in the sport. Czech Petr Korda tested positive for the Class One prohibited substance, nandrolone metabolites, an anabolic steroid, after his Wimbledon quarter-final defeat to Henman, but because of the extravagances of the system, it took six months for the result to come to light.

Korda had used the defence of 'exceptional circumstances' to an independent appeals committee, set up by the ITF to investigate, and the sport was horrified when the committee decided to impose a fine and wipe out the ranking points Korda had earned during the Championships, rather than throw him out for a year which they had the power to do. The ITF wanted to appeal the verdict of their own appeals committee, but Korda's lawyers won a High Court case preventing it.

Everywhere he went, Korda was dogged by persistent questions, but refused to answer. The exceptional circumstance was that he didn't know how the substance came to be in his bloodstream. As character witnesses before the appeals committee, he had called Boris Becker and Tony Pickard. How much damage the Korda case would do to the sport remained to be seen.

On the courts, the first port of call was the Middle East and a return to Doha. Rusedski, suggesting the 11.15p.m. start to his first round match was rather unusual, fell to Bernd Karbacher of Germany, his third straight defeat to the same player. Henman eased his way through to the Qatar Open final and ought to have been more than the equal of German, qualifier Rainer Schuttler. But, Schuttler, like Karbacher, had a hold over the Brits and his three set victory was his second in three meetings with Henman.

The British No.1 had already decided to side-step the Sydney tournament in which he had been the champion and runner-up in successive years, and get straight to Melbourne to compete in the eight-man Colonial Classic, played at the old Open venue of Kooyong. He was joined there pretty soon afterwards by Rusedski, beaten in Sydney by Gustavo Kuerten after winning the first set 6-1. 'I think this is the hardest part of the year,' he said. 'These courts favour the baseline player over the serve and volleyer, the ball sits up like a pancake.'

Henman didn't win a match in Kooyong in extreme heat and, exasperatedly, said he never wanted to play an exhibition again. Neither man could have been said to be entering the first Grand Slam of the year surfing a wave of confidence. Henman, breaking serve with increasingly contemptuous ease, brushed aside the challenge of Moroccan, Karim Alami, but found in the leggy Australian, Sandon Stolle, son of Fred, a far tougher nut to crack. Henman's description, 'a big, big struggle', was absolutely right, from which he eventually emerging in five sets after three hours and seven minutes.

Rusedski had just about edged another Aussie, Scott Draper in the opening round, and, for both he and Henman the draw was opening out. Rusedski played an American qualifier Paul Goldstein, Henman would meet Marc Rosset, who was a notorious peaks and troughs player. It was British tennis which would end up in the trough. Rusedski had a point to lead 4-0 in the first set but was consistently unnerved by an opponent who looked and played like a bag of nails. In all, Greg contributed 76 unforced errors to his own downfall and had little in the way of excuse.

His coach tried to take as much positive gloss from the setback as he could. 'Greg is a realist, he knows this wasn't good enough,' said Groeneveld. 'Just because the guy was returning his serve so well, didn't mean he had to get so flustered. We have to go back to the drawing board and see what's next. He's got to get back his hunger and dig these matches out. We have two and a half weeks before our next tournament and since we started together, it's been non-stop. I still have full confidence in Greg, I see his possibilities, it's a matter of finding the right ingredients and putting them all together.' I hoped he would find them quickly, for his own sake.

Henman's defeat to Rosset was equally lamentable, especially as he led with two mini breaks, 5-2 in the first set tie-break, and broke first in both the second and third sets. A straight sets defeat was hard to swallow, Henman burst into the press room some five minutes after the match, chided the press corps and tried, unsuccessfully, to catch a flight home that evening.

The most open Open for a number of years was won by the Russian, Yevgeny Kafelnikov, who had engaged a new coach in American Larry Stefanki, and played as if his confidence was soaring – in such a stark contrast to the British pair. Still, there was a lot to play for. Henman had been even more disgusted with himself a year before and look where he ended up.

Rusedski was every bit as determined. He maintained his confidence by keeping in close contact with his most fervent supporter, his father. Rusedski was happy to give his family the credit it is clear they deserve. 'My Dad knows my results even quicker than some of those at the events,' he said. 'He has got all the stats about me, he knows everything. I keep my whole family in touch with my tennis and my personal life. What my parents did for me is more amazing than anything I might accomplish in the sport. It's what drives me on to be even better.

'They never really let me know what they were doing, but you could tell something was happening. They didn't put any pressure on me, they never said "You've got to make it", or "Look at what we're doing for you." There are other people who have dreams for their kids who phone up my parents all the time and ask them how they did what they did for me. I've been very lucky.'

What was interesting was that Groeneveld, now well established and promising to sign for a further year as Rusedski's coach, had only spoken to Tom Rusedski once in six months. Maybe this was a sign that father felt that son finally had the coach who would give them both what they really wanted. I decided to put a few bob on Greg Rusedski at 8–1 for the 1999 Wimbledon. His contentment was confirmed with the February announcement – in *Hello!* magazine – that he was getting engaged to Lucy Connor.

At the end of this venture, I spoke to a number of those who spent all their time in the game and wondered if they had a chance to ask Rusedski one question, what it would be. The consensus was that they would want to know whether with hindsight, he would have chosen differently in 1995 when Britain needed a tennis saviour and one came from Montreal bearing gifts.

When I asked Greg, the response came searing towards me, like a howitzer serve. 'When I make a decision, good or bad, I go for it, that's what makes me what I am,' he said. 'It was never a difficult choice to come here. It was the right thing to do in all the categories. I am where I want to be. I couldn't ask for anything better. I have come through my trial. From 1995 onwards, I knew exactly what it all entailed. I won't look back with any regret. I'm happy with it now and I will be happy with it for the rest of my life.'

And we had our answer.

The country couldn't have asked for two more credible, yet more diverse role models. 'We are different,' Rusedski emphasised, 'as tennis players as well as people. On the court, Tim relies on his natural ability, the way he flows. For myself, even if I'm having a bad time, I try to find a way to win, and usually, even on those bad days, I *find* a way. I want someone who's pushing me on, but keeping me level headed. We have two British players in the top ten, but wouldn't it be better to say we have a world No.1 and a Wimbledon champion?

'Tim are I are both playing for the same country, we live in the same country, the rivalry is going to be there, that's the way life is. We are great for British tennis, I don't think there's any denying that. If I achieve what I want to achieve, I'll be very happy, if it means getting there ahead of Tim, I'll have to do that. If it means getting ahead of Sampras, I'll have to get ahead of Sampras.'

Obviously, they were the two most powerful people in the sport in Britain. Well, no, apparently not. In an article in *Ace* magazine late in the year Tim was included in the top ten, but his picture was placed at the end of the list behind Sir Geoffrey Cass, David Lloyd, John Crowther (the chief executive of the LTA), BBC commentator John Barrett and Sir Cliff Richard. Really?

And where was Greg? Had anyone in the game done more for British tennis in such a short space of time? Had anyone made more people look at themselves, attracted more people want to take up the sport (in a far-reaching poll of kids across the country, more of them wanted to be Greg than Tim), drawn more applause, both sympathetic and appreciative, shown more courage, had brought his fiercest rival up by his bootlaces, and shown the way it has to be done to succeed in the sport? To my mind, by virtue of all of this and much more, Rusedski had become *the* most powerful man in the British game, no doubt. His was the standard whether he was truly a Brit or not.

Tim Henman Tour Statistics

DATE	EVENT	TOURNAMENT	INDOOR/OUTDOOR	SURFACE	DRAW	RANK
5/1/98	Dora	ATP	Outdoor	Hard	32	S017

R32	Sanchez, Javier	7–5	6–1	
R16	Raoux, Guillaume	7–5	6–4	
Q	Korda, Petr	5–7	6–4	4–6

YEAR TO DATE – 1998

Won/Lost	Singles/Doubles	Earnings
2 / 1	S&D	US$41,045

THIS EVENT ONLY

Points	Singles/Doubles	Earnings
68	Singles	US$27,970

DATE	EVENT	TOURNAMENT	INDOOR/OUTDOOR	SURFACE	DRAW	RANK
12/1/98	Sydney	ATP	Outdoor	Hard	32	S019

R32	Woodforde, Mark	6–2	3–6	6–4
R16	Portas, Albert	7–6	6–4	
Q	Enqvist, Thomas	3–6	7–5	6–4
S	Rafter, Patrick	7–6	7–5	
F	Kucera, Karol	5–7	4–6	

YEAR TO DATE – 1998

Won/Lost	Singles/Doubles	Earnings
6 / 2	S&D	US$67,045

THIS EVENT ONLY

Points	Singles/Doubles	Earnings
195	Singles	US$26,000

DATE	EVENT	TOURNAMENT	INDOOR/OUTDOOR	SURFACE	DRAW	RANK
19/1/98	Australian OP	Grand Slam	Outdoor	Hard	128	S018

R128	Golmard, Jerome	3–6	7–6	2–6	6–3	9–11

YEAR TO DATE – 1998

Won/Lost	Singles/Doubles	Earnings
6 / 3	S&D	US$75,160

THIS EVENT ONLY

Points	Singles/Doubles	Earnings
1	Singles	US$6,293

DATE	EVENT	TOURNAMENT	INDOOR/ OUTDOOR	SURFACE	DRAW	RANK
2/2/98	Split	ATP	Indoor	Carpet	32	S018

R32	Schuttler, Rainer	3–6	6–1	3–6

YEAR TO DATE – 1998

Won/Lost	Singles/Doubles	Earnings
6 / 4	S&D	US$78,880

THIS EVENT ONLY

Points	Singles/Doubles	Earnings
1	Singles	US$3,720

DATE	EVENT	TOURNAMENT	INDOOR/ OUTDOOR	SURFACE	DRAW	RANK
9/2/98	Dubai	ATP	Outdoor	Hard	32	S018

R32	Becker, Boris	5–7	0–6

YEAR TO DATE – 1998

Won/Lost	Singles/Doubles	Earnings
6 / 5	S&D	US$96,490

THIS EVENT ONLY

Points	Singles/Doubles	Earnings
1	Singles	US$10,080

DATE	EVENT	TOURNAMENT	INDOOR/ OUTDOOR	SURFACE	DRAW	RANK
16/2/98	Antwerp	ATP	Indoor	Hard	32	S017

R32	Norman, Magnus	5–7	3–6

YEAR TO DATE – 1998

Won/Lost	Singles/Doubles	Earnings
6 / 6	S&D	US$104,040

THIS EVENT ONLY

Points	Singles/Doubles	Earnings
1	Singles	US$6,550

DATE	EVENT	TOURNAMENT	INDOOR/ OUTDOOR	SURFACE	DRAW	RANK
23/2/98	London	ATP	Indoor	Carpet	32	S021

R32	Krajicek, Richard	6–7	7–6	7–5
R16	Schuttler, Rainer	4–6	6–3	6–4
Q	Kafelnikov, Yevgeny	6–4	4–6	2–6

YEAR TO DATE – 1998

Won/Lost	Singles/Doubles	Earnings
8 / 7	S&D	US$123,640

THIS EVENT ONLY

Points	Singles/Doubles	Earnings
91	Singles	US$18,600

DATE	EVENT	TOURNAMENT	INDOOR/ OUTDOOR	SURFACE	DRAW	RANK
9/3/98	Indian Wells	ATP	Outdoor	Hard	56	S019

R64	Black, Wayne	3–6	4–6

YEAR TO DATE – 1998

Won/Lost	Singles/Doubles	Earnings
8 / 8	S&D	US$136,630

THIS EVENT ONLY

Points	Singles/Doubles	Earnings
1	Singles	US$7,690

DATE	EVENT	TOURNAMENT	INDOOR/ OUTDOOR	SURFACE	DRAW	RANK
19/3/98	Lipton	ATP	Outdoor	Hard	96	S020

R128	Bye				
R64	Stafford, Grant	6–4	6–2		
R32	Moya, Carlos	6–1	6–4		
R16	Korda, Petr	6–4	6–4		
Q	Kuerten, Gustavo	6–2	6–4		
S	Rios, Marcelo	2–6	6–4	0–6	

YEAR TO DATE – 1998

Won/Lost	Singles/Doubles	Earnings
12 / 9	S&D	US$242,230

THIS EVENT ONLY

Points	Singles/Doubles	Earnings
259	Singles	US$100,000

DATE	EVENT	TOURNAMENT	INDOOR/ OUTDOOR	SURFACE	DRAW	RANK
3/4/98	GBR v UKR	Davis Cup	Indoor	Carpet	4	S015

R2	Medvedev, Andrei	6–2	6–7	6–4	1–6	6–1
R5	Rybalko, Andrei	6–1	2–6	6–2		

YEAR TO DATE – 1998

Won/Lost	Singles/Doubles	Earnings
14 / 9	S&D	US$242,230

THIS EVENT ONLY

Points	Singles/Doubles	Earnings
0	Singles	0

DATE	EVENT	TOURNAMENT	INDOOR/ OUTDOOR	SURFACE	DRAW	RANK
13/4/98	Japan Open	ATP	Outdoor	Hard	56	S015

R64	Bye		
R32	Nestor, Daniel	6–2	7–5
R16	Golmard, Jerome	6–4	6–1
Q	Gambill, Jan-Michael	3–6	6–4	3–6

YEAR TO DATE – 1998

Won/Lost	Singles/Doubles	Earnings
16 / 10	S&D	US$256,030

THIS EVENT ONLY

Points	Singles/Doubles	Earnings
55	Singles	US$13,800

DATE	EVENT	TOURNAMENT	INDOOR/ OUTDOOR	SURFACE	DRAW	RANK
20/4/98	Monte Carlo	ATP	Outdoor	Clay	56	S015

| R64 | Blanco, Galo | | 2–6 | 4–6 | | |

YEAR TO DATE – 1998

Won/Lost	Singles/Doubles	Earnings
16 / 11	S&D	US$263,720

THIS EVENT ONLY

Points	Singles/Doubles	Earnings
21	Singles	US$7,690

DATE	EVENT	TOURNAMENT	INDOOR/ OUTDOOR	SURFACE	DRAW	RANK
27/4/98	Munich	ATP	Outdoor	Clay	32	S017

| R32 | Knippschild, Jens | | 6–4 | 4–6 | 6–1 |
| R16 | Nydahl, Tomas | | 3–6 | 1–6 | |

YEAR TO DATE – 1998

Won/Lost	Singles/Doubles	Earnings
17 / 12	S&D	US$272,870

THIS EVENT ONLY

Points	Singles/Doubles	Earnings
21	Singles	US$8,400

DATE	EVENT	TOURNAMENT	INDOOR/ OUTDOOR	SURFACE	DRAW	RANK
4/5/98	Hamburg	ATP	Outdoor	Clay	56	S017

| R64 | Apell, Jan | | 6–3 | 6–2 |
| R32 | Arazi, Hicham | | 3–6 | 3–6 |

YEAR TO DATE – 1998

Won/Lost	Singles/Doubles	Earnings
18 / 13	S&D	US$292,670

THIS EVENT ONLY

Points	Singles/Doubles	Earnings
21	Singles	US$14,500

DATE	EVENT	TOURNAMENT	INDOOR/ OUTDOOR	SURFACE	DRAW	RANK
11/5/98	Rome	ATP	Outdoor	Clay	64	S017

| R64 | Santoro, Fabrice | | 6–1 | 6–0 |
| R32 | Rios, Marcelo | | 3–6 | 1–6 |

YEAR TO DATE – 1998

Won/Lost	Singles/Doubles	Earnings
19 / 14	S&D	US$308,170

THIS EVENT ONLY

Points	Singles/Doubles	Earnings
38	Singles	US$14,000

DATE	EVENT	TOURNAMENT	INDOOR/ OUTDOOR	SURFACE	DRAW	RANK
25/5/98	French Open	Grand Slam	Outdoor	Clay	128	S018

R12	Sargsian, Sargis	2–5	Retired

YEAR TO DATE – 1998			THIS EVENT ONLY		
Won/Lost	Singles/Doubles	Earnings	Points	Singles/Doubles	Earnings
19 / 15	S&D	US$317,943	1	Singles	US$9,773

DATE	EVENT	TOURNAMENT	INDOOR/ OUTDOOR	SURFACE	DRAW	RANK
8/6/98	Queen's	ATP	Outdoor	Grass	56	S018

R64	Bye			
R32	Sargsian, Sargis	6–3	6–4	
R16	Ivanisevic, Goran	6–1	6–7	6–4
Q	Tieleman, Laurence	6–2	6–7	4–6

YEAR TO DATE – 1998			THIS EVENT ONLY		
Won/Lost	Singles/Doubles	Earnings	Points	Singles/Doubles	Earnings
21 / 16	S&D	US$337,593	66	Singles	US$17,500

DATE	EVENT	TOURNAMENT	INDOOR/ OUTDOOR	SURFACE	DRAW	RANK
22/6/98	Wimbledon	Grand Slam	Outdoor	Grass	128	S018

R128	Novak, Jiri	7–6	7–5	5–7	4–6	6–2
R64	Nainkin, David	6–3	5–7	6–4	6–2	
R32	Black, Byron	6–4	6–4	3–6	7–5	
R16	Rafter, Patrick	6–3	6–7	6–3	6–2	
Q	Korda, Petr	6–3	6–4	6–2		
S	Sampras, Pete	3–6	6–4	5–7	3–6	

YEAR TO DATE – 1998			THIS EVENT ONLY		
Won/Lost	Singles/Doubles	Earnings	Points	Singles/Doubles	Earnings
26 / 17	S&D	US$519,380	523	Singles	US$181,787

DATE	EVENT	TOURNAMENT	INDOOR/ OUTDOOR	SURFACE	DRAW	RANK
27/7/98	Los Angeles	ATP	Outdoor	Hard	32	S012

R32	Stafford, Grant	6–3	6–0		
R16	Tarango, Jeff	7–6	7–5		
Q	Black, Byron	5–7	6–1	6–4	
S	Raoux, Guillaume	7–5	6–3		
F	Agassi, Andre	4–6	4–6		

YEAR TO DATE – 1998

Won/Lost	Singles/Doubles	Earnings
30 / 18	S&D	US$545,380

THIS EVENT ONLY

Points	Singles/Doubles	Earnings
134	Singles	US$26,000

DATE	EVENT	TOURNAMENT	INDOOR/ OUTDOOR	SURFACE	DRAW	RANK
3/8/98	Canadian Open	ATP	Outdoor	Hard	56	S012

R64	Bye				
R32	Canas, Guillermo	3–6	7–6	6–2	
R16	Costa, Albert	7–6	6–2		
Q	Vacek, Daniel	6–3	5–7	6–1	
S	Rafter, Patrick	2–6	4–6		

YEAR TO DATE – 1998

Won/Lost	Singles/Doubles	Earnings
33 / 19	S&D	US$645,380

THIS EVENT ONLY

Points	Singles/Doubles	Earnings
193	Singles	US$100,000

DATE	EVENT	TOURNAMENT	INDOOR/ OUTDOOR	SURFACE	DRAW	RANK
10/8/98	Cincinnati	ATP	Outdoor	Hard	56	S011

R64	Muster, Thomas	4–6	5–7	

YEAR TO DATE – 1998

Won/Lost	Singles/Doubles	Earnings
33 / 20	S&D	US$653,070

THIS EVENT ONLY

Points	Singles/Doubles	Earnings
1	Singles	US$7,690

DATE	EVENT	TOURNAMENT	INDOOR/ OUTDOOR	SURFACE	DRAW	RANK
17/8/98	New Haven	ATP	Outdoor	Hard	56	S010

R64	Bye				
R32	Santopadre, Vincenzo	6–2	6–3		
R16	Sanguinetti, Davide	4–6	6–3	6–3	
Q	Krajicek, Richard	7–5	2–6	6–7	

YEAR TO DATE – 1998

Won/Lost	Singles/Doubles	Earnings
35 / 21	S&D	US$670,870

THIS EVENT ONLY

Points	Singles/Doubles	Earnings
61	Singles	US$17,800

DATE	EVENT	TOURNAMENT	INDOOR/ OUTDOOR	SURFACE	DRAW	RANK
31/8/98	U.S. Open	Grand Slam	Outdoor	Hard	128	S013

R128	Draper, Scott	6–3	7–6	7–6	
R64	Mantilla, Felix	6–3	5–7	7–5	6–4
R32	Kohlmann, Michael	6–3	7–5	1–6	6–4
R16	Philippoussis, Mark	5–7	6–0	4–6	1–6

YEAR TO DATE – 1998

Won/Lost	Singles/Doubles	Earnings
38 / 22	S&D	US$720,870
0		

THIS EVENT ONLY

Points	Singles/Doubles	Earnings
150	Singles	US$50,00

DATE	EVENT	TOURNAMENT	INDOOR/ OUTDOOR	SURFACE	DRAW	RANK
14/9/98	Tashkent	ATP	Outdoor	Hard	32	S011

R32	Welgreen, Nir	6–1	6–4		
R16	Ran, Eyal	6–4	6–1		
Q	Pescosolido, Stefano	6–4	6–4		
S	Escude, Nicolas	3–6	6–3	6–4	
F	Kafelnikov, Yevgeny	7–5	6–4		

YEAR TO DATE – 1998

Won/Lost	Singles/Doubles	Earnings
43 / 22	S&D	US$790,420

THIS EVENT ONLY

Points	Singles/Doubles	Earnings
219	Singles	US$66,400

DATE	EVENT	TOURNAMENT	INDOOR/ OUTDOOR	SURFACE	DRAW	RANK
25/9/98	GBR v IND WGPO	Davis Cup	Outdoor	Hard	56	S011

R2	Bhupathi, Mahesh	4–6	6–3	6–3	6–3
R4	Paes, Leander	7–6	6–2	7–6	

YEAR TO DATE – 1998

Won/Lost	Singles/Doubles	Earnings
45 / 22	S&D	US$790,420

THIS EVENT ONLY

Points	Singles/Doubles	Earnings
0	Singles	0

DATE	EVENT	TOURNAMENT	INDOOR/ OUTDOOR	SURFACE	DRAW	RANK
28/9/98	Grand Slam Cup		Indoor	Hard	12	S011

R16	Bjorkman, Jonas	5–7	3–6

YEAR TO DATE – 1998

Won/Lost	Singles/Doubles	Earnings
45 / 23	S&D	US$890,420

THIS EVENT ONLY

Points	Singles/Doubles	Earnings
0	Singles	US$100,000

DATE	EVENT	TOURNAMENT	INDOOR/ OUTDOOR	SURFACE	DRAW	RANK
5/10/98	Basel	ATP	Indoor	Carpet	32	S011

R32	Stoltenberg, Jason	2–6	6–3	6–4	
R16	Arazi, Hicham	6–4	7–6		
Q	Kiefer, Nicolas	6–3	6–4		
S	Johansson, Thomas	6–3	2–6	7–6	
F	Agassi, Andre	6–4	6–3	3–6	6–4

YEAR TO DATE – 1998

Won/Lost	Singles/Doubles	Earnings
50 / 23	S&D	US$1,027,420

THIS EVENT ONLY

Points	Singles/Doubles	Earnings
316	Singles	US$137,000

DATE	EVENT	TOURNAMENT	INDOOR/ OUTDOOR	SURFACE	DRAW	RANK
12/10/98	Vienna	ATP	Indoor	Carpet	32	S010

R32	Gustafsson, Magnus	6–3	6–4	
R16	Enqvist, Thomas	6–7	6–3	6–3
Q	Sampras, Pete	0–6	3–6	

YEAR TO DATE – 1998

Won/Lost	Singles/Doubles	Earnings
52 / 24	S&D	US$1,045,620

THIS EVENT ONLY

Points	Singles/Doubles	Earnings
89	Singles	US$18,200

DATE	EVENT	TOURNAMENT	INDOOR/ OUTDOOR	SURFACE	DRAW	RANK
26/10/98	Stuttgart Ind	ATP	Indoor	Hard	48	S009

R64	Bye,			
R32	Woodforde, Mark	7–5	6–1	
R16	Gambill, Jan-Michael	6–7	6–1	6–7

YEAR TO DATE – 1998

Won/Lost	Singles/Doubles	Earnings
53 / 25	S&D	US$1,074,620

THIS EVENT ONLY

Points	Singles/Doubles	Earnings
46	Singles	US$29,000

DATE	EVENT	TOURNAMENT	INDOOR/ OUTDOOR	SURFACE	DRAW	RANK
2/11/98	Paris Indoor	ATP	Indoor	Carpet	48	S010

R64	Bye			
R32	Di Pasquale, Arnaud	6–3	6–3	
R16	Kafelnikov, Yevgeny	3–6	7–6	6–7

YEAR TO DATE – 1998

Won/Lost	Singles/Doubles	Earnings
54 / 26	S&D	US$1,104,770

THIS EVENT ONLY

Points	Singles/Doubles	Earnings
43	Singles	US$30,150

DATE	EVENT	TOURNAMENT	INDOOR/ OUTDOOR	SURFACE	DRAW	RANK
9/11/98	Stockholm	ATP	Indoor	Carpet	32	S010

R32	Tillstrom, Mikael	6–3	6–1	
R16	Ferreira, Wayne	7–6	6–3	
Q	Gustafsson, Magnus	6–3	3–6	7–6
S	Martin, Todd	6–4	1–6	2–6

YEAR TO DATE – 1998

Won/Lost	Singles/Doubles	Earnings
57 / 27	S&D	US$1,143,770

THIS EVENT ONLY

Points	Singles/Doubles	Earnings
129	Singles	US$39,000

DATE	EVENT	TOURNAMENT	INDOOR/ OUTDOOR	SURFACE	DRAW	RANK
23/11/98	Tour Sing CHP	ATP	Indoor	Hard	12	S010

R1	Rios, Marcelo	7–5	6–1	
R3	Corretja, Alex	7–6	6–7	6–2
R4	Rusedski, Greg	2–6	4–6	
S	Moya, Carlos	6–4	3–6	5–7

YEAR TO DATE – 1998

Won/Lost	Singles/Doubles	Earnings
59 / 29	S&D	US$1,448,770

THIS EVENT ONLY

Points	Singles/Doubles	Earnings
180	Singles	US$305,000

Greg Rusedski Tour Statistics

DATE	EVENT	TOURNAMENT	INDOOR/OUTDOOR	SURFACE	DRAW	RANK
5/1/98	Doha	ATP	Outdoor	Hard	32	S006

R32	Viloca, Juan Albert	6–4	6–4	
R16	Alami, Karim	6–2	7–5	
Q	Santoro, Fabrice	2–6	6–3	3–6

YEAR TO DATE – 1998

Won/Lost	Singles/Doubles	Earnings
2 / 1	S&D	US$27,970

THIS EVENT ONLY

Points	Singles/Doubles	Earnings
62	Singles	US$27,970

DATE	EVENT	TOURNAMENT	INDOOR/OUTDOOR	SURFACE	DRAW	RANK
19/1/98	Australian Open	Grand Slam	Outdoor	Hard	128	S006

R128	Witt, David	7–6	6–3	6–4	
R64	Stark, Jonathan	6–4	6–4	1–0	Retired
R32	Woodbridge, Todd	6–7	4–6	2–6	

YEAR TO DATE – 1998

Won/Lost	Singles/Doubles	Earnings
4 / 2	S&D	US$43,868

THIS EVENT ONLY

Points	Singles/Doubles	Earnings
45	Singles	US$15,898

DATE	EVENT	TOURNAMENT	INDOOR/OUTDOOR	SURFACE	DRAW	RANK
2/2/98	Split	ATP	Indoor	Carpet	32	S008

R32	Pozzi, Gianluca	6–3	6–4	
R16	Kroslak, Jan	6–4	6–3	
Q	Damm, Martin	6–1	6–4	
S	Rosset, Marc	6–7	7–6	7–6
F	Ivanisevic, Goran	6–7	6–7	

YEAR TO DATE – 1998

Won/Lost	Singles/Doubles	Earnings
8 / 3	S&D	US$75,368

THIS EVENT ONLY

Points	Singles/Doubles	Earnings
144	Singles	US$31,500

DATE	EVENT	TOURNAMENT	INDOOR/ OUTDOOR	SURFACE	DRAW	RANK
16/2/98	Antwerp	ATP	Indoor	Hard	32	S009

R32	Arazi, Hicham	7–6	3–6	6–3	
R16	Raoux, Guillaume	7–6	3–6	7–6	
Q	Johansson, Thomas	6–3	4–6	6–4	
S	Kucera, Karol	6–4	6–3		
F	Rosset, Marc	7–6	3–6	6–1	6–4

YEAR TO DATE – 1998

Won/Lost	Singles/Doubles	Earnings
13 / 3	S&D	US$237,868

THIS EVENT ONLY

Points	Singles/Doubles	Earnings
358	Singles	US$162,500

DATE	EVENT	TOURNAMENT	INDOOR/ OUTDOOR	SURFACE	DRAW	RANK
23/2/98	London	ATP	Indoor	Carpet	32	S005

R32	Goellner, Marc-Kevin	7–5	5–7	4–6

YEAR TO DATE – 1998

Won/Lost	Singles/Doubles	Earnings
13 / 4	S&D	US$243,068

THIS EVENT ONLY

Points	Singles/Doubles	Earnings
1	Singles	US$5,200

DATE	EVENT	TOURNAMENT	INDOOR/ OUTDOOR	SURFACE	DRAW	RANK
2/3/98	Rotterdam	ATP	Indoor	Carpet	32	S006

R32	Alami, Karim	6–7	7–6	7–6
R16	Reneberg, Richey	6–3	6–2	
Q	Krajicek, Richard	6–3	6–7	6–7

YEAR TO DATE – 1998

Won/Lost	Singles/Doubles	Earnings
15 / 5	S&D	US$263,798

THIS EVENT ONLY

Points	Singles/Doubles	Earnings
57	Singles	US$20,730

DATE	EVENT	TOURNAMENT	INDOOR/ OUTDOOR	SURFACE	DRAW	RANK
9/3/98	Indian Wells	ATP	Outdoor	Hard	56	S006

R64	Bye				
R32	Spadea, Vincent	4–6	6–3	6–4	
R16	Moya, Carlos	6–3	7–5		
Q	Enqvist, Thomas	2–6	7–6	6–4	
S	Muster, Thomas	7–6	6–1		
F	Rios, Marcelo	3–6	7–6	6–7	4–6

YEAR TO DATE – 1998

Won/Lost	Singles/Doubles	Earnings
19 / 6	S&D	US$453,798

THIS EVENT ONLY

Points	Singles/Doubles	Earnings
337	Singles	US$190,000

			INDOOR/			
DATE	EVENT	TOURNAMENT	OUTDOOR	SURFACE	DRAW	RANK
19/3/98	Lipton	ATP	Outdoor	Hard	96	S005

R128	Bye			
R64	Hrbaty, Dominik	6–3	6–1	
R32	Rosset, Marc	6–1	7–6	
R16	Enqvist, Thomas	2–6	2–6	

YEAR TO DATE – 1998 **THIS EVENT ONLY**

Won/Lost	Singles/Doubles	Earnings	Points	Singles/Doubles	Earnings
21 / 7	S&D	US$481,398	64	Singles	US$27,600

			INDOOR/			
DATE	EVENT	TOURNAMENT	OUTDOOR	SURFACE	DRAW	RANK
3/4/98	GBR v UKR EAZ	Davis Cup	Indoor	Carpet	4	S005

R1	Rybalko, Andrei	6–4	6–0	6–4	
R4	Medvedev, Andrei	6–1	6–4		

YEAR TO DATE – 1998 **THIS EVENT ONLY**

Won/Lost	Singles/Doubles	Earnings	Points	Singles/Doubles	Earnings
23 / 7	S&D	US$481,398	0	Singles	0

			INDOOR/			
DATE	EVENT	TOURNAMENT	OUTDOOR	SURFACE	DRAW	RANK
20/4/98	Monte Carlo	ATP	Outdoor	Clay	56	S005

R64	Bye			
R32	Becker, Bors	4–6	6–3	3–6

YEAR TO DATE – 1998 **THIS EVENT ONLY**

Won/Lost	Singles/Doubles	Earnings	Points	Singles/Doubles	Earnings
23 / 8	S&D	US$495,898	1	Singles	US$14,500

			INDOOR/			
DATE	EVENT	TOURNAMENT	OUTDOOR	SURFACE	DRAW	RANK
27/4/98	Munich	ATP	Outdoor	Clay	32	S005

R32	Gross, Oliver	4–6	0–6

YEAR TO DATE – 1998 **THIS EVENT ONLY**

Won/Lost	Singles/Doubles	Earnings	Points	Singles/Doubles	Earnings
23 / 9	S&D	US$500,898	1	Singles	US$5,000

DATE	EVENT	TOURNAMENT	INDOOR/ OUTDOOR	SURFACE	DRAW	RANK
4/5/98	Hamburg	ATP	Outdoor	Clay	56	S005

R64	Bye			
R32	Alvarez, Emilio	7–6	0–6	6–3
R16	Ivanesvic, Goran	4–6	2–6	

YEAR TO DATE – 1998			THIS EVENT ONLY			
Won/Lost	Singles/Doubles	Earnings	Points	Singles/Doubles	Earnings
24 / 10	S&D	US$528,896	42	Singles	US$28,000

DATE	EVENT	TOURNAMENT	INDOOR/ OUTDOOR	SURFACE	DRAW	RANK
11/5/98	Rome	ATP	Outdoor	Clay	64	S005

R64	Ulihrach, Bohdan	5–7	6–7

YEAR TO DATE – 1998			THIS EVENT ONLY			
Won/Lost	Singles/Doubles	Earnings	Points	Singles/Doubles	Earnings
24 / 11	S&D	US$536,298	1	Singles	US$7,400

DATE	EVENT	TOURNAMENT	INDOOR/ OUTDOOR	SURFACE	DRAW	RANK
25/5/98	French Open	Grand Slam	Outdoor	Clay	128	S004

R128	Van Herck, Johan	4–6	4–6	4–6

YEAR TO DATE – 1998			THIS EVENT ONLY			
Won/Lost	Singles/Doubles	Earnings	Points	Singles/Doubles	Earnings
24 / 12	S&D	US$546,071	1	Singles	US$9,773

DATE	EVENT	TOURNAMENT	INDOOR/ OUTDOOR	SURFACE	DRAW	RANK
8/6/98	Queen's	ATP	Outdoor	Grass	56	S004

R64	Bye			
R32	Golmard, Jerome	6–7	6–4	6–1
R16	Tieleman, Laurence	2–2	Retired	

YEAR TO DATE – 1998			THIS EVENT ONLY			
Won/Lost	Singles/Doubles	Earnings	Points	Singles/Doubles	Earnings
25 / 13	S&D	US$557,071	26	Singles	US$10,250

DATE	EVENT	TOURNAMENT	INDOOR/ OUTDOOR	SURFACE	DRAW	RANK
22/6/98	Wimbledon	Grand Slam	Outdoor	Grass	128	S005

R128	Draper, Mark	6–4	2–6	4–5	Retired

YEAR TO DATE – 1998

Won/Lost	Singles/Doubles	Earnings
25 / 14	S&D	US$567,987

THIS EVENT ONLY

Points	Singles/Doubles	Earnings
1	Singles	US$10,916

DATE	EVENT	TOURNAMENT	INDOOR/ OUTDOOR	SURFACE	DRAW	RANK
17/8/98	Indianapolis	ATP	Outdoor	Hard	56	S007

R64	Bye		
R32	Larsson, Magnus	7–6	6–3
R16	Clavet, Francisco	6–1	7–6
Q	Corretja, Alex	4–6	3–6

YEAR TO DATE – 1998

Won/Lost	Singles/Doubles	Earnings
27 / 15	S&D	US$585,787

THIS EVENT ONLY

Points	Singles/Doubles	Earnings
83	Singles	US$17,800

DATE	EVENT	TOURNAMENT	INDOOR/ OUTDOOR	SURFACE	DRAW	RANK
24/8/98	Long Island	ATP	Outdoor	Hard	32	S006

R32	Norman, Magnus	6–3	6–4
R16	Meligeni, Fernando	6–2	7–6
Q	Vacek, Daniel	6–2	6–3
S	Rafter, Patrick	4–6	6–7

YEAR TO DATE – 1998

Won/Lost	Singles/Doubles	Earnings
30 / 16	S&D	US$601,237

THIS EVENT ONLY

Points	Singles/Doubles	Earnings
101	Singles	US$15,450

DATE	EVENT	TOURNAMENT	INDOOR/ OUTDOOR	SURFACE	DRAW	RANK
31/8/98	U.S. Open	Grand Slam	Outdoor	Hard	128	S006

R128	Ferreira, Wayne	4–6	7–6	5–7	7–6	6–4
R64	Ulihrach, Bohdan	4–6	6–3	4–6	6–2	7–5
R32	Siemerink, Jan	6–1	4–6	7–5	2–6	4–6

YEAR TO DATE – 1998

Won/Lost	Singles/Doubles	Earnings
32 / 17	S&D	US$631,231

THIS EVENT ONLY

Points	Singles/Doubles	Earnings
101	Singles	US$30,000

DATE	EVENT	TOURNAMENT	INDOOR/OUTDOOR	SURFACE	DRAW	RANK
25/9/98	GBR v IND WGPO	Davis Cup	Indoor	Hard	5	S015

| R1 | Paes, Leander | | 2–6 | 6–3 | 3–6 | 6–2 | 11–9 |

YEAR TO DATE – 1998

Won/Lost	Singles/Doubles	Earnings
33 / 17	S&D	US$631,237

THIS EVENT ONLY

Points	Singles/Doubles	Earnings
0	Singles	0

DATE	EVENT	TOURNAMENT	INDOOR/OUTDOOR	SURFACE	DRAW	RANK
28/9/98	Toulouse	ATP	Indoor	Hard	32	S014

R32	Goellner, Marc-Kevin	7–6	7–6
R16	Medvedev, Andrei	6–4	6–3
Q	Clement, Arnaud	6–4	6–1
S	Kiefer, Nicolas	6–4	6–1
F	Siemerink, Jan	4–6	4–6

YEAR TO DATE – 1998

Won/Lost	Singles/Doubles	Earnings
37 / 18	S&D	US$662,737

THIS EVENT ONLY

Points	Singles/Doubles	Earnings
138	Singles	US$31,500

DATE	EVENT	TOURNAMENT	INDOOR/OUTDOOR	SURFACE	DRAW	RANK
5/10/98	Basel	ATP	Indoor	Carpet	32	S014

R32	Pretzsch, Akel	6–2	6–2
R16	Prinosil, David	6–7	5–7

YEAR TO DATE – 1998

Won/Lost	Singles/Doubles	Earnings
38 / 19	S&D	US$678,737

THIS EVENT ONLY

Points	Singles/Doubles	Earnings
25	Singles	US$16,000

DATE	EVENT	TOURNAMENT	INDOOR/OUTDOOR	SURFACE	DRAW	RANK
12/10/98	Vienna	ATP	Indoor	Carpet	32	S017

R32	Kafelnikov, Yevgeny	6–3	3–6	7–6
R16	Muster, Thomas	6–4	6–3
Q	Rafter, Patrick	6–3	7–6
S1	Kucera, Karol	6–7	4–6

YEAR TO DATE – 1998

Won/Lost	Singles/Doubles	Earnings
41 / 20	S&D	US$713,437

THIS EVENT ONLY

Points	Singles/Doubles	Earnings
204	Singles	US$34,700

DATE	EVENT	TOURNAMENT	INDOOR/ OUTDOOR	SURFACE	DRAW	RANK
26/10/98	Stuttgart Ind	ATP	Indoor	Hard	48	S013

R64	Bye			
R32	Stoltenberg, Jason	7–6	6–7	7–6
R16	Rafter, Patrick	7–6	6–7	6–4
Q	Bjorkman, Jonas	3–6	2–6	

YEAR TO DATE – 1998

Won/Lost	Singles/Doubles	Earnings
43 / 21	S&D	US$768,437

THIS EVENT ONLY

Points	Singles/Doubles	Earnings
137	Singles	US$55,000

DATE	EVENT	TOURNAMENT	INDOOR/ OUTDOOR	SURFACE	DRAW	RANK
2/11/98	Paris Indoor	ATP	Indoor	Carpet	48	S013

R64	Bye			
R32	Kiefer, Nicolas	6–3	6–4	
R16	Stoltenberg, Jason	7–6	6–4	
Q	Gustafsson, Magnus	6–3	6–2	
S	Kafelnikov, Yevgeny	6–3	4–6	6–4
F	Sampras, Pete	6–4	7–6	6–3

YEAR TO DATE – 1998

Won/Lost	Singles/Doubles	Earnings
48 / 21	S&D	US$1,161,437

THIS EVENT ONLY

Points	Singles/Doubles	Earnings
548	Singles	US$393,000

DATE	EVENT	TOURNAMENT	INDOOR/ OUTDOOR	SURFACE	DRAW	RANK
9/11/98	Stockholm	ATP	Indoor	Hard	32	S011

R32	Haas, Tommy	6–1	6–4	
R16	Spadea, Vincent	6–1	6–4	
Q	Nestor, Daniel	7–6	1–6	6–3
S	Johansson, Thomas	5–7	6–7	

YEAR TO DATE – 1998

Won/Lost	Singles/Doubles	Earnings
51 / 22	S&D	US$1,200,437

THIS EVENT ONLY

Points	Singles/Doubles	Earnings
116	Singles	US$39,000

DATE	EVENT	TOURNAMENT	INDOOR/ OUTDOOR	SURFACE	DRAW	RANK
23/11/98	Tour Sing CHP	ATP	Indoor	Hard	12	S011

R3	Costa, Albert		7–6	6–1
R4	Henman, Tim		6–2	6–4

YEAR TO DATE – 1998

Won/Lost	Singles/Doubles	Earnings
53 / 22	S&D	US$1,460,437

THIS EVENT ONLY

Points	Singles/Doubles	Earnings
180	Singles	US$260,000